LONGMAN STUDY GUIDES

GCSE Spanish

John Bates

LONGMAN

LONGMAN STUDY GUIDES

SERIES EDITORS: **Geoff Black and Stuart Wall**

Titles available

Biology
Business Studies
Chemistry
Design and Technology
Economics
English
English Literature
French
Geography
German
Information Technology
Mathematics
Mathematics: Higher Level
Music
Physics
Psychology
Religious Studies
Science
Sociology
Spanish
World History

Addison Wesley Longman Limited,
Edinburgh Gate, Burnt Mill, Harlow,
Essex CM20 2JE, UK
and Associated Companies throughout the World.

First published 1994
Second edition 1998

British Library Cataloguing-in-Publication Data
A catalogue record for this book is available from the British Library.

ISBN 0582-304997

Set by 8 in 9.75/12pt Sabon

Printed in Great Britain by Henry Ling Ltd, at The Dorset Press, Dorchester, Dorset

CONTENTS

Editors' preface iv
Acknowledgements v
Information about this book vi

1 Preparing for the examination 1

2 The examinations 7

3 Topics, tasks and vocabulary 13

4 Listening 70

5 Speaking 97

6 Reading 120

7 Writing 149

8 Coursework 172

9 Grammar 179

Index 192

EDITORS' PREFACE

Longman Study Guides have been written by the people who set and mark the exams – the examiners. Examiners are aware that, due to lack of practice and poor preparation, some students achieve only the lowest grades: they are not able effectively to show the examiner what they know. These books give excellent advice about exam practice and preparation, and organizing a structured revision programme, all of which are essential for examination success. Remember: the examiners are looking for opportunities to *give* you marks, not take them away!

Longman Study Guides are designed to be used throughout the course. The self-contained chapters can be read in any order appropriate to the stage you have reached in your course. The examiner guides you through the essential parts of each topic, making helpful comments throughout.

We believe that this book, and the series as a whole, will help you establish and build your basic knowledge and examination technique skills. For additional help with exam practice and revision techniques, Addison Wesley Longman has published a series called **Longman Exam Practice Kits**, which are available from all good bookshops, or direct from Addison Wesley Longman.

GEOFF BLACK AND STUART WALL

ACKNOWLEDGEMENTS

I am grateful to the following examining boards for permission to reproduce questions, which in almost all cases are specimen questions for the 1998 examination.

Edexcel Foundation (London Examinations); Midland Examining Group (MEG); Northern Examinations and Assessment Board (NEAB); Northern Ireland Council for the Curriculum, Examinations and Assessment (NICCEA); Southern Examining Group (SEG); Welsh Joint Education Committee (WJEC).

The name 'Edexcel' is used throughout the book for references to London Examinations: a division of Edexcel Foundation.

With the exception of Recording 1, all SEG questions are specimen questions.

I am also grateful to Alasdair McKeane, for allowing me to use his work on coursework and the task list; to John Connor, for all his work on the vocabulary and the task list; to my wife, Carmen, for the checking of many details.

Note: The suggested answers provided in this book (including all hints about answers), while in accordance with normal GCSE examining practice, are the author's own and are not 'official answers' issued by the examining boards.

INFORMATION ABOUT THIS BOOK

This book has been written as a course companion for use throughout your GCSE course in Spanish. The first two chapters concentrate on study skills and examination requirements. You should read these chapters carefully as they give invaluable advice about preparing for the examinations in Listening, Reading, Speaking and Writing; about preparing coursework and details about assessment and grading. This information will be useful to you throughout your GCSE course.

Chapter 3 then turns to the topics, tasks and vocabulary that you will be expected to know for your GCSE papers. Tick the 'learnt' and 'tested' boxes in the topic checklist on pages 14–25, so that you are aware of exactly what you have and haven't revised, and what topics you need further practice on. Try to learn the vocabulary in small, manageable chunks and test yourself afterwards to check that you can remember what you have just learnt.

Chapters 4 to 8 then look at the main assessment methods for GCSE Spanish: Listening, Reading, Speaking, Writing and Coursework. Each of these chapters includes:

- an outline of how to approach the assessment and improve skills
- example examination questions with student answers
- further questions for you to practise on.

The practice questions have been divided into G, F, E tasks; D, C tasks; and B, A, A* tasks. This will help you to find your own level, but do have a go at the harder questions too – you may surprise yourself! Note that there is an audio-tape available for the Listening chapter, containing all the extracts set in the chapter. If you do not have the tape, however, then ask a friend or parent to read the transcripts found on pages 91–95 to you.

The final chapter looks at Grammar. This chapter can be used as a reference tool while working through the other chapters, and during your two-year course. However, you should also check that you understand the grammatical points raised in the chapter as this will help you to improve your Spanish (not only in Writing, but Listening, Reading and Speaking too).

The ideal way to use this book is to use it throughout your course as a **study guide**.

- After covering a new topic area at school, e.g. 'Tourism', learn the vocabulary and phrases for that topic given in Chapter 3 and check if there are any similar topics covered in the role-play sections in Chapter 5 'Speaking'.
- If you have been taught some new grammar, for example the Perfect Tense, then check that you understand it fully by reading through the explanations and examples given in Chapter 9 'Grammar' and practise applying it.
- Before attempting any written homework, look through Chapter 7 to see examples of similar questions and styles of writing, and to learn ways of improving your written work.
- Understanding the types of questions you are likely to face and what will be expected of you in the different examinations will help to improve your grade. Read the chapters on Listening, Reading, Speaking and Writing carefully. Look at the sample student answers and examiner's comments to typical questions, and then try the 'Practice questions' at the end of each chapter.
- Fill in the 'Language task list' during your two year course so that you can see which topics you need to do some more work on.

Alternatively, you could use this book as a quick **revision guide**, and work from it intensively in the period before your examination. Quick revision will help you, but remember that there is no substitute for hard work during your course.

Chapter 1

Preparing for the Examination

GETTING STARTED

In this chapter we shall look at ways of preparing for GCSE examinations. We shall first consider study skills of a general nature which should help you to make best use of your time in the period leading up to the GCSE, and which can generally be applied to other subjects as well. Then we shall consider briefly the four language skills of **listening, speaking, reading** and **writing.** Finally we shall consider a few general techniques that are important in the examination room itself.

TOPIC	STUDY	REVISION 1	REVISION 2
Attitude to the course			
Organization			
Planning your revision			
How to revise			
Learning Spanish			
In the examination			

WHAT YOU NEED TO KNOW

Attitude to the course

Success in GCSE is based firmly on what you have done during the course. In particular, a **positive attitude** and a **desire to learn** are essential. It is no good taking things easy on the assumption that you will be able to do some work at the end and then do well in the examination. You cannot learn everything you need in the last two weeks before the examination. Remember also that, since performance in Spanish is a skill, it needs to be practised regularly – and in all practice you must aim for success. Never be satisfied with work of a lower standard than you know you are capable of producing.

Organization

- **Have a routine.** Having set times when you do your work takes away much of the strain of actually making up your mind to get started.
- **Have a suitable place to study.** Keep it tidy so that you are not put off by the clutter.
- **Do work as it is set.** Don't let a backlog build up – and don't allow your regular work in Spanish to be squeezed out by the demands of coursework in other subjects.
- **Make sure you learn some new words each week.** Set yourself a target – e.g. 20 new words on a particular topic (such as eating in a restaurant) each week.
- **Revise work regularly.** Check that you can remember the vocabulary or grammar points you learned last month, last year, etc.
- **Learn from what you have done.** Check every piece of work that has been marked for you and make sure you have learnt any lessons from the marking. Work out where your weaknesses are and then plan what to do to eliminate them.
- **Plan times for relaxation and leisure interests.** These are important. If there is something you particularly want to do that requires a change in your study routine, plan it in advance so that your work gets done and, equally importantly, you enjoy the activity without having to worry about work.

Planning your revision

- **Plan well ahead.** Set specific times of the week when you concentrate on Spanish GCSE.
- **Make sure you know what each examination involves.** Check the language skills chapters in this book. Your teachers and the examining boards themselves can provide further information, if needed.
- **Use questions from specimen papers and examinations of previous years for practice.** You will find many such questions in this book.
- **Make the most of your strengths.** Be sure to revise thoroughly the things you are good at so that you get high marks for them.
- **Work at your weaknesses.** However, don't let them depress you. Remember that you can usually make up for weakness in one skill by doing particularly well in another.
- **Identify the sort of questions that are likely to be set.** Many of the tasks are very similar from one year to another – because there is a limit to the number of different things you are likely to have to do in any situation. (How many different tasks can you think of that you might reasonably have to perform in a shop?)
- **Make sure you are familiar with your dictionary.** There are differences in the way dictionaries present certain items. You will obviously need to know whether your school will provide the dictionary you use in the examination or whether you will be using your own. Then make sure you understand how that particular dictionary works. There is advice on using a dictionary in Chapter 3.

How to revise

Concentration is often the main problem with revision. If you are not careful, you can sit in front of a book, with your eyes moving steadily over the pages, only to realize after half-an-hour that you have not been thinking about what you are studying at all. Your mind has been on the television programme you watched last night, or on your plans for the coming weekend or an argument you have had. Mechanically passing your eyes over the page in that way is not revision and is of no use at all.

So how can you maintain concentration? You need to be *actively* involved in what you are doing.

- **Write notes.** One way is by writing notes, but that means notes that actively engage your mind. Again it is all too easy to copy notes mechanically, without thinking about them at all, with your mind somewhere completely different. So make sure that you set yourself tasks that make you think before you write.
- **Test yourself on the material you are revising.** Then make sure you go back and learn thoroughly what you didn't know.
- **Keep a checklist of what you have revised.** Make a list of what you are sure you now know. It will be helpful in planning your future revision and it should also give you a sense of achievement. In Chapter 3 there are boxes to tick as you learn the vocabulary for specific tasks. You can use this idea in other areas as well.
- **Set targets.** Set yourself sensible targets and give yourself small rewards when you achieve them. If you can successfully complete a particular item of revision in forty minutes, give yourself a break. (And if you complete it with thorough knowledge in thirty minutes – give yourself an extra ten minutes' break! Remember, what is important is what you learn, not how many hours you have spent at your desk!)
- **Practise vocabulary by using it in likely tasks.** Think how you might have to use the words, rather than simply what they mean. Imagine you are a customer in a shop, or trying to change money, etc.
- **Vary your activities and what you revise.** This will allow you to maintain concentration for longer.
- **Work with a friend.** Practise speaking together. Test each other, both orally and in writing.

Don't work late the night before an examination and don't indulge in panic revision just before the examination – that can often prevent you recalling effectively what you revised earlier. What you don't know by the day before the exam is almost always best left alone. Remember that in most examinations you will have a dictionary and will be able to check any words you have forgotten. Provided you have a reasonable working vocabulary, you do not need to worry at all if you forget the occasional word.

Learning Spanish

General

1. Although the four skills are tested separately, they are very closely linked in real life. This means, for example, that any work you do to improve your listening techniques will also have a positive 'spin-off' effect on the other three skills.
2. Vocabulary-learning is a chore, but it is a necessary part of your preparation. If you do not have a sound basis of vocabulary, you will simply not have time in the examination to look up in the dictionary all the words you do not know. Make sure you begin vocabulary-learning early and learn steadily, over the weeks, remembering to test yourself as you learn. Chapter 3 will help you to work your way through the topic areas you have to study in depth.
3. Grammar is an important part of any language. Although the emphasis in the GCSE is less 'academic' than in earlier examinations, the more accurate you are the higher the marks you will gain – and this is particularly true at Higher Tier. Grammar is important in helping us to understand what we hear and read, as well as in helping us to express ourselves clearly. Again, be methodical:
   (a) go over exercises you have done in class, then do them again and see if you can improve on your earlier performances;
   (b) use the Grammar section at the end of this book;
   (c) draw up a practical checklist for use before and during the examination.
4. Working with a friend can often be a helpful change from working on your own. This is especially important for speaking and vocabulary work.

Listening

This is at first sight the most difficult skill to practise on your own, but there are still plenty of things you can do. In Chapter 4 we go into detail about some of these, but the following will serve as an introduction:

- **Make use of language programmes on radio and television.** There is an increasing number of language programmes on radio and television. Listen or watch them whenever you can. Make recordings where that is possible, so that you can listen to them again. You will need to check details yourself, because broadcast series are constantly changing.

- **Listen to cassettes.** Most courses now have cassettes to accompany them, so make sure you hear them at school. You may be able to borrow listening material (both course material and past examination recordings) from your teacher or from your local library. An audio cassette is available with this book. It will help you to develop your listening (and speaking) skills.
- **Listen to Spanish radio stations.** Depending on where you live, you may be able to pick up Spanish radio stations. Or you could try Radio Spectrum International's Spanish Service, broadcasting on Mondays to Saturdays from 3 p.m. to 4 p.m. and on Sundays from 5 p.m. to 6 p.m., on 558 khz medium wave. (You will hear an interesting mixture of Spanish and South American accents.) It's a good idea to tune in occasionally to some Spanish language station – and don't worry if you can't understand very much at first. Just see, first of all, if you can recognize the occasional word. If you can do that, fairly quickly you will find that you recognize more and more and you will develop a sense of positive achievement. (If, instead, you concentrate on the fact that there is much you do not understand, you will make much less progress.)
- **Use any Spanish-speaking contacts you have.** Speak to Spanish or South American people. Talk to any friends or relatives who speak Spanish. Ask penfriends to record some Spanish for you – you can help them with their English. Blank cassettes are cheap!

Speaking

We deal in depth with preparations for Speaking in Chapter 5, but you should bear the following in mind:

- **Use the task and vocabulary lists.** The language tasks and vocabulary lists in Chapter 3 will provide you with a lot of essential material for the Speaking tests. Make sure you know what tests you have to do and which topic areas they cover. Try to anticipate likely activities for role-plays and areas for conversation.
- **Learn thoroughly the key expressions.** They are especially useful for the role-plays. Several of them occur remarkably often in the examinations – because they are used so often in real life.
- **Get used to the sound of your own voice.** The Speaking tests will almost certainly be recorded.
- **Get as much practice as you can.** Talk with your teacher, friends – anyone who speaks Spanish.
- **Make full use of this book and your textbook.** Cover all the examples they provide.

Reading

Reading is in some ways the easiest skill to revise, because material is more readily available. At GCSE you are required to read a wide range of texts in different styles, so the more you read the better.

- **Make full use of your course textbook.** It will no doubt contain much reading material, and the more modern courses provide an excellent range of texts suitable for GCSE.
- **Re-read articles you have read before.** This is one of the easiest ways of revising vocabulary. As you see words in a familiar context, you are often reminded of their meaning without having to look them up in a list or dictionary.
- **Note down vocabulary.** Make a note of any key words you did not know without looking them up. This is an invaluable step on the way to learning vocabulary.
- **Use readers.** There are some interesting readers in schools and libraries. Find out what there is and take advantage of what is 'on the doorstep'.
- **Read language magazines.** There are a number of short magazines especially designed for foreign-language learners. Ask your teacher which are most readily available in your school.
- **Read Spanish newspapers and magazines.** Do not expect to understand everything,

but, even in quite difficult texts, you will find many words you recognize and many more you can understand from the context. Advertisements in particular give many clues about the meanings of words, so that you do not have to look them up in a dictionary.

- **Use the Internet.** If you have access to the Internet, there is a great deal of material in Spanish that you can read on screen or have printed out.

Writing

Grammar and spelling will be important but the main thing is to get the message across. The more accurate you are, though, the more marks you will gain, especially in the Higher Tier.

- **Go over exercises done in class.** Try them again. See how you can improve on your first attempt.
- **Work your way through the writing tasks in this book and your course textbook.** Then check them through again.
- **Use the grammar section.** Chapter 9 contains the grammar you need in order to do well.

In the examination

Memory aids

Don't forget your 'supports', such as mnemonics, tables, key aids and checklists, which you have developed during your preparation for the written examinations. Once you have been told you can begin, make a quick note of your 'supports' *before* you start answering the questions.

Read the questions carefully

Read the questions carefully and make sure you answer ALL parts of the question, that you cover ALL tasks. This applies to ALL FOUR SKILLS!

Presentation

Whatever people may say to the contrary, a tidy, well-presented script which is easy on the eye and easy to read does create a favourable impression on examiners. It does not mean that they will award you more marks, but it will certainly do you no harm, and if an examiner cannot read clearly what you have written, then he or she cannot award marks!

Timing

Timing is critical. First check you know exactly how long you have for each test.

You will have been working to timed exercises in your preparation for the examination so you should have a clear idea of how long you will need for a particular exercise. Make sure you distribute your time in the examination wisely so that you don't spend too long on one question and then have to rush things at the end. You should also include in your schedule enough time to *re-read* and *check* your answers. This is especially important for the Writing tests, but it is still important for the other skills. In Chapter 7 there are suggestions for drawing up your own grammar checklist and using it in the examination.

Planning answers

In the Writing papers, especially in the Higher Tier, you will need to plan carefully what to write, by making notes of key vocabulary, structures and idioms, before you write your answer.

You will have to keep to fairly strict word limits, and in some cases the space provided for your answer will not allow you to write much, e.g. for postcards.

You must also remember that you have to cover all the tasks, so you have to leave yourself enough words and room to do this.

In both Foundation and Higher Tier Writing you will be attempting to 'show off' what you know, so it's a great help to jot down a few interesting items of vocabulary and some idioms before you start writing your actual answer – but do make sure they are not completely irrelevant to the task you have been set!

Answer all the questions

There may be occasions when you are genuinely stuck on a particular question. Do not waste time over it. Write yourself a note of the question number and go on to the next question. Don't forget to come back to the unanswered question later though!

If all else fails, don't just leave a blank space – make a sensible guess based on what seems possible. Remember, you never lose out by 'having a go'.

Re-read and check

Use your checklist wisely, make sure you have in fact covered all you were required to do.

And finally ...

Work your way thoroughly through the book and persevere. It will be worth it. GOOD LUCK!

Chapter 2

The examinations

GETTING STARTED

This chapter sets out the aims of GCSE Spanish and the nature of the examinations. It briefly outlines what the examining boards expect you to know, including the differences between Full and Short Courses, and the way in which the examinations are organized in Tiers for the different skills. It also includes information about the availability of Coursework options and when you are allowed to use a dictionary. Finally, it shows how your entry for different Tiers affects the grades you can be awarded.

TOPIC	STUDY	REVISION 1	REVISION 2
Aims of GCSE Spanish			
The nature of the examination			
The defined content			
The GCSE Full Course			
The GCSE Short Course			
Assessment			
Dictionaries			
Grades and entry levels			
Examining boards			

WHAT YOU NEED TO KNOW

Aims of GCSE Spanish

There are differences in the way in which the different GCSE examining boards set out their aims in their Spanish syllabuses. Some give more detail than others, but it is clear that differences are more a matter of presentation than of principle. The aims that are clearly common to all are:

1. To develop the ability to understand and use Spanish effectively for purposes of practical communication.
2. To form a sound base of the skills, language and attitudes required for further study, work and leisure.
3. To offer insights into the culture and civilization of countries where the language is spoken.
4. To develop an awareness of the nature of language and language learning, including an understanding of the grammar of Spanish.
5. To allow candidates to make imaginative and creative use of Spanish and to understand the language when used in imaginative or creative contexts.
6. To provide enjoyment and intellectual stimulation.
7. To encourage positive attitudes to foreign language learning and to speakers of foreign languages and a positive approach to other cultures and civilizations.
8. To promote learning skills of a more general application (e.g. analysis, memorizing, drawing inferences, use of reference materials including dictionaries, use of information technology).

Other aims mentioned by certain boards include.

- Understanding language in its cultural context.
- Promoting in candidates a better understanding of themselves and of their own culture through comparison with the customs of the Spanish-speaking world.
- Developing the ability to engage in pair work, group work and independent learning.

Obviously not all of these aims can be directly tested in the GCSE examinations, where the emphasis is very much on understanding and on effective practical communication in Spanish.

The nature of the examination

The examination is based mainly on situations that you might find yourself in when dealing with Spanish speakers. The tasks set are generally ones that you might possibly have to carry out in real life. Reading and listening material is normally authentic Spanish material (possibly edited), rather than artificial texts invented purely to test English-speaking (or Welsh-speaking) candidates.

A key aspect of the GCSE is that it should test what candidates know, understand and can do. The emphasis is on success and the tasks set are therefore realistic in the demands they make on candidates. Marks are awarded for what is actually achieved, rather than being deducted for every mistake (which was often the case in earlier examinations). There are sections which everyone, no matter what their level of ability, should be capable of doing successfully.

The defined content

Each of the examining boards has published a **Defined Content**, which includes:

- A list of **areas of experience and topics** to be covered.
- A list of the **language tasks** students should be able to perform.
- A minimum core **vocabulary list**.
- A list of the **grammar** candidates are expected to know.
- A list of common **rubrics or instructions** used in setting the questions.

Candidates (and their teachers) can be sure that they will not be tested on any unforeseen grammar.

All the examining boards include in the introduction to their minimum core vocabulary list the following statement: '**The assessment tasks at Foundation Tier will be based on the minimum core vocabulary list but candidates should also expect to encounter unfamiliar**

vocabulary.' In most of the examinations candidates will have a Spanish–English, English–Spanish dictionary available to help them to deal with unfamiliar words.

The GCSE Full Course

The GCSE Full Course develops further the National Curriculum Areas of Experience prescribed for Key Stage 3 and adds two new areas. The five Areas of Experience are:

A. *Everyday Activities*
including: the language of the classroom
home life and school
food, health and fitness

B. *Personal and Social Life*
including: self, family and personal relationships
free time and social activities
holidays and special occasions

C. *The World Around Us*
including: home town and local area
the natural and made environment
people, places and customs

D. *The World of Work*
including: further education and training
careers and employment
language and communication in the workplace

E. *The International World*
including: tourism at home and abroad
life in other countries and communities
world events and issues

The GCSE Short Course

Short Courses in Spanish (intended to require half the study time of the Full Course) are offered by Edexcel, MEG, NEAB and WJEC. Candidates following a Short Course in Spanish study *two* of the Areas of Experience. Area B (Personal and Social Life) is compulsory for all four boards. For MEG, NEAB and WJEC the second area studied is Area D (The World of Work). Edexcel papers allow candidates to choose either Area D or Area E (The International World).

Assessment

The four language skills of listening, speaking, reading and writing are assessed separately and carry equal weight. The tests in the different skills are divided into two tiers, so that there are normally eight tests:

- Foundation Listening
- Foundation Speaking
- Foundation Reading
- Foundation Writing
- Higher Listening
- Higher Speaking
- Higher Reading
- Higher Writing

The Foundation Tier covers Grades G–C and the Higher Tier covers Grades D–A*. You enter for one tier only in each skill, but it is possible to enter different tiers in different skills, so that particular strengths and weaknesses can be catered for. The Speaking tests will be conducted by your own teacher and will be tape-recorded.

For all examining boards Speaking tests take place between March and May and Listening, Reading and Writing tests take place between late May and the first week in July. Details of the final examination components are shown in Table 2.1. (Details of the SEG scheme are given below in Table 2.3).

Coursework

Edexcel, MEG, NEAB and WJEC all offer a written coursework alternative to the Writing test. In addition, Edexcel offers a spoken coursework alternative to the Speaking test, but candidates are *not* allowed to take both the written and spoken coursework options.

The coursework option is not available in the WJEC Short Course.

In the SEG scheme, all four skills are involved in coursework at some point, with two of the four modules being assessed by means of coursework.

Advice on coursework is given in Chapter 8, but the information and practice given in Chapters 4 to 7 are also important for those doing coursework. Coursework options are shown in Table 2.2.

Table 2.1 GCSE Examining Board final examination components

Examining Board	Edexcel		MEG		NEAB		NICCEA		SEG		WJEC	
Level	F	H	F	H	F	H	F	H	F	H	F	H
Listening Time allowed (minutes)	25	35	40	40	30	40	30	30	20	20	45	45
Speaking Time allowed (minutes)	8–10	10–12	10–12	12–15	8–10	10–12	10	10	5	8	10	12
Role-plays	2	2	2	2	2	2	2	2	1	1	2	2
Conversation	C	C	C	C	C	C	C	C	C	C	C	C
Presentation	P	P	P	P	P	P						
Reading Time allowed (minutes)	30	45	50	50	30	50	40	40	30	30	45	45
Writing Time allowed (minutes)	30	50	50	50	40	60	45	45	30	30	45	45

Key:
F = Foundation
H = Higher

Table 2.2 Coursework options

	Edexcel	MEG	NEAB	NICCEA	SEG	WJEC
Listening	–	–	–	–	M1	–
Speaking	Yes*	–	–	–	M1 + M3	–
Reading	–	–	–	–	M1	–
Writing	Yes*	Yes	Yes	–	M3	Yes

* Candidates entered for Edexcel certification are permitted to take only one of the coursework options.

M: In the SEG modular scheme coursework is compulsory in Modules 1 and 3 as shown.

SEG modular assessment

Table 2.3 SEG modular scheme

	Module 1 (Full range)	Module 2 (2 Tiers)	Module 3 (Full range)	Module 4 (2 Tiers)	TOTAL
Listening	C 5%	EMT 10%	–	TE 10%	25%
Speaking	C 5%	–	C 5%	TE 15%	25%
Reading	C 5%	EMT 10%	–	TE 10%	25%
Writing	–	–	C 10%	TE 15%	25%
TOTAL	15%	20%	15%	50%	100%

C = Coursework
EMT = End-of-module test
TE = Terminal examination

While all the other examining boards assess candidates by means of a final examination, with a coursework option which can account for 25% of the marks, the SEG scheme is assessed in four modules:

- Module 1 (Coursework): Spring Term, first year of course.
- Module 2 (End-of-module test): Summer Term, first year of course.
- Module 3 (Coursework): Spring Term, second year of course.
- Module 4 (Terminal examination): Summer Term, second year of course.
- Details are shown in Table 2.3.

Dictionaries

Bilingual (Spanish–English, English–Spanish), dictionaries are permitted in all Reading and Writing components. They are also permitted during the preparation stage of Speaking components. In Listening tests, NEAB permits the use of dictionaries during a five-minute reading period at the beginning and a five-minute period at the end. WJEC allows dictionaries for a ten-minute reading period at the beginning and also at the end of the test. In all cases, dictionaries may not be used while the tape-recording is being played. Details about use of dictionaries are summarized in Table 2.4.

Table 2.4 Use of dictionaries

	Edexcel	MEG	NEAB	NICCEA	SEG	WJEC
Listening	No	No	B5 + E5	No	No	B10 + E
Speaking	Prep	Prep	Prep	Prep	Prep	Prep
Reading	Yes	Yes	Yes	Yes	Yes	Yes
Writing	Yes	Yes	Yes	Yes	Yes	Yes
Written coursework	Yes	Yes	Yes	N/A	Yes	Yes
Speaking coursework	Prep	N/A	N/A	N/A	Prep	N/A

Yes Dictionaries may be used at any time during the test.
Prep Dictionaries may be used during the preparation period for the Speaking test.
B5 Dictionaries may be used while looking at the questions for 5 minutes before the tape is played.
B10 Dictionaries may be used while looking at the questions for 10 minutes before the tape is played.
E Dictionaries may be used after the end of the recording.
E5 Dictionaries may be used for five minutes after the end of the recording.

Grades and entry levels

There are two tiers of entry: Foundation Tier and Higher Tier. Candidates are allowed to enter for only one tier in any skill (Listening, Speaking, Reading or Writing), but it is possible to enter for different tiers in different skills (e.g. Foundation Listening and Writing with Higher Speaking and Reading).

A candidate who enters for Foundation Tier in all four skills can be awarded any grade up to C. A candidate who enters for Higher Tier in all four skills can be awarded any grade from D to A*, but could be ungraded if he or she fails to meet the minimum requirement for Grade D. Grade A* is available only to candidates who enter for the Higher Tier in all four skills.

Questions within the examination papers are targeted at particular levels of performance and all boards have some degree of overlap within their papers, using questions targeted at Grades D and C in both Foundation and Higher Tiers. For this reason we have divided the tasks in the different components into three groups:

- **Tasks aimed at Grades G, F and E (Foundation Tier only).**
- **Tasks aimed at Grades D and C (Foundation and Higher Tiers).**
- **Tasks aimed at Grades B, A and A* (Higher Tier only).**

An awareness of these three different groups of tasks will be helpful in understanding the way Chapters 4, 5, 6 and 7 are organized.

Examining boards

Details of the examining board addresses and telephone numbers follow.

Edexcel

Edexcel Foundation
Stewart House, 32 Russell Square, London WC1B 5DN
Telephone: 0171 393 4444; Fax: 0171 393 4445.

MEG

Midland Examining Group
1 Hills Road, Cambridge CB1 2EU
Telephone: 01223 553311; Fax: 01223 460278.

NEAB

Northern Examinations and Assessment Board
Devas Street, Manchester M15 6EX
Telephone: 0161 953 1180; Fax: 0161 273 7572.

NICCEA

Northern Ireland Council for the Curriculum, Examinations and Assessment
29 Clarendon Road, Belfast BT1 3BG
Telephone: 01232 261200; Fax: 01232 261234.

SEG

Southern Examining Group
Stag Hill House, Guildford GU2 5XJ
Telephone: 01483 506506; Fax: 01483 300152.

WJEC

Welsh Joint Education Committee
245 Western Avenue, Cardiff CF5 2YX
Telephone: 01222 265000; Fax: 01222 575994.

IGCSE

International General Certificate of Secondary Education
University of Cambridge Local Examinations Syndicate
1 Hills Road, Cambridge CB1 2EU
Telephone: 01223 553311; Fax: 01223 460278.

When contacting the examining boards you will need to ask for the Publications Department and request an order form to be sent to you. Be prepared to send a cheque or postal order with your order.

Chapter 3

Topics, tasks and vocabulary

GETTING STARTED

The National Curriculum Programme of Study for Modern Foreign Languages specifies the areas of experience that are to be covered in any GCSE course, but it does not specify the vocabulary to be used. The National Criteria for GCSE require each examining board to publish, for Foundation Tier only, a minimum core vocabulary list. The boards normally restrict the vocabulary that they test for Grades G, F and E to their published list, but for all tasks aimed above that level you will need a wider range of words than the minimum core vocabulary. If you learn the words in the vocabulary lists in this chapter you will be well prepared to perform very successfully at either Foundation or Higher Tier.

The National Criteria also state that rubrics (the instructions given on the question papers) should normally be in the language in which the candidate is expected to respond. This means that all instructions on Speaking and Writing papers and at least 80 per cent of the instructions on Listening and Reading papers are likely to be in Spanish. At the end of this chapter is a list of key words and phrases used in Spanish rubrics and you should make sure you could understand those expressions if you found them on a question paper.

The chapter includes some advice on using a dictionary and a section on how to learn vocabulary effectively. Unless you know most of the words that occur in an examination, you will not be able to cope, even with the help of a dictionary. The main message in learning vocabulary is to do a little but often.

TOPIC	STUDY	REVISION 1	REVISION 2
The Areas of Experience			
Settings			
Language tasks by topic			
Using a dictionary			
Learning vocabulary			
Vocabulary lists			
Key words and expressions			
Examination rubrics			

WHAT YOU NEED TO KNOW

The Areas of Experience

The **Areas of Experience** to be covered are specified in the National Curriculum for Modern Foreign Languages. They are:

A. Everyday Activities
B. Personal and Social Life
C. The World Around Us
D. The World of Work
E. The International World

These were listed, together with some of the topics within them, in Chapter 2, where we also set out which are required for the GCSE Short Course.

Later in this chapter you will find the vocabulary you will need in order to deal with the areas of experience. To avoid too much repetition, I have listed about 400 key words and expressions separately at the beginning of the vocabulary lists.

Settings

It is often helpful to consider the places where, in real life, you might be required to carry out the language tasks and use the vocabulary. The most likely settings are:

- School
- Home
- Town
- Place of work
- Places of entertainment
- Places of interest
- Private transport
- Public transport
- Tourist information office
- Shops and markets
- Cafés and restaurants
- Hotels, campsites etc.
- Country, seaside
- Dentist's, doctor's, chemist's
- Garage, petrol station
- Bank, exchange office
- Lost property office, police station

Language tasks by topic

A comprehensive list of the things you will be expected to do is given below. It may appear somewhat off-putting at first, but you will soon see that there are many things, such as giving your name and age, that you can already do well. It also gives you a clear point of reference as to what else you need to learn!

You need to work your way through the list systematically and check that you can perform all the tasks. To help you to check your progress through the tasks, two boxes are provided next to them in which you can tick off (or even date) items as you learn them and again when you have been tested at a later date (either by yourself or by a friend or a by a member of your family).

Language problems	*Learned*	*Tested*
▶ Say whether or not you understand.	☐	☐
▶ Ask for and understand the spelling of names, place names, etc.	☐	☐
▶ Ask if someone speaks English or Spanish.	☐	☐
▶ State how well or how little you speak and understand Spanish.	☐	☐
▶ Ask what things are called in Spanish.	☐	☐
▶ Ask what words or phrases mean.	☐	☐
▶ Say you do not know (something).	☐	☐
▶ Say you have forgotten (something).	☐	☐
▶ Apologize.	☐	☐
▶ Ask whether, or state that, something is correct.	☐	☐

	Learned	Tested
▶ Say for how long you have been learning Spanish and any other languages you know.	☐	☐
▶ Ask someone to explain something, to correct mistakes.	☐	☐
▶ Ask how something is pronounced.	☐	☐

A1 School

	Learned	*Tested*
▶ Describe your school/college and its facilities: state the type, size and location of your school and describe the buildings.	☐	☐
▶ Describe daily routines: when school begins, ends; how many lessons there are and how long they last; break times and lunch times; homework; how you travel to and from school.	☐	☐
▶ Discuss your school year and holidays: subjects studied and preferences; clubs, sports, trips and other activities.	☐	☐

A2 Home life

	Learned	*Tested*
▶ Discuss where and under what conditions you and others live.	☐	☐
▶ Say whether you live in a house, flat, etc., and ask others the same.	☐	☐
▶ Describe your house, flat, etc. and its location.	☐	☐
▶ Mention or enquire about availability of the most essential pieces of furniture, amenities, services.	☐	☐
▶ Say whether you have a room of your own and describe your room or the room where you sleep.	☐	☐
▶ Say what jobs you do around the home.	☐	☐
▶ Ask where places and things are in a house.	☐	☐
▶ Say you need soap, toothpaste, or a towel.	☐	☐
▶ Invite someone to come in, sit down.	☐	☐
▶ Thank somebody for hospitality.	☐	☐
▶ Offer and ask for help to do something about the house.	☐	☐
▶ Ask permission to use or do things when you are the guest of a Spanish-speaking family.	☐	☐
▶ Give and seek information about members of the family.	☐	☐
▶ Describe members of the family and their occupations.	☐	☐
▶ Give and seek information about daily routine.	☐	☐
▶ Say what time you usually get up and go to bed, have meals, how you spend your evenings and weekends.	☐	☐
▶ Express hunger and thirst.	☐	☐
▶ Ask about time and place of meals.	☐	☐
▶ Ask for food and table articles (including asking for more, a little, a lot).	☐	☐
▶ React to offers of food (accept, decline, apologize, express pleasure).	☐	☐
▶ Express appreciation and pay compliments.	☐	☐
▶ Respond to a toast (e.g. *Salud*).	☐	☐

A3 Health, fitness and welfare

General	*Learned*	*Tested*
▶ Refer to parts of the body where you are in pain or discomfort.	☐	☐

Hygiene

▶ Obtain toiletries and other things you need.	☐	☐

Illness and injury

▶ State how you feel (well, ill, better, hot, cold, hungry, thirsty, tired) and ask others how they feel.	☐	☐
▶ Say you would like to rest or go to bed.	☐	☐
▶ Call for help.	☐	☐
▶ Warn about danger.	☐	☐
▶ Say you would like to lie down.	☐	☐
▶ Respond to an enquiry about how long an ailment or symptom has persisted.	☐	☐
▶ Say you would like to see a doctor.	☐	☐
▶ Deal with contact with the medical services.	☐	☐
▶ Say whether you take medicine regularly, and if so, what.	☐	☐
▶ Say whether or not you are insured.	☐	☐
▶ Tell others about medical facilities, surgery hours.	☐	☐

At the chemist's

▶ Report minor ailments (e.g. temperature, cold, sunburn) and injuries.	☐	☐
▶ Ask for items in a chemist's and ask if they have anything for particular ailments.	☐	☐

Accidents

▶ Ask or advise someone to phone the doctor, police, fire brigade, ambulance, consulate, acquaintance, etc.	☐	☐
▶ Ask for someone's name and address.	☐	☐
▶ Suggest filling in a road accident form.	☐	☐
▶ Describe an accident.	☐	☐
▶ Ask or say whether it is serious.	☐	☐
▶ Deny responsibility and say whose fault it was.	☐	☐

A4 Food and drink

General	*Learned*	*Tested*
▶ Discuss your likes, dislikes and preferences and those of others.	☐	☐
▶ Discuss your typical meals, meal times and eating habits.	☐	☐
▶ Buy food and drink (see C4 'Shopping').	☐	☐
▶ Explain to a visitor what a dish is, or what it contains.	☐	☐

Café, restaurant and other public places

	Learned	Tested
▶ Attract the attention of the waiter/waitress.	☐	☐
▶ Order a drink, snack or meal.	☐	☐
▶ Ask for a particular fixed-price menu.	☐	☐
▶ Say how many there are in your group.	☐	☐
▶ Ask for a table (for a certain number of people).	☐	☐
▶ Ask about the availability of certain dishes and drinks.	☐	☐
▶ Ask for an explanation or a description of something on the menu.	☐	☐
▶ Express opinions about a meal or dish.	☐	☐
▶ Accept or reject suggestions.	☐	☐
▶ Ask if the service charge is included.	☐	☐
▶ Ask about the location of facilities (e.g. toilets, telephone).	☐	☐

B1 Self, family and friends	*Learned*	*Tested*
▶ Give your identity and information about others (e.g. members of your family or host family).	☐	☐
▶ Seek information from others on the following points:		
– Names (including spelling out the name of your home town).	☐	☐
– Address and telephone number.	☐	☐
– Ages and birthdays.	☐	☐
– Nationality.	☐	☐
– Religion.	☐	☐
– Family and relatives	☐	☐
▶ Give general descriptions including sex, marital status, physical appearance, character or disposition of yourself and others.	☐	☐
▶ Describe your likes and dislikes (with regard to other people and other topics in the syllabus).	☐	☐
▶ Describe your pets and other livestock and undomesticated creatures.	☐	☐

B2 Free time and social activities	*Learned*	*Tested*
▶ Discuss pocket money and part-time work.	☐	☐
▶ Talk about hobbies.	☐	☐
▶ Discuss sporting activities.	☐	☐
▶ Describe different sorts of film, play and concert.	☐	☐
▶ Discuss a performance, giving your opinion.	☐	☐
▶ Know what sorts of TV programme there are.	☐	☐
▶ Discuss your viewing habits.	☐	☐
▶ Give your opinion on different programmes.	☐	☐
▶ Give reasons for your opinions.	☐	☐

- Deal with situations at the box office for:
  - A play. ☐ ☐
  - A sporting event. ☐ ☐
  - A concert. ☐ ☐
  - A film. ☐ ☐

B3 Meeting people	*Learned*	*Tested*
▶ Greet someone and respond to greetings.	☐	☐
▶ Ask how someone is and reply to similar enquiries.	☐	☐
▶ Say you are pleased to meet someone.	☐	☐
▶ Introduce yourself.	☐	☐
▶ Introduce an acquaintance to someone else.	☐	☐
▶ Give, receive and exchange gifts.	☐	☐

B4 Arranging a meeting or an activity	*Learned*	*Tested*
▶ Find out what a friend wants to do.	☐	☐
▶ Ask what is on TV or at the cinema.	☐	☐
▶ Express preferences for an activity (e.g. watching TV, going out, visiting a friend).	☐	☐
▶ Invite someone to go out (stating when and where).	☐	☐
▶ Suggest going to a particular place, event or on a visit.	☐	☐
▶ Accept or decline invitations.	☐	☐
▶ Express pleasure.	☐	☐
▶ State likes and dislikes.	☐	☐
▶ State that something is possible, impossible, probable or certain.	☐	☐
▶ Ask about, suggest or confirm a time and place to meet.	☐	☐
▶ Ask about and state the cost (of entry, etc.).	☐	☐

B5 Holidays

General	*Learned*	*Tested*
▶ Say where you normally spend your holidays; how long they last; with whom you go on holiday; what you normally do; and understand others giving the above information.	☐	☐
▶ Describe a previous holiday; where you went; with whom you went; how you went, and for how long; where you stayed; what the weather was like; what you saw and did; what your general impressions were; and understand others giving the same information.	☐	☐
▶ Describe your holiday plans.	☐	☐
▶ Say whether you have been abroad (e.g. to a Spanish-speaking country) and give details if applicable.	☐	☐
▶ Supply information about travel documents.	☐	☐

Tourist information office

	Learned	Tested
▶ Ask for and understand information about a town or region (maps, brochures of hotels and campsites).	☐	☐
▶ Ask for and understand details of excursions, shows, places of interest (location, costs, times).	☐	☐
▶ Give information about your own area, or one you have visited, to others (e.g. prospective tourists).	☐	☐
▶ React to (i.e. welcome or reject) suggestions about activities and places of interest.	☐	☐
▶ Write a short letter asking for information and brochures about a town or region and its tourist attractions.	☐	☐

B6 Festivals and special occasions

(For vocabulary see B1, B5, C6)

	Learned	*Tested*
▶ Talk about special occasions and anniversaries (e.g. your own and other family birthdays, weddings).	☐	☐
▶ Give information and express opinions about festivals/special occasions in your own area.	☐	☐
▶ Give information about special excursions and visits.	☐	☐

C1 Home town and local environment

	Learned	*Tested*
▶ Give information about your home town or village and surrounding areas.	☐	☐
▶ Seek information from others, with respect to:		
– Location.	☐	☐
– Character.	☐	☐
– Amenities, attractions, features of interest, entertainment.	☐	☐
▶ Express a simple opinion about your own town or someone else's town.	☐	☐
▶ Give full descriptions of your home town/village or that of others, and of the surrounding area and region.	☐	☐
▶ Outline possibilities for sightseeing.	☐	☐

C2 Finding the way

	Learned	*Tested*
▶ Attract the attention of a passer-by.	☐	☐
▶ Ask where a place is.	☐	☐
▶ Ask the way (to a place).	☐	☐
▶ Ask if it is a long way (to a place).	☐	☐
▶ Ask if a place is nearby.	☐	☐
▶ Ask if there is a place or an amenity nearby.	☐	☐
▶ Understand directions.	☐	☐
▶ Ask if there is a bus, train, tram or coach.	☐	☐
▶ Ask someone to repeat what they have said.	☐	☐

	Learned	Tested
▶ Say you do not understand.	☐	☐
▶ Thank people.	☐	☐
▶ Give directions to strangers.	☐	☐
▶ State and enquire about distances.	☐	☐

C3 Weather

	Learned	*Tested*
▶ Describe or comment upon current weather conditions.	☐	☐
▶ Ask about weather conditions in the country you are visiting.	☐	☐
▶ Describe the general climate of your own country and ask about the climate in another country.	☐	☐
▶ Understand simple predictions about weather conditions.	☐	☐
▶ Understand spoken and written weather forecasts.	☐	☐

C4 Shopping

	Learned	*Tested*
▶ Ask for information about supermarkets, shopping centres, markets, shops.	☐	☐
▶ Ask where specific shops and departments are.	☐	☐
▶ Discuss shopping habits.	☐	☐
Shops and markets		
▶ Ask whether particular goods are available.	☐	☐
▶ Ask for particular items (mentioning e.g. colour, size, whom it is for, etc.).	☐	☐
▶ Find out how much things cost.	☐	☐
▶ Say an item is (not) satisfactory or too expensive, small, big, etc.	☐	☐
▶ Say you will (not) take or prefer something.	☐	☐
▶ Express quantity required (including weights, volumes, containers).	☐	☐
▶ Find out opening and closing times.	☐	☐
▶ Say that is all you require.	☐	☐
▶ Enquire about costs and prices.	☐	☐
▶ Pay for items.	☐	☐
▶ State whether you have enough money.	☐	☐
▶ Understand currencies used in Spanish-speaking countries, including written and printed prices.	☐	☐
▶ Ask for small change.	☐	☐
▶ Return unsatisfactory goods and ask for a refund or replacement.	☐	☐

C5 Services

Post Office	*Learned*	*Tested*
▶ Ask where a post office or letter box is.	☐	☐
▶ Ask how much it costs to send letters, post cards or parcels to a particular country or within the country.	☐	☐

- Say whether you would like to send letters, postcards or parcels. ☐ ☐
- Buy stamps of a particular value. ☐ ☐
- Find out opening and closing times. ☐ ☐
- Say that is all you require. ☐ ☐
- Give and seek information about where phone calls can be made. ☐ ☐

Bank or foreign exchange office

- Say you would like to change traveller's cheques or money (including sterling). ☐ ☐
- Ask for coins or notes of a particular denomination. ☐ ☐
- Give proof of identity (e.g. show passport). ☐ ☐
- Cope with any likely eventuality that may arise while using a bank or foreign exchange office to change currency or cheques. ☐ ☐

Lost property

- Report a loss or theft, stating what you have lost, when and where it was lost or left, describing the item (size, shape, colour, make, contents). ☐ ☐
- Express surprise, pleasure, disappointment, anger. ☐ ☐

Having things repaired or cleaned

- Report an accident, damage done or breakdown. ☐ ☐
- Ask if shoes, clothes, camera, etc. can be repaired. ☐ ☐
- Explain what is wrong. ☐ ☐
- Ask for, and offer, advice about getting something repaired or cleaned. ☐ ☐
- Find out how long it will take, what it will cost, when it will be ready. ☐ ☐
- Thank, complain, express disappointment, pleasure. ☐ ☐
- Suggest the need for repair or cleaning and report or comment on any action taken. ☐ ☐

C6 Getting around

Public transport — *Learned* *Tested*

- Ask if there is a train, bus, ship, hovercraft or plane to a particular place. ☐ ☐
- Buy tickets, stating:
  - – Destination. ☐ ☐
  - – Single or return. ☐ ☐
  - – Class of travel. ☐ ☐
  - – Proposed times of departure and arrival. ☐ ☐
- Ask about the cost of tickets. ☐ ☐
- Ask about times of departure and arrival. ☐ ☐
- Ask and check whether it is:
  - – The right platform. ☐ ☐
  - – The right station. ☐ ☐
  - – The right line or bus, tram, coach or stop. ☐ ☐
- Ask about the location of facilities, e.g. bus stop, waiting room, information office, toilets. ☐ ☐

- Ask if and/or where it is necessary to change buses, trains, trams or coaches. ☐ ☐
- Ask or state whether a seat is free. ☐ ☐
- Understand information given in brochures and tables. ☐ ☐
- Write a letter about requirements for travel arrangements and give this information to others. ☐ ☐
- Ask how to get to a place by bus, train, tram, tube or coach and give this information to others. ☐ ☐
- Reserve a seat. ☐ ☐
- Ask for information, timetables or a plan. ☐ ☐
- Ask about price reductions and supplements. ☐ ☐
- Make arrangements for taking, leaving or sending luggage. ☐ ☐
- Deal with an element of the unexpected in travel arrangments (e.g. delayed or cancelled departures, mislaid tickets, documents, lost luggage). ☐ ☐

Travel by air or sea

- Buy a ticket. ☐ ☐
- Ask about the cost of a flight or crossing. ☐ ☐
- Say where you would like to sit. ☐ ☐
- Ask about times of departure and arrival. ☐ ☐
- Inform someone about your proposed times of arrival and departure. ☐ ☐
- Check which is the right flight, ferry or hovercraft. ☐ ☐
- Ask about the location of facilities. ☐ ☐
- Say whether you wish to declare anything at the customs. ☐ ☐

Private transport

- Buy petrol by type, volume or price. ☐ ☐
- Ask for the tank to be filled up. ☐ ☐
- Ask the cost. ☐ ☐
- Ask someone to check oil, water and tyres. ☐ ☐
- Ask where facilities are. ☐ ☐
- Ask about availability of facilities nearby. ☐ ☐
- Obtain and give information about routes, types of roads, traffic rules, parking facilities. ☐ ☐
- Report a breakdown, giving location and other relevant information. ☐ ☐
- Report a road accident. ☐ ☐
- Ask for technical help. ☐ ☐
- Pay and ask for a receipt. ☐ ☐

D1 Further education and training *Learned* *Tested*

- Discuss what sort of education you have had, propose to continue with, and at what types of educational establishment. ☐ ☐
- Talk about examinations. ☐ ☐

See also A1 School

D2 Careers and employment	*Learned*	*Tested*
▶ Discuss your plans and hopes for the future including:		
– Immediate plans for the coming months.	☐	☐
– Plans for the time after the completion of compulsory education.	☐	☐
– Where you would like to work, giving reasons as appropriate.	☐	☐
– Occupations.	☐	☐
▶ Say whether you have a part time job, if so what job, what working hours, how much you earn.	☐	☐

D3 Travel to work and school	*Learned*	*Tested*
▶ Say how you get to school/place of work (means of transport, if any; duration of journey).	☐	☐
▶ Understand and give information about other journeys.	☐	☐

D4 Advertising and publicity	*Learned*	*Tested*
▶ Understand a range of small ads and other posters, and broadcast advertising.	☐	☐

D5 Communication	*Learned*	*Tested*
▶ Ask for a telephone number and give your own telephone number.	☐	☐
▶ Answer a phone call, stating who you are.	☐	☐
▶ Make a phone call and ask to speak to someone.	☐	☐
▶ Ask someone to telephone you.	☐	☐
▶ Find out if others can be contacted by telephone.	☐	☐
▶ Tell others you will telephone them.	☐	☐
▶ Ask for coins.	☐	☐
▶ Ask for a reversed charge call.	☐	☐
▶ Buy a phone card.	☐	☐

D6 Language at work *(For vocabulary see A1, D2 and p. 31)*	*Learned*	*Tested*
▶ Understand instructions and signs in school or the workplace.	☐	☐
▶ Fill in simple forms relating to jobs.	☐	☐
▶ Write a simple letter of application for a job.	☐	☐
▶ Ask someone to repeat what they said.	☐	☐

E1 Life in other countries	*Learned*	*Tested*
▶ Understand names of countries, nationalities and languages commonly encountered.	☐	☐
▶ Describe a part of a country where the target language is spoken.	☐	☐
▶ Describe foodstuffs from other countries (see A4 'Food and drink').	☐	☐

E2 Tourism	*Learned*	*Tested*
▶ Discuss past and future holidays.	☐	☐
▶ Give opinions.	☐	☐
▶ Deal with the tourist office.	☐	☐

E3 Accommodation

General	*Learned*	*Tested*
▶ Describe accommodation you use or have used.	☐	☐
▶ Write a short letter asking about the availability and price of accommodation at a hotel, campsite or youth hostel and about amenities available.	☐	☐
▶ Write a short letter booking such accommodation.	☐	☐
▶ Read and understand relevant information about accommodation (e.g. brochures).	☐	☐
▶ Make complaints.	☐	☐
Hotel		
▶ Ask if there are rooms available.	☐	☐
▶ State when you require a room/rooms and for how long.	☐	☐
▶ Say what sort of room is required.	☐	☐
▶ Ask the cost (per night, per person, per room).	☐	☐
▶ Say it is too expensive.	☐	☐
▶ Ask to see the room(s).	☐	☐
▶ Accept or reject a room.	☐	☐
▶ Check into a hotel.	☐	☐
▶ Say that you have (not) reserved accommodation.	☐	☐
▶ Identify yourself.	☐	☐
▶ Ask if there is a particular facility (e.g. restaurant) in or near the hotel.	☐	☐
▶ Ask where the facilities are, e.g. telephone, car park, lift, lounge.	☐	☐
▶ Ask if meals are included.	☐	☐
▶ Ask what meals are available.	☐	☐
▶ Ask the times of meals.	☐	☐
▶ Ask for the key.	☐	☐
▶ Say you would like to pay.	☐	☐
Youth hostel		
▶ Ask if there is any room.	☐	☐
▶ State when and for how long the rooms are required.	☐	☐
▶ State how many males and females require accommodation.	☐	☐
▶ Say you have (not) reserved.	☐	☐
▶ Identify yourself.	☐	☐
▶ Ask the cost (per night, per person or facility).	☐	☐
▶ Ask if there is a particular facility in or near the hostel.	☐	☐
▶ Ask where the facilities are.	☐	☐
▶ Say you would like to pay.	☐	☐
▶ Ask about meal times.	☐	☐
▶ Ask about opening and closing times.	☐	☐
▶ Say you have a sleeping bag.	☐	☐
▶ Say you wish to hire a sleeping bag.	☐	☐

Campsite

- Ask if there is any room. ☐ ☐
- State when and for how long you will be staying. ☐ ☐
- Say you have (not) made a reservation. ☐ ☐
- Identify yourself. ☐ ☐
- Say how many tents, caravans, people or vehicles it is for. ☐ ☐
- Say how many children and adults are in the group. ☐ ☐
- Ask the cost (per night, per person, per tent, caravan, vehicle or facility). ☐ ☐
- Say it is too expensive. ☐ ☐
- Ask if there is a particular facility on or near the site. ☐ ☐
- Ask where the facilities are. ☐ ☐
- Buy essential supplies. ☐ ☐
- Ask about rules and regulations. ☐ ☐

Holiday home in Spain

- Describe your holiday home. ☐ ☐
- Discuss advantages and disadvantages. ☐ ☐
- Deal with reservation problems. ☐ ☐

E4 The wider world; world events and issues

Learned *Tested*

- Talk and understand about Spanish-speaking and other countries. ☐ ☐
- Talk and understand about people and nationalities. ☐ ☐
- Follow the recounting or discussion of current issues and events of general news value and of interest to 16 year-old students. ☐ ☐
- Express an opinion or reaction to such events or issues. ☐ ☐

Using a dictionary

It is tempting to think that the availability of a dictionary makes the learning of vocabulary unnecessary, but this is definitely not the case. Unless you know most of the words in a text already, working through it with a dictionary becomes a very slow and boring task. There is certainly not time in an examination to look up most of the words and do everything else you have to do. In any case, when looking up a word, we use our understanding of the rest of the sentence to help us know which of the alternatives in the dictionary we should choose. So you really do need to learn vocabulary.

Using the Spanish–English section

Before referring to your dictionary, always check:

- **Do you really need to understand the word?** If you can answer the questions without knowing the English equivalent, don't waste time in an examination looking it up.
- **Can you work out the meaning in any other way?** There is a section in Chapter 6 (p. 125) on coping with words you do not know. Practise the strategies listed there and you will save a considerable amount of time in the examination.

When looking up a verb, you will have to look for the infinitive. *Aprovechó* will not be listed, but you should be able to work out that the infinitive is *aprovechar* and look that up.

Similarly, **when looking up an adjective**, you will need to look for the masculine (singular) form. *Pintorescas* will not be listed; *pintoresco* will.

When you look up a word and find several English words listed, use your common sense to decide which is the most likely meaning. If somebody planning to go to the cinema buys *una entrada*, it should not take you long to work out whether this is an entrance, a porch or a ticket!

Using the English–Spanish section

This really can be a very dangerous area. Any teacher or examiner of Spanish will be able to tell you of the dangers, with examples such as the student who said he bought *un murciélago* in order to play cricket. (*Un murciélago* is a bat – of the flying animal type.) Even worse are the cases of students who feel they should look up every word and try to translate word for word, even to the extent of using *testamento* (last will and testament) when they should be using the **Future Tense!** So when is it right to use the English–Spanish section of a dictionary? It can be very useful:

- To check the spelling of a word you know.
- To check the gender of a word (is *ciudad* masculine or feminine?).
- To look for words you know but have just forgotten (if when you see the word you think 'Of course, I should have remembered that!' you have almost certainly found the correct word).

When you need a Spanish word that you do not know and have never used before, you should first try the strategies for coping with problems that are included in Chapters 5 and 7. If you do have to use the dictionary in the examination in order to find a new word, it is often a good idea to check the word you find by looking it up in the Spanish–English section. You may find that the English equivalents given there show that the word has a rather different meaning from the one you had in mind.

Knowing your dictionary

Make sure you know how your dictionary works. There are important differences.

1. **Which version of the Spanish alphabet does your dictionary use?** Remember that *ñ* is a separate letter from *n*, so that the combination *-ña-* will always come after the combination *-nu-*, for example. Traditionally *ch* has been treated as a separate letter from *c*. This has meant that a word such as *chaleco* would be listed in the *Ch* section, after all the words in the *C* section, such as *curva*. Similarly, *ll* has been treated as a separate letter from *l*, so that, for example, *llamar* would be in the *Ll* section, after all the *L* words, such as *luz*. Recently, however, it has become quite normal for *-ch-* to be treated in the same way as in English, occurring between *-ce-* and *-ci-*. Similarly, *-ll-* quite often now shown between *-li-* and *-lo-*. Check your dictionary *now* to see which form of alphabetical order it uses for Spanish words. That will save you wasting a lot of time looking for words in the wrong part of the dictionary.
2. **Make sure you understand the abbreviations it uses** to tell you what sort of word is listed.

   For a feminine word such as *lengua* does it use *nf* or simply *f* to tell you that this is a feminine noun?

   For a word such as *inteligente* does it use *adj* or no symbol at all to show that this is an adjective?

   For a word such as *comer* does it use *v* or *vt* or nothing at all to show that this a verb?

   As an example, try looking up the word *dent* in the English–Spanish section. You will almost certainly find both *abollar* and *abolladura*. Use the abbreviations to work out which means *a dent* and which means *to dent*.
3. **Check whether your dictionary makes extensive use of 'headwords'.** Try looking up the word *lento* in the Spanish–English section. In many dictionaries you will find it exactly where you would expect to, in its correct alphabetical place. In others you will find it only as part of the entry for the 'headword', *lentitud*. You need to know which way your dictionary works.
4. **Make sure you know where the verb section is.** Do you understand it? Above all can you identify the verb tenses? You will certainly not need all the tenses given in your dictionary, so check the Grammar section (Chapter 9) to be sure which you are likely to need.

Learning vocabulary

This is, for most people, one of the tedious tasks of language learning but it has to be done, and it has to be done over the weeks and months if you are to acquire a working knowledge of 1500–2200 words by the time you take your examination. So how can you make sure that the hard work you do is effective?

- **Learn vocabulary regularly** – ideally every day (and certainly at least twice a week).
- **Work in short sessions.** For most people, about 10 minutes at one go is enough. After that, words don't seem to lodge in the memory so well. Three 10-minute spells of vocabulary learning are far more effective than one 30-minute session. So do 10 minutes now, then do something else and come back to the vocabulary, maybe half-an-hour or an hour later.
- **Be systematic.** Keep a record of what you have learnt, so that you can plan your future learning successfully.
- **Work by topic and by specific areas within each topic.** It is much easier to remember words learnt in a group which is linked with one type of situation (e.g. ordering food in the restaurant) than to recall a list of words whose only link is that they begin with the letter 'a'.
- **Test yourself regularly as you learn** (or ask someone else to test you), so that you can concentrate on the words you still don't know well enough. Some words can be learnt almost on sight; others prove far more difficult. So don't spend the same amount of time on each word!
- **Start by making sure you know the English for the Spanish words**, then reverse the process and make sure you can give the Spanish when you see or hear the English.
- **Say each word aloud at some point** (or at least think how you would pronounce it, listen to it in your mind). Remember you have to speak the words as well as write them – so make sure you can say them correctly.
- **Think how you might use the word in a real situation.** Putting it into a sentence is one of the most effective ways of 'fixing' a word in the memory.
- If you **record the words on a cassette**, leaving a gap between the English word and its Spanish equivalent, you can use your cassette recorder or personal stereo as a means of testing yourself at odd times, such as when you are getting dressed, doing your hair or even travelling. Your aim is to say (or think) the correct Spanish word during the gap before you hear it on the cassette.
- Many people who enjoy **using computers** find the computer can be a great help in learning words and their spellings, using the word processor and, if it has one, the spelling checker. (You must take care to enter Spanish words correctly in the spelling checker!)

And when you are learning vocabulary, don't forget that, if you are to use a word correctly, you will need to know:

- The **correct spelling**, including accents.
- Whether it is **masculine or feminine** – so learn the gender with the word;
- If it is a **radical-changing verb** – so learn the letters (*ue*), (*ie*) or (*i*) that are printed after the radical-changing verbs in the vocabulary lists (and check the Grammar section if you are unsure how radical-changing verbs work!).

If you say or write words incorrectly but in a way that a Spanish-speaker with no knowledge of English would understand, you will be given credit for effective communication, though you will not gain good marks for quality of language – and that can be quite important at Higher Tier if you are aiming for a high grade.

VOCABULARY LISTS

Key words and expressions

Underlying all the topic areas are certain key words and expressions that are not necessarily related to any specific topic but which are likely to be essential in dealing with almost any. In this section I have set out the most common expressions that you will need to know and that have not been included in the topic sections which follow.

ser *to be*
estar *to be*
tener *to have*
hay *there is / there are*

ir *to go*
venir *to come*
entrar *to enter, go in*
salir *to go out, to depart*
llegar *to arrive*
subir *to go up*
bajar *to go down*
quedar *to stay*
estar en casa *to be at home*
ir a casa *to go home*
volver(ue) a casa *to return home*

ocurrir *to occur, to happen*
pasar *to happen*
suceder *to happen*
tener lugar *to take place*

bueno *good*
malo *bad*
mejor *better*
peor *worse*
grande *big*
pequeño *small*
mayor *greater, older*
menor *lesser, younger*
más *more*
menos *less, fewer*
más grande *bigger*
más pequeño *smaller*
mucho/a *much, a lot (of)*
muchos/as *many, a lot of*
poco/a *not much*
pocos/as *few*
todo/a/os/as *all*
demasiado/a *too much*
demasiados/as *too many*
medio/a *half (a)*
bastante(s) *enough*
bien *well*
mal *badly*
muy *very*

aquí *here*
allí *there*
ahí *there (near the person being addressed)*
en alguna parte *somewhere*
en ninguna parte *nowhere*
en todas partes *everywhere*
por todas partes *everywhere*

aunque *although*
como *as*
pero *but*
porque *because*
y *and*

a *to*
en *at, on, in*
sobre *on*
cerca (de) *near*
lejos (de) *far (from)*
debajo de *under*
encima de *above, on top of*
delante (de) *in front (of)*
detrás (de) *behind*
al lado de *beside*
con *with*
sin *without*
para *for*
por *by, through, because of*
casi *almost*
también *also*

alguien *someone*
algo *something*
alguno / algún / alguna . . . *some . . .*
ninguno / ningún / ninguna *not one, none*
cada (uno / una) *each (one)*
nada *nothing*
nadie *nobody*
todos *all, everyone*
todo el mundo *everybody*

Emotions

enfadarse *to be angry*
(no) estar contento *to be (un)happy*
gozar de *to enjoy*
inquietarse por *to worry about*
llorar *to cry, weep*
odiar *to hate*
preocuparse (por) *to worry (about)*
pasarlo bien *to enjoy oneself*
querer (ie) *to wish, to love*
reírse *to laugh*
sentir (ie) *to regret, to be sorry*
tener miedo (de) *to be afraid (of)*
alegre *happy*
triste *sad*
preocupado (por) *worried (about)*
de buen humor *in a good mood*
de mal humor *in a bad mood*
lo siento (mucho) *I'm (very) sorry*

Common greetings and courtesies

Buenos días *Good morning*
Buenas tardes *Good afternoon, Good evening*
Buenas noches *Good night*
Hola *Hello*
Adiós *Good-bye*
Hasta luego *See you later*
Hasta mañana *See you tomorrow*
Por favor *Please*
Gracias *Thank you*
De nada *Don't mention it*
See also B3 Meeting people

Time

el año *year*
el día *day*
la estación *season (of the year)*
la fecha *date*
la hora *hour*
el mes *month*
el minuto *minute*
el momento *moment*
la semana *week*
el rato *short while*
el segundo *second*
el siglo *century*
el tiempo *time*

este año *this year*
el año pasado *last year*
el año que viene *next year*
el año siguiente *the following year*
al día siguiente *on the following day*
esta semana *this week*
el fin de semana *(at) the weekend*
quince días *a fortnight*
¿Cuánto tiempo . . . ? *for how long . . . ?*
durante mucho tiempo *for a long time*

la mañana *morning*
la tarde *afternoon, early evening*
la noche *late evening, night*
la madrugada *early morning*
durar *to last*
por la mañana *in the morning*
a las diez de la mañana *at 10 o'clock in the morning*

la primavera *spring*
el verano *summer*
el otoño *autumn*
el invierno *winter*

enero *January*
febrero *February*
marzo *March*
abril *April*
mayo *May*
junio *June*
julio *July*
agosto *August*
se(p)tiembre *September*
octubre *October*
noviembre *November*
diciembre *December*

¿Qué fecha es? *what is the date?*
Es el 5 de marzo *it is the 5 March*
¿A cuántos estamos? *what is the date?*
¿Estamos a 5 de marzo *it is the 5 March*
a principios de enero *at the beginning of January*
a mediados de octubre *in mid-October*
a fines de diciembre *at the end of December*

lunes *Monday*
martes *Tuesday*
miércoles *Wednesday*
jueves *Thursday*
viernes *Friday*
sábado *Saturday*
domingo *Sunday*

el domingo *on Sunday*
los viernes *on Fridays*
el jueves que viene *next Thursday*
el lunes por la mañana *on Monday morning*
el sábado que viene por la tarde *next Saturday afternoon*

el día de Año Nuevo *New Year's Day*
el día de Reyes *Epiphany, Twelfth Night*
la Semana Santa *Holy Week, Easter*
las vacaciones de Semana Santa *the Easter holidays*
el Viernes Santo *Good Friday*
la Nochebuena *Christmas Eve*
el día de Navidad *Christmas Day*
la Nochevieja *New Year's Eve*

hoy *today*
mañana *tomorrow*
pasado mañana *the day after tomorrow*
ayer *yesterday*
anteayer *the day before yesterday*
anoche *last night*
mañana por la mañana *tomorrow morning*
hoy día *these days*

actualmente *at the present time*
ahora *now*
ahora mismo *right now, straightaway*
al mismo tiempo *at the same time*
antes *before, earlier*
de nuevo *again*
de repente *suddenly*
después *afterwards, later*
en seguida *at once, immediately*
entonces *then, at that time*
finalmente *finally*
luego *then, next*
más tarde *later*
por fin *finally, at last*
pronto *soon*
tarde *late*
temprano *early*
todavía *still*
todavía no *not yet, still not*
ya *already, by now*
ya no *no longer*
al final *at the end, in the end*
al principio *at the beginning*
hace tres horas *three hours ago*

a menudo *often*
a veces *sometimes*
de vez en cuando *from time to time*

generalmente *generally*
normalmente *normally*
nunca *never*
casi nunca *hardly ever*
pocas veces *rarely*
raramente *rarely*
siempre *always*
todos los días *every day*
una vez al año *once a year*

a partir de *(starting) from*
antes de *before*
desde *since, from*
después de *after*
durante *during, for*
hasta *until*
como *as*
cuando *when*
en cuanto *as soon as*
mientras *while*

Time of day

¿A qué hora . . . ? *At what time . . . ?*
a la una *at one o'clock*
a las dos *at two o'clock*
a las tres y media *at half past three*
a las cinco y cuarto *at quarter past five*
a las doce menos cuarto *at quarter to twelve*
a las diez y veinte *at twenty past ten*
a las ocho menos diez *at ten to eight*
a las siete y pico *just after seven*
¿Qué hora es? *What time is it?*
Es la una *It is one o'clock*
Son las dos *It is two o'clock*
¿Qué hora era? *What time was it?*
Eran las seis y veinte *It was twenty past six*
aproximadamente *about, approximately*
a eso de . . . *at about . . .*
en punto *exactly*
dar *to strike*
daban las cinco *it was striking five*
las siete de la tarde *seven o'clock in the evening*
la una de la madrugada *one o'clock in the morning*

Speed

a gran velocidad *at great speed*
a toda velocidad *at full speed*
de prisa *quickly*
despacio *slowly*
lentamente *slowly*
rápidamente *rapidly*
lento *slow*
rápido *quick*
tener prisa *to be in a hurry*
darse prisa *to hurry*
a noventa kilómetros por hora *at 90 kilometres per hour*

Numbers

0	cero
1	uno, un, una
2	dos
3	tres
4	cuatro
5	cinco
6	seis
7	siete
8	ocho
9	nueve
10	diez
11	once
12	doce
13	trece
14	catorce
15	quince
16	dieciséis
17	diecisiete
18	dieciocho
19	diecinueve
20	veinte
21	veintiuno/a
22	veintidós
23	veintitrés
24	veinticuatro
25	veinticinco
26	veintiséis
27	veintisiete
28	veintiocho
29	veintinueve
30	treinta
31	treinta y uno/a
32	treinta y dos
40	cuarenta
41	cuarenta y uno/a
50	cincuenta
60	sesenta
70	setenta
80	ochenta
90	noventa
100	ciento / cien
101	ciento uno
200	doscientos/as
300	trescientos/as
400	cuatrocientos/as
500	quinientos/as
600	seiscientos/as
700	setecientos/as
800	ochocientos/as
900	novecientos/as
1000	mil
2000	dos mil
100 000	cien mil
1 000 000	un millón
2 000 000	dos millones

Notes:

(*a*) Dos, tres, *and* seis *take an accent when added to the end of another word* (dieciséis; veintidós; veintitrés; veintiséis).

(*b*) *The word* y *occurs only between the tens and units from 31 to 99.*

(*c*) Cien *is used before a noun* (*e.g.* cien personas) *but not before an additional part of the number* (*e.g.* ciento cincuenta y seis).
(*d*) Millón *and* millones *take* de *before a noun, but not before a continuation of the number* (*e.g.* tres millones de personas *but* cuatro millones trescientos mil).

Ordinal numbers

1° primero/a *first*
2° segundo/a *second*
3° tercero/a *third*
4° cuarto/a *fourth*
5° quinto/a *fifth*
6° sexto/a *sixth*
7° séptimo/a *seventh*
8° octavo/a *eighth*
9° noveno/a *ninth*
10° décimo/a *tenth*

Question words

¿Adónde . . . ? *Where . . . to?*
¿Cómo . . . ? *How . . . ?*
¿Cómo? *I beg your pardon? / What? (asking someone to repeat)*
¿Cómo te llamas? *What is your name?*
¿Cómo se llama? *What is his/her name?*
¿Cómo es (tu casa)? *What is (your house) like?*
¿Cómo son (las habitaciones)? *What are (the rooms) like?*
¿Cuál? *Which one?*
¿Cuál de . . . ? *Which one of . . . ?*
¿Cuándo . . . ? *When . . . ?*
¿Cuánto/a . . . ? *How much . . . ?*
¿Cuántos/as . . . ? *How many . . . ?*
¿Dónde . . . ? *Where . . . ?*
¿Por qué . . . ? *Why . . . ?*
¿Qué . . . ? *What . . . ?*
¿Qué libro . . . ? *Which book . . . ? What book . . . ?*
¿Quién . . . ? *Who . . . ? (singular)*
¿Quiénes . . . ? *Who . . . ? (plural)*
¿A quién . . . ? *To whom. . . . ? Who . . . to? Whom . . . ?*
¿De quién es / son . . . ? *Whose is / are . . . ?*

Common colours

amarillo/a *yellow*
azul *blue*
blanco/a *white*
color naranja *orange*
gris *grey*
marrón *brown*
negro/a *black*
rojo/a *red*
rosa *pink*
verde *green*
¿De qué color es / son . . . ? *What colour is / are . . . ?*

Knowledge, meaning and understanding

la duda *doubt*
el error *error, mistake*
la palabra *word*
la pregunta *question*
la mentira *lie*
la verdad *truth*
comprender *to understand*
conocer *to be acquainted with*
corregir (i) *to correct*
creer *to believe, to think*
decir *to say, tell*
entender (ie) *to understand*
escribir *to write, to spell*
escribirse *to be spelt*
escuchar *to listen (to)*
equivocarse *to be wrong, to make a mistake*
explicar *to explain*
hablar *to speak*
llamarse *to be called*
mentir (ie) *to lie*
oír *to hear*
negar (ie) *to deny*
pensar (ie) *to think*
preguntar *to ask*
pronunciar *to pronounce*
querer decir *to mean*
repetir (i) *to repeat*
saber *to know, to know how to*
ver *to see*
(no) tener razón *to be right (wrong)*
correcto/a *correct*
verdadero/a *real*

¿Cómo se escribe? *How is it spelt?*
¿Cómo se llama esto? *What is this called?*
¿Cómo se pronuncia esta palabra? *How do you pronounce this word?*
¿Conoce usted Londres? *Do you know London?*
¿Está bien esto? *Is this right?*
Es verdad *It is true*
¿Habla usted inglés? *Do you speak English?*
Hable más despacio por favor *Speak more slowly, please*
Llevo tres años estudiando el español *I have been studying Spanish for three years*
¿Me puede explicar . . . ? *Can you explain to me . . . ?*
¿Me puede corregir esto, por favor? *Could you correct this for me please?*
No entiendo *I don't understand*
No es verdad *It is untrue*
No sé *I don't know*
¿Qué quiere decir . . . ? *What does . . . mean?*
Repita usted, por favor *Please would you repeat that*
¿Sabes dónde está mi reloj? *Do you know where my watch is?*
Se me ha olvidado *I have forgotten*

A1 School

Buildings and types

el aula (*feminine*) *classroom*
la biblioteca *library*
la cantina *canteen*
el césped *lawn*
el colegio *secondary school, college*
la enfermería *infirmary*
la escuela *primary school*
el gimnasio *gymnasium*
el instituto *state secondary school*
el laboratorio *lab(oratory)*
el patio *playground*
la sala de profesores *staffroom*
el salón de actos *School hall*
el taller *workshop*
la universidad *university*
los vestuarios *changing rooms*
lejos *far*
mixto/a *mixed*
privado/a *private*
público/a *public*

School routine

el/la amigo/a *friend*
el boletín *school report*
el boli *ball-point pen*
el bolígrafo *ball-point pen*
la cartera *school satchel, briefcase*
la clase *lesson*
la comida *meal*
el concierto *concert*
el cuaderno *exercise*
los deberes *homework*
el ejemplo *example*
la enseñanza *education*
el error *mistake*
el/la estudiante *student*
la frase *sentence*
la goma *rubber*
el horario *timetable*
el intercambio *exchange*
el interno *boarder*
el lápiz *pencil*
el libro *book*
el libro de texto *textbook*
la nota *mark*
el ordenador *computer*
el papel *paper*
el permiso *permission*
la pizarra *blackboard, whiteboard*
el problema *problem*
el/la profe *teacher*
el profesor *teacher*
la profesora *teacher*
el recreo *break*
la regla *ruler, rule*
la respuesta *answer*
la secretaría *office*
la tiza *chalk*
el uniforme *uniform*
las vacaciones *leave, time off, holidays*
el vocabulario *vocabulary*
asistir a *to be present at*
calcular *to calculate*
cantar *to sing*
contar (ue) *to count*
corregir (i) *to correct*
criticar *to criticise*
durar *to last*
escoger *to choose*
faltar *to lack, to be missing*
hacer los deberes *to do one's homework*
hacer progresos *to make progress*
hacer un ejercicio *to do an exercise*
hacer un experimento *to do an experiment*
hacer una pregunta *to ask a question*
jugar (ue) *to play*
leer *to read*
nadar *to swim*
olvidar(se) *to forget*
practicar *to train, practise*
prestar atención *to pay attention*
repasar *to revise*
repetir (i) *to repeat*
supervisar *to supervise*
traducir *to translate*
ausente *absent*
clásico/a *classical*
difícil *difficult*
fácil *easy*
presente *present*
primero/a *first*
severo/a *strict*
COU *Year 13*
después *after*
luego *then, next*
Mañana es día de fiesta *Tomorrow is a holiday*
sexto de EGB *Year 7*

Subjects

el alemán *German*
la asignatura *subject*
la biología *biology*
la cerámica *pottery*
las ciencias *science*
las (ciencias) económicas *economics*
la cocina *cookery*
el comercio *commerce*
la costura *needlework*
los deportes *sport*
el dibujo *drawing*
la economía doméstica *home economics*
la educación física *physical education*
la electrónica *electronics*
el español *Spanish*
la física *physics*
el francés *French*
la geografía *geography*

la gimnasia *gymnastics*
el griego *Greek*
la historia antigua *ancient history*
la historia moderna *modern history*
los idiomas *modern languages*
la informática *information technology*
el inglés *English*
la instrucción cívica *civics, social studies, PSE*
el italiano *Italian*
el latín *Latin*
la literatura *literature*
las matemáticas *mathematics*
la música *music*
la química *chemistry*
la religión *religious education*
el ruso *Russian*
los trabajos manuales *crafts*
gustar (me gusta, etc.) *to like*
odiar *to hate*
preferir (ie) *to prefer*
aburrido/a *boring*
complicado/a *complicated*
divertido/a *amusing*
fenomenal *great, terrific*
interesante *interesting*
tonto/a *stupid*
Mi asignature preferida es *My favourite subject is*
Mi mejor asignatura es el inglés *My best subject is English*

Examinations

el diploma *diploma*
el examen *examination*
el resultado *result*
el título *certificate*
aprobar (ue) *to pass*
copiar *to cheat*
examinarse *to take an exam*
suspender *to fail an exam*
He aprobado el bachillerato *I have passed my 'bachillerato' (A Levels)*
He aprobado el examen *I have passed my exam*
Me han suspendido en el bachillerato *I have failed my 'bachillerato'* (*A Levels*)
Me han suspendido en física *I have failed my physics exam*
Voy a examinarme este verano *I will take my exams this summer*

A2 Home life

el alojamiento *accommodation*
el alquiler *rent*
el bloque (de viviendas) *building*
la casa *house*
el chalé *detached house* (*suburban*)
el chalé adosado *semi-detached house*
el confort *comfort*
la diferencia *difference*
el edificio *building*
la entrada *entrance*
el exterior *outside*
el granero *barn*
la granja *farm*
el interior *inside*
la llave *key*
la manzana *a block* (*of buildings*)
el metro cuadrado *square metre*
los meubles *furniture*
la pintura *painting*
el piso *flat, storey*
la planta baja *ground floor*
el propietario *owner*
el rascacielos *skyscraper*
el ruido *noise*
la situación *situation*
la terraza *terrace*
la torre *tower*
la vista *view*
la vivienda protegida *council flat*
adorar *to love*
alojarse *to lodge*
alquilar *to rent*
amueblar *to furnish*
aumentar *to increase*
comprar *to buy*
decorar *to decorate*
empapelar *to paper*
gustar (*impersonal*) *to like*
limpiar *to clean*
llamar (a la puerta) *to knock (on the door)*
mudarse (de casa) *to move house*
tocar el timbre *to ring the doorbell*
vender *to sell*
vivir *to live*
agradable *pleasant*
antiguo/a *old, former, ex . . .*
bonito/a *pretty*
caro/a *expensive*
cómodo/a *comfortable*
de lujo *luxurious*
elegante *smart*
estrecho/a *narrow*
fatal *awful*
fenomenal *great*
feo/a *ugly*
grande *large*
guapo/a *pretty*
hermoso/a *beautiful, fine*
limpio/a *clean*
moderno/a *modern*
necesario/a *necessary*
práctico/a *practical*
raro/a *odd, strange*
ruidoso/a *noisy*
sorprendente *surprising*
sucio/a *dirty*
típico/a *typical*

tranquilo/a *peaceful, calm, quiet*
útil *useful*
viejo/a *old*
abajo *downstairs*
arriba *upstairs*
de hormigón *of concrete*
de ladrillo *of brick*
de madera *of wood*
de metal *made of metal*
de plástico *made of plastic*
en buenas condiciones *in good condition*
en casa de *at the house of*
en malas condiciones *in bad condition*
lejos de *far from*
no demasiado caro/a *not too expensive*
no muy caro/a *not very expensive*

Las habitaciones *Rooms*

General

el aparcamiento *parking place, car park*
el ascensor *lift*
el aseo *toilet*
el balcón *balcony*
la cocina *kitchen*
el comedor *dining room*
el cuarto *room*
el cuarto de baño *bathroom*
el cuarto de estar *lounge, sitting room*
el (cuarto) trastero *lumber room*
el desván *loft*
el dormitorio *bedroom*
la entrada *entrance*
la escalera *staircase*
el garaje *garage*
el jardín *garden*
el pasillo *corridor*
el patio *courtyard*
el salón *living room*
el servicio *toilet*
el sótano *cellar, basement*
el suelo *floor*
el techo *roof*
el vestíbulo *hall*
el wáter / el w.c. *toilet*
el agua (no) potable *(non) drinking water*
la barandilla *banister*
la bombilla *electric light bulb*
la calefacción central *central heating*
la cerradura *lock*
la contraventana *shutter*
la electricidad *electricity*
el enchufe *power point*
la estufa eléctrica *electric radiator*
el gas *gas*
la lámpara *lamp*
la luz *light*
el mantenimiento *maintenance*
los muebles *furnishings, fittings*
la pared *wall*
el plano *plan*
la puerta *door*
el radiador *central heating radiator*
el techo *ceiling*
la ventana *window*
abrir *to open*
apretar (ie) *to lean, press*
cerrar (ie) *to close*
cortar *to cut*
encender (ie) *to light*
enchufar *to plug in*
hacer bricolaje *to do odd jobs*
reparar *to repair*
utilizar *to use*
amueblado *fitted, furnished*
allí está *there is . . .*
aquí está *here is . . .*
Apaga el gas, por favor *Turn off the gas, please*
Cierra la puerta, por favor *Close the door, please*
Pulsa el botón *Press the button*

El dormitorio *The bedroom*

la alfombra *carpet*
la almohada *pillow*
el armario *wardrobe, cupboard*
la cadena estereofónica *stereo*
la cama *bed*
el colchón *mattress*
la cortina *curtain*
el despertador *alarm clock*
el espejo *mirror*
el estante *shelf*
la lámpara *lamp*
el magnetofón *tape recorder (cassette recorder)*
la manta *blanket*
la moqueta *wall-to-wall carpet*
el ordenador *computer*
el póster *poster*
la sábana *sheet*
el tocadiscos *record player*
el transistor *transistor*
compartir *to share*
Comparto mi dormitorio con mi hermano/a *I share my bedroom with my brother/sister*
Tengo mi propio dormitorio *I have my own bedroom*
varios *several*

La cocina *The kitchen*

el agua caliente/fría (*feminine*) hot/cold water
el armario *cupboard*
la aspiradora *vacuum cleaner*
el cazo *saucepan*
las cerillas *matches*
la cocina de gas *gas cooker*
la cocina eléctrica *electric cooker*
el congelador *freezer*
el cubo de la basura *dustbin*

la cuchara *spoon*
el cuchillo *knife*
el fregadero *sink*
la fuente *large dish*
el grifo *tap*
el horno *oven*
la lavadora *washing machine*
el lavaplatos *dishwasher*
la mesa *table*
la nevera *refrigerator*
la plancha *iron*
el plato *plate*
la sartén *frying pan*
la taza *cup*
el tazón *bowl*
el tenedor *fork*
la vajilla *crockery*
el vaso *glass*
la vela *candle*
apagar *to turn off*
encender (ie) *to light, switch on*
fregar (ie) los platos *to wash dishes*
lavar la ropa *to wash clothes*
tirar *to throw (out)*

El cuarto de baño *The bathroom*

el agua fría/caliente (*feminine*) *cold/hot water*
la bañera, el baño *bath*
el bidé *bidet*
el cepillo de dientes *toothbrush*
el champú *shampoo*
la ducha *shower*
el enchufe de la máquina de afeitar *electric razor socket*
el espejo *mirror*
la esponja *sponge*
el jabón *soap*
el lavabo *wash-basin*
la maquinilla de afeitar *razor*
el paño *flannel*
la pasta de dientes *toothpaste*
la toalla *towel*

El comedor *The dining room*

el aparador *sideboard, dresser*
la chimenea *fireplace, hearth*
el cuadro *picture*
la garrafa *glass jug, carafe*
el mantel *table-cloth*
la mesa *table*
el plato *dish*
el reloj *clock*
la servilleta *serviette*
la silla *chair*

El cuarto de estar *The living room*

la cadena estereofónica *stereo*
el cenicero *ashtray*
el cuadro *picture*
la foto *photo*
la librería *bookcase*
el magnetofón *tape recorder*
la mesita *coffee table*
el piano *piano*
la planta *plant*
el sillón *armchair*
el sofá *sofa*
la televisión *television*
el vídeo *video recorder*

El vestíbulo *Hall*

la llave *key*
la pared *wall*
la puerta (de entrada) (*front*) *door*
la puerta de la calle *front door*
el teléfono *telephone*

El jardín *Garden*

el árbol *tree*
el árbol frutal *fruit tree*
el arbusto *bush*
la flor *flower*
la fruta *fruit*
la hierba *grass*
la jardinería *gardening*
la legumbre *vegetable*
las malas hierbas *weeds*
la planta *plant*
cortar la hierba *to cut the grass*
cultivar *to cultivate, grow*
regar (ie) *to water*
Corté la hierba *I cut the grass*
Cultivo legumbres *I grow vegetables*

A3 Health and fitness

la boca *mouth*
el brazo *arm*
la cabeza *head*
el corazón *heart*
el dedo *finger*
el diente *tooth*
la espalda *back, shoulder*
el estómago *stomach*
la garganta *throat*
el hueso *bone*
la lengua *tongue*
la mano *hand*
la muela (*molar*) *tooth*
la nariz *nose*
el oído *ear*
el ojo *eye*

el pecho *chest*
el pie *foot*
la piel *skin*
la pierna *leg*
la rodilla *knee*
la sangre *blood*
el tobillo *ankle*
el vientre *stomach*

La higiene ***Hygiene***
el algodón *cotton wool*
el baño *bath*
el cepillo de dientes *toothbrush*
el maquillaje *make-up*
la pasta de dientes *toothpaste*
la toalla (de manos) *(hand) towel*
acostarse (ue) *to go to bed*
afeitarse *to shave*
ducharse *to have a shower*
lavarse *to wash*
limpiarse los dientes *to brush one's teeth*
maquillarse *to put on make-up*
limpio/a *clean*
sucio/a *dirty*

Enfermedades y lesiones ***Illness and injury***
el antiséptico *antiseptic*
la aspirina *aspirin*
la ambulancia *ambulance*
la cita *appointment*
la clínica *clinic*
el consultorio *cabinet, consulting room*
la crema *cream*
la crisis *crisis*
la cucharada *spoonful*
el/la dentista *dentist*
la diarrea *diarrhoea*
el/la doctor/a *doctor*
el dolor *pain*
la enfermedad *illness*
el/la enfermo/a *patient*
el farmacéutico *chemist*
la farmacia *chemist's shop*
la fiebre *fever, high temperature*
las gafas *spectacles*
los gastos *expenses*
la gripe *flu*
el hinchazón *swelling*
el hospital *hospital*
la indigestión *indigestion*
la insolación *sun stroke, sunburn*
el jarabe *cough medicine*
el medicamento *medicine, treatment*
la medicina *medicine (as a subject)*
el/la médico/a *doctor*
el nacimiento *birth*
la operación *operation*
la pastilla *tablet*
la pastilla para la garganta *throat pastille*
la picadura *sting, bite*
la píldora *pill*
el problema *problem*
la receta *prescription*
el remedio *remedy*
el resfriado *cold*
la salud *health*
el seguro *insurance (policy)*
la tirita *plaster, elastoplast*
el tubo *tube*
la voz *voice*
aconsejar *to advise*
ahogarse *to drown*
aliviar *to relieve*
caer(se) *to fall*
callarse *to be silent*
consultar *to consult*
cortarse el dedo *to cut one's finger*
curar *to heal, cure*
descansar *to rest*
dormir (ue) *to sleep*
estar bien *to be well*
estar enfermo/a *to be ill*
estar malo/a *to be ill*
estar mareado/a *to feel sick*
estar mejor *to be better*
gritar *to shout*
hacerse daño *to hurt oneself*
ingresar en el hospital *to be admitted to hospital*
llorar *to weep*
morder (ue) *to bite*
morir (ue) *to die*
picar *to sting, bite (insect)*
preocuparse *to worry*
quemarse la mano *to burn one's hand*
recibir un golpe *to get a knock*
romperse el brazo *to break one's arm*
sangrar *to bleed*
sentirse (ie) bien *to feel well*
sentirse (ie) mal *to feel ill*
sufrir *to suffer*
tener calor *to be warm*
tener frío *to be cold*
tener hambre *to be hungry*
tener sed *to be thirsty*
tener un resfriado *to have a cold*
tomar la temperatura *to take one's temperature*
torcerse el tobillo *to twist, sprain one's ankle*
toser *to cough*
tragar *to swallow*
vomitar *to vomit*
asegurado/a *insured*
cansado/a *tired*
capaz *capable*
doliente *ill, suffering*
en forma *on form*
enfermo/a *ill*
estreñido/a *constipated*
flojo/a *weak*
grave *serious*
gravemente *seriously*

herido/a *injured*
inquieto/a *anxious*
mejor *better*
muerto/a *dead*
sensible *sensitive*
vivo/a *alive*
Ana se ha torcido el tobillo *Ana has twisted her ankle*
Está sufriendo *She's not well*
Estoy mareado/a *I feel sick*
Le duele la cabeza *S/he has a headache*
Le ha picado un mosquito *A mosquito has bitten him*
Me duele el estómago *I have a stomach ache*
Me he quemado la mano *I have burnt my hand*
Me siento mejor ahora *I'm feeling better now*
No me siento bien *I am not well*
Se ha hecho daño en la pierna *She has hurt her leg*
Se ha roto el brazo *She has broken her arm*
Tengo calor *I'm warm*
Tengo fiebre *I have a high temperature*
Tiene hambre *He's hungry*
Una insolación es muy peligrosa *Sunstroke is very dangerous*

Los accidentes *Accidents*

el accidente *accident*
el bombero *fireman*
el choque *collision*
el/la ciclista *cyclist*
la comisaría *police station*
el/la conductor(a) *driver*
el consulado *consulate*
la culpa *fault, blame*
el daño *damage*
la declaración *statement*
la dirección *direction, address*
la disculpa *excuse*
el/la motociclista *motorcyclist*
el peatón *pedestrian*
el peligro *danger*
el permiso *permission*
el policía *policeman*
la policía *police (force)/policewoman*
la prioridad *priority*
el problema *problem*
el responsable *leader*
el riesgo *risk*
el sentido *direction*
las señas *address*
el testigo *witness*
el transeúnte *passer-by*
el vehículo *vehicle*
acusar *to accuse*
adelantar *to overtake*
atropellar *to knock down*
ayudar *to help*
chocar contra *to knock, bump into*
conducir *to drive*
correr *to run*
cruzar *to cross*
darse prisa *to hurry*
declarar *to declare*
disculparse, pedir (i) perdón *to apologize*
disminuir velocidad *to slow down*
enfadarse *to get angry*
esperar *to wait (for)*
gritar *to shout*
informar *to inform*
llamar *to call*
llorar *to weep, to cry*
matar *to kill*
mirar *to watch, to look at*
pagar *to pay (for)*
parar(se) *to stop*
perdonar *to forgive*
prestar atención a *to pay attention to*
protestar *to protest*
quemar *to burn*
rellenar *to fill*
reparar *to repair*
respetar *to repair*
tener derecho a *to have the right to*
torcer (ue) *to turn*
arrepentido/a *very sorry*
falso/a *false, wrong*
grave *serious*
herido/a *injured*
mojado/a *wet*
seguro/a *safe*
sorprendente *surprising*
urgente *urgent*
de acuerdo *agreed*
gravemente *seriously*
inmediatamente *straight away*
sin embargo *however*
suavemente *gently*
¡Atención! *Look out!*
¡Ay de mí! *Oh dear! Alas!*
¡Dios mío! *Oh dear!*
¡Fuego! *Fire!*
¡Oye! / ¡Oiga! *Hey!*
¡No se preocupe! *Never mind!*
¡Perdón! *Sorry!*
¡Socorro! *Help!*
Plus vocabulary from C6 Getting around

A4 Food and drink

Meat, fish, fruit and vegetables

Meat

el asado *roast meat*
el bistec *beef steak*
la carne *meat*
la carne picada *minced meat*
el cerdo *pork*
la chuleta *chop*
el cocido *stew*
el conejo *rabbit*

el cordero *lamb, mutton*
la costilla *rib*
el filete *(fillet) steak*
la hamburguesa *hamburger*
el jamón serrano *cured ham*
el jamón de York *(York) ham, (Boiled ham)*
el lomo *loin*
el pato *duck*
el pollo *chicken*
la salchicha *sausage*
la ternera *beef, veal*

Fish

el bacalao *cod*
los boquerones *(fresh) anchovy*
la caballa *mackerel*
los calamares *squid*
el camarón *shrimp*
el cangrejo *crab*
las gambas *prawns*
el lenguado *sole*
los mariscos *shellfish*
el mejillón *mussel*
la merluza *hake*
la ostra *oyster*
el pescado *fish*
el pulpo *octopus*
la sardina *sardine*
la trucha *trout*

Fruit

el albaricoque *apricot*
la cereza *cherry*
la ciruela *plum*
la frambuesa *raspberry*
la fresa *strawberry*
el limón *lemon*
la manzana *apple*
el melocotón *peach*
el melón *melon*
la nuez *nut*
la pera *pear*
la piña *pineapple*
el plátano *banana*
la sandía *water melon*
la uva *grape*

Vegetables

la alcachofa *artichoke*
el arroz *rice*
la cebolla *onion*
el champiñón *mushroom*
la col *cabbage*
las coles de Bruselas *Brussels sprouts*
la coliflor *cauliflower*
la ensalada *salad, lettuce*
las espinacas *spinach*
los guisantes *peas*
la judía *bean*
la lechuga *lettuce*
la legumbre *vegetable*
la patata *potato*
las patatas fritas *chips, crisps*
el pepino *cucumber*
el pimiento *pepper*
el tomate *tomato*
las verduras *green vegetables*
la zanahoria *carrot*

Other food

el ajo *garlic*
el almuerzo *lunch*
el azúcar *sugar*
la barra de pan *stick of bread*
el bocadillo *sandwich (Spanish bread)*
la cena *dinner, evening meal*
el chocolate *chocolate*
el chorizo *cured hard pork and paprika sausage*
el churro *churro, fritter*
la comida *meal*
el cruasán *crescent roll, croissant*
el desayuno *breakfast*
el dulce *sweet*
el entremés *starter*
el flan *caramel cream*
la galleta *biscuit*
el gazpacho *gazpacho, cold soup*
el helado *ice cream*
el huevo *egg*
la mahonesa/mayonesa *mayonnaise*
la mantequilla *butter*
la merienda *picnic*
la mermelada *jam*
la mostaza *mustard*
la nata *cream*
la paella *paella*
el pan *bread*
el panecillo *bread roll*
el pastel *(individual) cake*
el postre *dessert*
las provisiones *food*
el queso *cheese*
la sal *salt*
la salsa *sauce*
el sandwich *sandwich (sliced bread)*
la sopa *soup*
la tapa *bar snack*
la tarta *cake, tart*
la torta *flan*
la tortilla *omelette*
la tostada *slice of toast*
la vainilla *vanilla*
el vinagre *vinegar*
el yogur *yoghurt*

Drinks

el agua (mineral) *(feminine)* *(mineral) water*

el aperitivo *aperitif*
la bebida *drink*
el café *coffee*
el café con leche *white coffee*
el café solo *black coffee*
la caña *glass of draught beer*
la cerveza *beer*
el chocolate (caliente) *(hot) chocolate*
la Coca-cola *Coca-cola*
el coñac *brandy*
la horchata *horchata, tiger nut milk*
el jerez *sherry*
la leche *milk*
el licor *liqueur, spirit*
la limonada *lemonade*
la naranjada *orangeade*
el refresco *cold (soft) drink*
el ron *rum*
la sangría *sangría, fruit punch*
la sidra *cider*
el té *tea*
el vino blanco/tinto *white/red wine*
el zumo de fruta *fruit juice*
el zumo de limón *fresh lemon juice*
el zumo de naranja *fresh orange juice*

Other expressions

la bandeja *tray*
el bar *bar*
la botella *bottle*
la cafetera *coffee pot*
la camarera *waitress*
el camarero *server, waiter*
el cántaro *pitcher, jug*
la cena *dinner*
el/la cocinero/a *cook*
el cuarto *quarter (litre)*
el cubierto *table place, cover charge*
la cuchara *spoon*
el cuchillo *knife*
la cuenta *the bill*
el dueño *owner*
la especialidad *speciality*
las felicitaciones *congratulations*
el gas *gas*
el gusto *flavour*
el jarro *jug*
el menú *menu*
la mesa *table*
el olor *smell*
la persona *person*
el platillo *saucer*
el plato *dish, plate*
el plato principal *main dish*
la propina *tip*
la receta *recipe*
el restaurante *restaurant*
el sabor *taste, flavour*
el servicio *service*
los servicios *toilet*
la taza *cup*
el tazón *bowl*
el teléfono *telephone*
el tenedor *fork*
la tetera *teapot*
el vaso *glass*
apreciar *to appreciate*
aprobar (ue) *to approve*
beber *to drink*
cenar *to have dinner*
comer *to eat*
costar (ue) *to cost*
deber *to owe*
desaprobar (ue) *to disapprove*
encontrar (ue) *to find*
felicitar *to congratulate*
gustar *to like*
insultar *to insult*
ofrecer *to offer*
pasar *to pass*
pedir (i) *to order*
preferir (ie) *to prefer*
preparar *to prepare*
protestar *to protest*
quejarse (de) *to complain (about)*
querer (ie) *to want, wish*
recomender (ie) *to recommend*
servir (i) *to serve*
tener ganas de *to wish to*
tener hambre/sed *to be hungry/thirsty*
tomar *to take, have, eat, drink*
traer *to bring*
apetitoso/a *appetizing*
asado/a *roast*
azucarado/a *sweet*
caliente *hot*
delicioso/a *delicious*
dulce *mild, sweet*
en su punto *done to a turn*
excelente *excellent*
frío *cold*
incluido *included*
muy pasado/a *well cooked, well done*
picante *tart, biting, spicy*
poco hecho *rare, underdone*
salado/a *salty*
satisfecho/a *satisfied*
variado/a *varied*
completamente *completely*
enteramente *entirely*
exactamente *exactly*
igual *equal*
medio *half*
servicio (no) incluido *service (not) included*
solo *alone*
Aquí tiene Vd. *Here you are*
Basta *That's enough*
Gracias *Thank you*
Me gusta . . . *I like . . .*
(No) quiero *I would (not) like*
¡Salud! *Cheers! Your health!*

Attracting the waiter's attention

Attracting attention

¡Oiga, camarero! *Waiter!*
¡Señorita! *Waitress!*

Asking for a table

¿Hay una mesa para _____ personas? *Have you a table for _____ people?*
Lo siento *(No,) I'm sorry*
una mesa libre *free table*
reservar una mesa *to reserve a table*
Sí, por aquí *Yes, over here*

Ordering a meal

el menú de mil quinientas pesetas *menu at 1500 pesetas*
bebidas en suplemento *drinks extra*
café incluido *coffee included*
claro *of course*
en lugar de *in place of*
en vez de *instead of*
escoger *to choose*
medio pasado *medium*
muy pasado *well done*
para él/ella/ellos/ellas *for him/her/them*
para empezar . . . *to begin with . . .*
poco hecho *rare, underdone*
por supuesto *of course*
servicio 15 por ciento (no) incluido *service 15% (not) included*
Bueno, pues, voy a tomar . . . *Right, I'll have . . .*
¿Cómo quiere Vd. el bistec? *How would you like your steak?*
Eso es todo, gracias *That will be all, thank you*
¿Ha(n) escogido? *Have you chosen?*
Hay un suplemento *There is an extra charge*
Lo siento, pero no nos queda *I'm very sorry, we have none left*
Luego . . . *Then... / To follow . . .*
¿Qué bebida quiere? *What drink would you like?*
¡Qué lástima! *What a pity!*
¿Qué quiere Vd.? *What would you like?*
¿Qué quiere(s)? *What do you want?*
¿Qué toma(s)? *What are you having?*
¿Qué va a tomar? *What will you have?*
¿Qué van a tomar? *What would you like?*
Quiero el menú, por favor *I'd like the menu, please*
Quiero un bistec, por favor *I'd like a steak, please*
Quiero . . . *I would like . . .*
¿Se puede pedir? *May we order?*
Sí, ¿y después? *Yes, and after that?*
Voy a tomar . . . *I'll have . . .*
¿Vas a tomar un aperitivo? *Are you having an aperitif?*
¿Y para terminar? *And to finish?*
Y ¿para Vd., señorita? *And for you, miss?*

Requesting extras and clarification

Additions

¿Puede limpiar la mesa, por favor? *Could you clean the table please?*
¿Puede traernos más . . . ? *Could we have some more . . . ?*
¿Todo está bien? *Is everything all right?*
Haga el favor de cambiarme . . . *Would you change . . . ?*
Nos falta . . . *We are short of . . .*
Por favor, queremos . . . *Please could we have . . . ?*
Sí, claro *Yes, of course*
Voy a traerlo/la *I'll go and get you one*

Clarifications

Es un plato servido con . . . *It's a dish served with . . .*
Es un vino de la región *It's a local wine*
Es una salsa *It's a sauce*
Hay . . . y . . . *There are . . . and . . .*
No, el servicio no está incluido *No, service is not included*
No, el vino no está incluido *No, the wine is not included*
Sí, claro *Yes, of course*
Sí, el servicio está incluido *Yes, service is included*
Sí, las bebidas están incluidas *Yes, drinks are included*
Tardará . . . minutos *It'll take . . . minutes*
¿Cuánto tiempo va a tardar? *How long will it take?*
¿El servicio está incluido? *Is service included?*
¿El vino está incluido? *Is the wine included?*
¿Estará dentro de poco? *Will it soon be ready?*
¿Hay más . . . ? *Have you any more . . . ?*
¿Qué es . . . ? *What is . . . ?*
¿Qué hay de . . . ? *What have you got in the way of . . .?*
¿Quedan . . . ? *Are there any . . . left?*
¿Va a tardar mucho? *Will it take long?*

Requesting the bill and dealing with payment

pagar la cuenta *to settle the bill*
¿Admiten tarjetas de crédito? *Do you accept credit cards?*
Aquí tiene Vd. el cambio *Here is your change*
La cuenta, por favor *The bill, please*
No se admiten cheques *We don't accept cheques*
Son . . . pesetas *That makes . . . pesetas*
Vd. está equivocado/a *You are mistaken*
Son . . . pesetas *That makes . . . pesetas*

Among friends

Te invito *I'll treat you*
Voy a pagar yo *I'll pay/This is on me*

B1 Self, family and friends

el apellido *surname*
la firma *signature*
la identidad *identity*
el nombre *first name*
escribir *to write*
escribirse *to be written, to be spelt*
firmar *to sign*
llamarse *to be called*
Me llamo . . . *My name is . . .*
¿Cómo se escribe? *How do you spell that?*
Señor *Mr, sir*
Señora *Mrs, madam*
Señorita *Miss*
Sr/Sra/Srta *Mr/Mrs/Miss*

Home address

la aldea *village*
la avenida *walk, lane, avenue*
la calle *street, road*
el camino *road, lane*
la carta *letter*
la casa *house*
el código postal *postcode*
el condado *county*
la dirección *address*
el domicilio *home*
el número *number*
el país *country*
el paseo *avenue*
el piso *flat*
la planta baja *ground floor*
la plaza *square*
el/la portero/a *caretaker*
el pueblo *village, small town*
el sobre *envelope*
tener teléfono *to be on the phone*
vivir (en) *to live (in)*
abajo *downstairs, below*
arriba *upstairs, above*
en casa (de) *at (the) home (of)*
fuera de *outside*
¿Cuál es tu número de teléfono? *What is your phone number?*
Mi número de teléfono es el 01 78 56 . . . *My telephone number is 01 78 56 . . .*
Vivo en Bristol *I live in Bristol*
Vivo en el primer piso *I live on the first floor*
Vivo en Gales *I live in Wales*
Vivo en Inglaterra *I live in England*
Vivo en la planta baja *I live on the ground floor*
For use of telephone see also D5 Communication

Ages and birthdays

el adulto *adult*
el año *year*
el cumpleaños *birthday*
el edad *age*
la fecha *date*
la fecha de nacimiento *date of birth*
el lugar de nacimiento *place of birth*
el mes *month*
el nacimiento *birth*
nacer *to be born*
tener ____ años *to be ____ years old*
mayor *older, 18 and over*
menor *younger, under 18*
nacido(a) el ____ en ____ *born on the ____ at ____*
¿Cuál es la fecha de tu cumpleaños? *What is the date of your birthday?*
Nací el veinte de febrero de mil novecientos setenta y tres en Londres *I was born on 20th February 1973 in London*
Tengo dieciséis años *I am sixteen*

Nationality

el carnet de identidad *identity card*
la documentación *item of identification*
el extranjero *foreigner*
el pasaporte *passport*
venir (de) *to come (from)*
¿De dónde? *where from?*

Character and disposition

el amor *love*
el carácter *character*
la confianza *confidence*
el cuidado *care, worry*
la esperanza *hope*
el humor *humour*
la imaginación *imagination*
la opinión *opinion*
el sentimiento *feeling*
la suerte *luck*
aconsejar *to advise*
asombrar *to amaze*
asustar *to frighten*
atreverse a *to dare*
demostrar (ue) *to prove*
desconfiar de *to distrust*
esperar *to hope*
estar avergonzado/a *to be ashamed*
estar equivocado/a *to be wrong*
gustar *to like*
llevarse bien con *to understand one another, to get on well*
llorar *to weep*
parecer *to appear, seem*
reflejar *to think, reflect*
reír *to laugh*
sonreír *to smile*
tener derecho a *to have the right to*
tener ganas de *to wish to*
agradable *pleasant*
amable *kind*
asqueroso/a *disgusting*
capaz de *capable of*
célebre *famous*
celoso/a *jealous*
cómico/a *funny*

cortés, fino/a *polite*
decepcionado/a *disappointed*
desagradable *disagreeable, unpleasant*
divertido/a *amusing*
encantador/a *charming*
enérgico/a *active*
enfadado/a *angry*
famoso/a *famous*
fenomenal *great, marvellous*
gracioso/a *funny*
honrado/a *honest*
importante *important*
infeliz *unhappy*
insoportable *unbearable*
listo/a *clever*
loco/a *mad*
natural *natural*
nervioso/a *nervous, tense*
normal *normal*
optimista *optimistic*
orgulloso/a *proud*
perezoso/a *lazy*
pesimista *pessimistic*
pobre *poor*
preocupado/a *anxious*
raro/a *bizarre, strange*
rico/a *rich*
seguro/a *certain*
serio/a *serious*
simpático/a *nice*
sorprendente *surprising*
terco/a *obstinate*
terrible *awful*
tímido/a *shy*
tranquilo/a *calm, quiet*
travieso/a *naughty*
vivo/a *lively*
a mi parecer *in my opinion*
algo *rather*
bastante *fairly*
francamente *frankly*
generalmente *usually, generally*
naturalmente *naturally*
realmente *really*
tan *so*
¿Cómo encuentras _____ ? *How do you find _____ ?*
¿Cómo es ____ ? *What's _____ like?*
El profe se enfadó *The teacher got angry*
Estás equivocado/a *You are wrong*
Estoy de buen humor hoy *I'm in a good mood today*
Estoy harto/a *I'm fed up*
Estoy harto/a del francés *I'm fed up with French*
Juan me parece muy simpático *John seems to me to be really nice*
Me llevo bien con mi hermano *I get on well with my brother*
Tengo confianza en él *I have confidence in him*
Tengo ganas de comer *I want to eat*
Tengo miedo *I'm afraid*
Tengo permiso para salir esta tarde *I have permission to go out this evening*

Physical appearance

la barba *beard*
el bigote *moustache*
los cabellos *hair*
las gafas *spectacles*
los ojos *eyes*
el pelo *hair*
encontrar (ue) *to find*
llevar *to wear, carry*
parecerse a *to resemble*
reconocer *to recognize*
bajo *short (of person)*
bonito/a *pretty*
bronceado/a *tanned*
corto/a *short*
delgado/a *thin*
delicado/a *weak, fragile, delicate*
deportivo/a *good at sports, keen on sports*
elegante *elegant*
feo/a *ugly*
fuerte *strong*
gordo/a *big, fat*
guapo/a *handsome, beautiful*
joven *young*
largo/a *long*
marrón *brown*
moreno/a *chestnut* (*hair*)
pálido/a *pale*
pelirrojo/a *red* (*hair*)
rizado/a *curly*
rubio/a *fair*
semejante *alike, similar*
verde *green*
completamente *completely*
totalmente *totally, quite*
La encuentro bonita *I think she's pretty*
Lleva gafas *She wears glasses*
Parece deportivo *He looks athletic*
Tiene el pelo largo *He has long hair*
For colours see under 'Key words and expressions', p. 31

The family, relatives and friends

la abuela *grandmother*
el abuelo *grandfather*
los abuelos *grandparents*
el/la amigo/a *friend*
el bebé *baby*
el chico *boy*
el/la compañero/a *friend, class/workmate*
el/la corresponsal *pen-friend*
la familia *family*
la gente *people*
la hermana *sister*
la hermanastra *stepsister*
el hermanastro *stepbrother*

el hermano *brother*
la hija *daughter*
la hija política *daughter-in-law*
la hijastra *stepdaughter*
el hijastro *stepson*
el hijo *son*
el hijo político *son-in-law*
el hombre *man*
los jóvenes *young people*
la madrastra *stepmother*
la madre *mother*
la mamá *mummy*
el marido *husband*
la mujer *woman, wife*
la nieta *grand-daughter*
el nieto *grandson*
los nietos *grandchildren*
el/la niño/a *child*
el/la novio/a *fiancé(e), boyfriend, girlfriend*
el padrastro *stepfather*
el padre *father*
los padres *parents*
el papá *daddy*
el/la primo/a *cousin*
la religión *religion*
la sobrina *niece*
el sobrino *nephew*
la suegra *mother-in-law*
el suegro *father-in-law*
la tía *aunt*
el tío *uncle*
los tíos *uncle(s) and aunt(s)*
la viuda *widow*
el viudo *widower*
casarse con *to marry*
divorciar(se) *to divorce*
casado/a *married*
católico/a *Catholic*
divorciado/a *divorced*
familiar *of the family*
hindú *Hindu*
mayor *elder*
menor *younger*
musulmán *Muslim*
protestante *Protestant*
separado/a *separated*
soltero/a *single*
último/a *last*
Fui con mi madre a ver a unos parientes *I went with my mother to see relations*
Ian es mi hermano mayor *Ian is my elder brother*
Mi abuela es viuda *My grandmother is a widow*
Mi hermana se casó con un americano *My sister married an American*
Mi hermano está casado *My brother is married*
Mi tío es soltero *My uncle is a bachelor*
Mis padres están divorciados *My parents are separated/divorced*
Soy hijo único *I'm an only child*
For people's jobs see D2 Careers and employment

Likes and dislikes
encontrar (ue) *to find*
gustar, querer *to like, to love*
llevarse bien con *to get on well with*
odiar *to hate*
preferir (ie) *to prefer*

Pets
el animal *animal*
el cobayo *guinea-pig*
el conejo *rabbit*
el gato *cat*
el hámster *hamster*
el loro *parrot*
el pájaro *bird*
el periquito *budgerigar*
el perro *dog*
el pez de colores *goldfish*
el ratón *mouse*
la tortuga *tortoise*
¿Tienes un animal en casa? *Have you got a pet?*

Other livestock
el burro *donkey*
el caballo *horse*
la cabra *goat*
el cerdo *pig*
el cordero *lamb*
la gallina *hen*
el gallo *cockerel*
el ganso *goose*
la oveja *sheep*
el pato *duck*
el/la ternero/a *calf*
el toro *bull*
la vaca *cow*

Undomesticated creatures
la abeja *bee*
la araña *spider*
el caracol *snail*
el gorrión *sparrow*
el insecto *insect*
el pez *fish*
la rana *frog*
la serpiente *snake*
el zorro *fox*

Parts of animals
la cola *tail*
el hocico *mouth, muzzle*
la pata *foot, paw*
la piel *fur, skin*
la pluma *feather*

Daily routine
el almuerzo *lunch, midday meal*
la cena *dinner, evening meal*
la merienda *tea, snack*
acostarse (ue) *to go to bed*

afeitarse *to shave*
almorzar (ue) *to have lunch*
ayudar *to help*
bañarse *to have a bath*
barrer *to sweep*
beber *to drink*
cambiar *to change*
cambiar de ropa *to change*
cenar *to have dinner*
cocinar *to cook*
colgar (ue) *to hang up*
comer *to eat, to have lunch*
compartir *to share*
comprar *to buy*
cortar *to cut*
coser *to sew*
dar un paseo *to go for a walk*
dejar *to leave*
desayunar *to have breakfast*
descansar *to rest*
desnudarse *to undress*
despertarse (ie) *to wake up*
discutir *to discuss*
disputar *to argue*
divertirse (ie) *to enjoy oneself*
dormir (ue) *to sleep*
dormirse (ue) *to go to sleep*
ducharse *to have a shower*
estar listo/a (para) *to be ready (to)*
fregar (ie) *to wipe*
fregar (ie) los platos *to wash up*
guardar *to put away*
hacer bricolaje *to do odd jobs*
hacer de canguro *to look after the children/babysit*
hacer la cama *to make the bed*
hacer la comida *to prepare the meal*
hacer la compra *to do the shopping*
hacer los deberes *to do one's homework*
hacer los quehaceres domésticos *to do the housework*
hacer punto *to knit*
ir a buscar *to go and get*
ir a los servicios *to go to the toilet*
ir a ver *to go and see*
lavar la ropa *to do the washing*
lavarse *to get washed*
lavarse las manos, (etc.) *to wash one's hands, (etc.)*
levantarse *to get up, stand up*
limpiar *to clean*
marcharse *to go away*
molestar *to disturb*
necesitar *to need*
ofrecer *to offer*
oír música/la radio/discos *to listen to music/the radio/records*
parar(se) *to stop*
pasar la aspiradora *to do the hoovering*
peinarse *to brush one's hair*
pelar *to peel*
planchar *to iron*
poner la mesa *to lay the table*
prestar *to lend*
prohibir *to forbid*
querer (ie) *to want to*
quitar (la mesa) *to clear (the table)*
recibir *to receive*
reempezar (ie) *to start again*
regresar a casa *to return home*
reparar *to repair*
salir *to go out*
sentarse (ie) *to sit down*
servir (i) *to serve*
tirar *to throw (away)*
tomar el desayuno *to have breakfast*
tomar un café *to have a cup of coffee*
trabajar *to work*
traer *to bring*
utilizar *to use*
ver la televisión *to watch television*
vestirse (i) *to dress*
por lo general *usually*
Desayuno tostadas *I have toast for breakfast*
Me gusta ver la televisión *I like watching TV*
Me gustaría ducharme *I would like a shower*
Me he cambiado de ropa *I have changed*
Me he lavado las manos *I have washed my hands*
Me voy *I'm going*
Mi padre me ha prohibido salir esta tarde *My father has forbidden me to go out this evening*
Necesito lavarme *I need to wash*
Normalmente me acuesto a las diez *I usually go to bed at 10 o'clock*
Yo voy a hacer eso *I'll do that*
¿A qué hora te despiertas normalmente? *What time do you usually wake up?*
¿Puedes hacerme la compra? *Could you do the shopping for me?*
¿Puedes prestarme mil pesetas? *Can you lend me 1000 pesetas?*
¿Puedo ayudarte a arreglar tu dormitorio? *Can I help you tidy your room?*
¿Puedo echarte una mano? *Can I give you a hand?*
¿Quieres descansar? *Would you like to rest?*
¿Quieres pelar las zanahorias, por favor? *Will you please prepare (peel, scrape) the carrots?*
¡Vete! *Go away!*
Ve a ver quién está allí *Go and see who is there!*

B2 Free time and social activities

Pocket money and spare time jobs

la asignación *pocket money*
el cambio *small change*
la cartera *wallet*
el monedero *purse*
el precio *price*
el sueldo *pocket money*
ahorrar *to save*
comprar *to buy*
depositar *to deposit*
empezar (ie) *to begin*
ganar *to earn*
ganar _____ pesetas al día/por hora *to make _____ pesetas a day/an hour*
gastar *to spend*
pagar *to pay*
pedir prestado/a *to borrow (from)*
pertenecer a *to belong to*
prestar *to lend*
tener poco dinero *to be short of money*
terminar *to finish*
trabajar *to work*
caro/a *expensive*
gratis *free*
importante *important*
pobre *poor*
rico/a *rich*
Empiezo a las _______ y termino a las ________ *I begin at____o'clock and finish at ___ o'clock*
Estoy ahorrando para comprar . . . *I'm saving to buy . . .*
Gano mil pesetas por hora *I earn 1000 pesetas an hour*
Gano mucho *I earn a lot*
Lo he gastado todo *I have spent everything*
¿Me puedes prestar mil pesetas? *I'd like to borrow 1000 pesetas*
Tengo poco dinero *I'm short of money*
Trabajo los fines de semana *I work at weekends*

Hobbies

la actividad *activity*
el ajedrez *chess*
los alrededores *surroundings*
el baile *dance*
el club (de jóvenes) *(youth) club*
la colección *collection*
el coro *choir*
los deportes *sport*
el diario *newspaper*
el dibujo animado *cartoon*
el disco *record*
la discoteca *disco*
la diversión *entertainment*
la excursión *excursion*
la exposición *exhibition*
las festividades *festivities*
el instrumento *instrument*
el intercambio *exchange*
el jersey *jumper*
el juego *game*
la lectura *reading*
la música (pop/clásica) *(pop/classical) music*
el pasatiempo *hobby*
la pesca *fishing*
el programa *programme*
los ratos libres *free time*
la reunión *meeting*
la revista *magazine*
la sociedad *society, club*
el/la socio *member*
el telediario *TV news*
las vacaciones *holidays*
la visita *tour (of museum etc.)*
aburrirse *to get bored*
asistir a *to go to, attend*
bailar *to dance*
coleccionar *to collect*
discutir *to discuss, argue*
divertirse (i) *to enjoy oneself*
exponer *to exhibit*
gustar mucho *to like a lot*
interesar *to interest*
participar en *to take part in*
pescar *to fish*
pintar *to paint*
popular *popular*
preferir (ie) *to prefer*
realizar *to put into practice*
reír (i) *to laugh*
salir *to go out*
soñar (ue) (con) *to dream (of)*
tener tiempo para *to have the time to*
tocar la guitarra (etc.) *to play the guitar (etc.)*
ver *to watch*
visitar *to visit*
deportivo/a *athletic, keen on sports*
emocionante *exciting*
fenomenal *great, marvellous*
maravilloso/a *great, sensational*
mensual *monthly*
semanal *weekly*
solo/a *alone*
A veces juego al tenis *I sometimes play tennis*
Canto en un coro *I sing in a choir*
Hicimos la visita con guía *We had a guided tour*
Leo los diarios para informarme *I read the papers to learn about things*
Me gusta visitar castillos *I like going to castles*
Me interesa la fotografía *I'm interested in photography*
Odio el tenis *I hate tennis*
¿Qué hay como diversiones aquí? *What entertainments are there here?*
Soy socio de un club *I am a member of a club*
Toco la flauta *I play the flute*
Voy a la pesca bastante a menudo *I go fishing quite often*

Sporting activities

el árbitro *referee*
el atletismo *athletics*
el baloncesto *basketball*
la bici(cleta) *bicycle*
el campeón *champion*
el campeonato *championship*
el campo de deportes *sports ground*
la carrera *race*
el ciclismo *cycling*
el club (de deportes) *(sports) club*
la competición *competition*
el concurso *competition*
el críquet *cricket*
el deporte *sport*
los deportes de invierno *winter sports*
el deportista *sports player*
el empate *draw (scores equal)*
la entrada *(entrance) ticket*
el equipo *team*
la equitación *riding*
el estadio *stadium*
el footing *jogging*
el fútbol *football*
la gimnasia *gymnastics*
el hockey *hockey*
el jugador *player*
el juguete *toy*
la natación *swimming*
el partido *match*
el patinaje *skating*
la pista de patinaje *skating rink*
la pelota *ball (e.g. football)*
la piscina *swimming pool*
el polideportivo *sports centre*
el remo *oar*
el rugby *rugby*
el tenis (de mesa) *(table) tennis*
el terreno de juego *pitch*
el título *title*
el valor *courage, drive*
la vela *sailing*
el voleibol *volleyball*
bañarse *to swim, bathe*
correr *to run*
criticar *to criticize*
dar un paseo en barco *to go boating*
dar un paseo en bicicleta *to go for a bike ride*
defender (ie) *to defend*
descansar *to rest*
esquiar *to ski*
ganar *to win*
hacer ciclismo *to cycle*
jugar (ue) un partido de tenis, (etc.) *to play a game of tennis, (etc.)*
jugar (ue) al fútbol/tenis *to play football/tennis*
marcar un gol *to score a goal*
marcar un punto *to score a point*
montar a caballo *to go horse riding*
montar en bici(cleta) *to ride a bicycle*
nadar *to swim*
patinar *to skate*
perder (ie) *to lose*
practicar un deporte *to play a sport*
protestar *to protest*
sacar una entrada *to buy a ticket*
saltar *to jump*
ser hincha de *to support (a team)*
vencer *to beat*
¡Buena suerte! *Good luck! Play well!*
Me bañé en el río *I bathed in the river*
Me encanta nadar *I love swimming*
Perdimos el partido de rugby *We lost the rugby match*
Voy a esquiar muy a menudo *I often go skiing*

Entertainment

el actor *actor*
la actriz *actress*
el aire acondicionado *air conditioning*
el balcón *balcony*
el ballet *ballet*
la butaca *seat (at cinema, theatre)*
el circo *circus*
el/la cantante *singer*
el cine *cinema*
la comedia *comedy*
el concierto *concert*
la corrida *bullfight*
el cartel *poster*
los dibujos animados *cartoons*
la dirección *direction (of play, film)*
el entreacto, descanso *interval*
la entrada *(entry) ticket*
el espectáculo *show, spectacle*
la fila *row*
la información *information*
la música clásica *classical music*
la música pop *pop music*
la música rock *rock music*
la obra (de teatro) *play*
la ópera *opera*
la orquesta *orchestra*
la película *film*
la película de amor *love film*
la película de ciencia-ficción *science fiction film*
la película de miedo *horror film*
la película policíaca *police, crime film*
la plaza de toros *bull ring*
el programa *programme*
la radio *radio*
la sala (de fiestas) *(function) room, dance hall*
la sesión de la tarde *matinée*
la sesión de la noche *evening performance, showing*
la taquilla *box office*
la televisión *TV*
el teatro *theatre*
los toros *bullfight, bullfighting*
el vídeo *video*
el western *western*

empezar (ie) *to begin*
hacer cola *to queue*
reservar *to reserve, book in advance*
ser anunciado/a *to be advertised, billed*
tener lugar *to take place*
ver *to watch*
aburrido/a *boring*
cómico/a *comic*
divertido/a *amusing*
extraordinario/a *extraordinary*
fatal *awful*
fenomenal *great, terrific*
gracioso/a *funny*
horrible *terrible, awful*
interesante *interesting*
sensacional *sensational*
sorprendente *surprising*
subtitulado/a *subtitled*
versión española *Spanish language edition/version/soundtrack*
versión inglesa *English language edition/version/soundtrack*
¿A qué hora empieza? *What time does it begin?*
Dos entradas para esta noche *Two tickets for tonight*
¿Qué tal la película? *What was the film like?*

B3 Meeting people

Greetings, wishes and goodbyes

Adiós *Goodbye*
Bienvenido/a/os/as *Welcome*
Buen fin de semana *Have a good weekend*
Buen viaje *Have a good trip*
Buena suerte *Good luck*
Buenas noches *Goodnight*
Buenas tardes *Good evening, Good afternoon*
Buenos días *Good morning*
De nada *Don't mention it*
Felicidades *Happy birthday*
Feliz Año Nuevo *Have a good year/Happy New Year*
Gracias *Thank you*
Hasta el sábado (etc.) *Till Saturday (etc.)*
Hasta esta tarde *See you this evening*
Hasta la vista *See you later*
Hasta luego *See you later*
Hasta mañana *See you tomorrow*
Por favor *Please*
¡Enhorabuena! *Congratulations!*
¡Felices Pascuas (de Navidad)! *Happy Christmas!*
¡Hasta pronto! *See you soon!*
¡Hola! *Hi! Hello!*
¡Salud! *To your health, cheers*
¿Qué hay? *How are things?*
¿Qué tal? *How are you?*

Making acquaintances

el/la colega *colleague*
el discurso *speech*
la gente *people*
la hermanación *twinning (e.g. town twinning)*
la intención *intention*
el intercambio *exchange*
el placer *pleasure*
la proposición *suggestion*
las relaciones *relationships*
la sorpresa *surprise*
acompañar *to accompany*
agradecer *to thank*
asegurar *to assure, insure*
asombrar *to amaze*
conocer (a) *to make the acquaintance of (some one), to meet for the first time*
encontrar (ue) *to meet (by chance)*
felicitar *to congratulate*
ir a buscar *to go and get*
ponerse en contacto *to make contact with*
presentar *to present, introduce*
presentarse *to introduce oneself*
regresar *to return*
reparar en *to notice*
verse *to see one another*
amable *pleasant, friendly, kind*
encantado/a *delighted*
insoportable *unbearable, dreadful*
simpático/a *pleasant, friendly, kind*
de regreso *back*
Encantado/a *Pleased to meet you*
Me da mucho gusto verte *I am delighted to see you*
Mucho gusto (en conocerte) *Pleased to meet you*
Te doy la bienvenida *I welcome you*
Te presento a María *May I introduce María to you?*
Vamos a vernos mañana, ¿no? *We'll meet tomorrow, won't we?*

B4 Arranging a meeting or activity

la cita *meeting, date, appointment*
la invitación *invitation*
el parque *park*
el paseo *walk*
el tonto *fool*
aceptar *to accept*
acompañar *to accompany*
agradecer *to thank*
bailar *to dance*
citarse *to arrange to meet*
costar (ue) *to cost*
deber *to owe, ought to*
decidir *to decide*
disculparse *to apologise*
divertirse *to enjoy oneself*
encontrar (ue) *to meet (by chance)*

esperar *to wait (for)*
estar situado/a *to be situated*
exagerar *to exaggerate*
gustar *to like*
impedir (i) *to prevent*
invitar *to invite*
ir a ver *to go and see*
lamentar *to regret*
llegar *to arrive*
negarse (ie) a *to refuse to*
ofrecer *to offer*
olvidar(se) *to forget*
organizar una cita *to arrange to meet*
pedir (i) *to ask (for)*
preferir (ie) *to prefer*
prometer *to promise*
quedarse *to stay*
regresar *to return*
rehusar *to refuse*
suponer *to suppose*
tener derecho a *to have the right to*
tener ganas de *to want to*
tener lugar *to take place*
tener tiempo de *to have the time to*
venir *to come*
verse *to see one another*
visitar *to visit someone*
estupendo *great, terrific*
imposible *impossible*
libre *free*
posible *possible*
urgente *urgent*
Basta *That's enough*
Claro *Of course*
con (mucho) gusto *with pleasure, gladly*
de acuerdo *agreed, OK*
de nada *don't mention it*
en *on*
junto/a/os/as *together*
Me es igual, francamente *To be honest, I don't mind*
No importa *It doesn't matter*
No se preocupe *Don't worry*
No vale la pena *It's not worth it*
por cierto *of course*
tanto mejor *all the better*
A mi parecer era demasiado largo/a/serio/a *In my opinion it was too long/serious*
De acuerdo. ¿Dónde nos vemos? *OK. Where shall we meet?*
Delante del cine a las ocho *In front of the cinema at 8 o'clock*
Depende *It depends*
¿Es en versión original? *Is it in the original language/version?*
¡Fenomenal! *Great!*
La película/El concierto fue maravilloso/a/ interesante/aburrido/a/ fatal *The film/The concert was marvellous/interesting/boring/awful*
No, está doblada *No, it's dubbed*
Me gustaría ver una película de miedo *I'd like to see a horror film*
¡Oye! *Hey!*
¡Oye! ¡El gran baile es mañana! *Hey! The big dance is tomorrow!*
¿Por qué no salimos esta tarde? *Why don't we go out tonight?*
¿Qué día? *Which day?*
¿Qué fecha? *What date?*
¡Qué lástima! *What a shame!*
¡Qué lástima! Tengo demasiados deberes *What a shame! I have too much home work*
¿Qué película ponen/echan? *What film are they showing?*
¿Quieres ir al cine conmigo? *Would you like to go to the cinema with me?*
¿Qué te parece la película/la obra? *What do you think of the film/play?*
Vale/De acuerdo *Agreed*
¡Vaya! *Oh well!*
Ya la he visto *I've already seen it*

B5 Holidays

el acantilado *cliff*
la agencia de viajes *travel agency*
la arqueología *archaeology*
el barco de vela *sailing boat*
el bosque *forest*
las botas de esquí *ski boots*
el centro de información *information office*
el centro de vacaciones *holiday centre*
los cheques de viajero *travellers' cheques*
el cinturón salvavidas *life belt*
la crema solar *sun cream*
la escuela de idiomas *language school*
la escuela de verano *summer school*
el espectáculo *entertainment*
la estancia *stay*
el faro *lighthouse*
las festividades *festival, celebration*
el folleto *brochure*
la foto *photograph*
el grupo *group*
el guía *guide (person)*
la guía *guide (book)*
la hospitalidad *hospitality*
la información *information*
la insolación *sunstroke*
la lista *list*
la máquina fotográfica *camera*
la merienda *picnic lunch/picnic tea*
la mochila *rucksack*
el monumento *monument*
el mundo *world*
el museo *museum*
la Navidad *Christmas*
la oficina de turismo *tourist office*
el paraguas *umbrella*

el parasol *parasol*
el parque zoológico *zoo*
la película *film (for camera)*
la piscina *swimming pool*
la pista *track*
el plan *plan*
la playa *beach*
la publicidad *publicity*
el puerto *port*
la región *area*
la Semana Santa *Easter*
el Támesis *the Thames*
la terraza del café *café terrace*
el tipo *type*
la tumbona *couch, sunbed*
el/la turista *tourist*
el viaje *journey*
la visita *visit*
la visita escolar *school trip*
el windsurf *wind surfboard*
acoger *to welcome*
acordarse (ue) de *to remember*
ahogarse *to drown*
alquilar *to hire*
broncearse *to get brown*
divertirse (ie) *to enjoy oneself*
enseñar *to show*
estar de vacaciones *to be on holiday*
gustar *to please*
hacer deportes acuáticos *to do water sports*
hacer esquí acuático *to water-ski*
hacer las maletas *to pack*
hacer vela *to go sailing*
hacer windsurf *to go windsurfing*
hospedarse en un hotel *to stay at a hotel*
informarse to *find out*
ir al extranjero *to go abroad*
ir de vacaciones *to set out on holiday*
mostrar (ue) *to show*
organizar *to organize*
ponerse en marcha *to set out*
quedarse *to stay*
remar *to row*
secar *to dry*
suceder *to take place, happen*
tener buen tiempo *to have fine weather*
tener lugar *to take place*
tener mal tiempo *to have bad weather*
viajar *to travel*
volar (ue) *to take the plane, fly*
acogedor/a *welcoming*
pintoresco/a *picturesque*
a orillas del mar *by the sea*
al aire libre *in the open air*
durante las vacaciones *during the holidays*
en (el mes de) junio *in June*
en el campo *in the country*
en la sierra *in the mountains*
quince días *a fortnight*
todo el mundo *everyone*
tan *so*
Busqué conchas a orillas del mar *I looked for shells by the sea*
Fuimos de vacaciones en agosto *We went on holiday in August*
Nos hospedamos en un hotel en Dover *We stayed in a hotel in Dover*
¿Tiene un folleto sobre la región? *Have you a leaflet showing what is on in the area?*
Todo el mundo estaba de vacaciones *Everyone was on holiday*

C1 Home town and local environment

la acera *pavement*
el aeropuerto *airport*
las afueras *suburbs*
la agencia de viajes *travel agency*
los alrededores *surroundings, neighbourhood*
el ambiente *environment*
el aparcamiento *car park*
la autopista *motorway*
el Ayuntamiento *town hall*
el banco *bank*
el barrio *quarter, district*
la biblioteca *library*
el buzón *letter box*
la cabina telefónica *phone box*
el camping *campsite*
la capital *capital*
el castillo *castle*
la catedral *cathedral*
el centro comercial *shopping centre*
el centro de la ciudad *town centre*
el cine *cinema*
la ciudad *city*
la comisaría *police station*
Correos *post office*
el edificio *building*
el espacio *space*
la estación *station*
la estación de autobuses *bus station*
la estación de metro *underground station*
la estación de servicio *service station*
el estadio *stadium*
la fábrica *factory*
la feria *fair*
la fiesta *festival*
el/la habitante *inhabitant*
el hospital *hospital*
la iglesia *church*
la industria *industry*
le jardín público *park*
el letrero *notice*
el mercado *market*
el monumento *monument*
el museo *museum*
la oficina *office*

la Oficina de Turismo *tourist information office*
la parada del autobús *the bus stop*
una parada de autobús *a bus stop*
el parque *park*
el paso a nivel *level crossing*
el paso de peatones *pedestrian crossing*
el paso subterráneo *subway*
el peligro *danger*
la piscina *swimming pool*
la plaza *square*
el pueblo *small town, village*
el puente *bridge*
el puerto *port, harbour*
el ruido *noise*
el semáforo *traffic lights*
el siglo *century*
el sitio *place*
el suceso *event*
el teatro *theatre*
la tienda *shop*
la torre *tower*
el tráfico *traffic*
el/la vecino/a *neighbour*
la zona peatonal *pedestrian precinct*
Llevo tres años viviendo en Newcastle *I've been living in Newcastle for 3 years*
Siempre he vivido en Norwich *I've always lived in Norwich*

In the countryside

la aldea *village*
los alrededores *surroundings*
el bosque *wood*
la calidad *quality*
el campo *countryside*
los campos *fields*
la contaminación *pollution*
la excursión a pie *long walk*
la granja *farm*
la isla *island*
el lago *lake*
el lugar *place*
el mar *sea*
la montaña *mountain*
el mundo *world*
la naturaleza *nature*
el país *country, region*
el paisaje *countryside*
la playa *beach*
la polución *pollution*
la provincia *province*
la región *region*
el río *river*
la tierra *land, earth*
el valle *valley*

Positions

a la derecha (de) *on the right (of)*
a la izquierda (de) *on the left (of)*
a lo largo de *along*
abajo *downstairs, below*
al aire libre *in the open air*
alrededor de *around*
cerca de *near*
dondequiera *anywhere*
en casa de *at the home of*
en lo alto de *at the top of*
en medio de *in the middle of*
enfrente de *opposite*
(estar) situado/a *(to be) situated*
fuera de *outside*
lejos de *far from*
relacionado con *linked to*
rodeado de *surrounded by*

Descriptions

aburrido/a *boring*
acogedor/a *welcoming*
agradable *pleasant*
agrícola *agricultural*
animado/a *lively*
antiguo/a *old, ex-____*
apenas *hardly, scarcely*
contaminado/a *polluted*
encantador/a *charming*
feo/a *ugly*
histórico/a *historical*
importante *important*
industrial *industrial*
interesante *interesting*
limpio/a *clean*
natural *natural*
peligroso/a *dangerous*
pintoresco/a *picturesque*
profundo/a *deep*
raro/a *rare, unusual, strange*
sucio/a *dirty*
tranquilo/a *peaceful*
triste *sad*
variado/a *varied*
vecino/a *neighbouring*

C2 Finding the way

el camino *way/path/lane/route*
el cruce *crossroads*
la dirección *direction*
la distancia *distance*
la esquina *corner*
el mapa *map*
la oficina de cambio *exchange office*
el policía *policeman*
la rotonda *roundabout*
el semáforo *traffic lights*
los servicios *toilet*
ayudar *to help*
buscar *to look for*
cruzar *to cross*

informarse *to get information, to find out*
irse *to go away*
llegar *to arrive*
pasar delante de *to pass in front of*
prestar atención *to pay attention*
perderse (ie) *to get lost*
recomendar (ie) *to recommend*
regresar *to return*
subir a *to go up to, to get in (a vehicle)*
a la derecha *to the right*
a la izquierda *to the left*
a ____ metros *____ metres away*
a ____ minutos *____ minutes away*
al final de *at the end of*
al lado de *next to*
al este *to the east*
al norte *to the north*
al oeste *to the west*
al sur *to the south*
dondequiera *anywhere*
enfrente de *opposite*
hasta *as far as*
a lo largo de *along*
luego *then*
para ir a . . . *to get to . . .*
¿A qué distancia está de aquí? *How far is it from here?*
¿A cuántos kilómetros está la playa? *How far is it to the beach?*
¿Dónde está la Plaza Joaquín Cortés, por favor? *Where is Joaquín Cortés Square, please?*
¿Dónde puedo aparcar? *Where can I park?*
¿Por dónde se va a Salamanca, por favor? *The way to Salamanca, please?*
¿Qué día es la feria? *On which day is the travelling fair?*
7 kilómetros, más o menos *About 7 kilometres*
Dondequiera a lo largo de esta calle *Anywhere along this road*
Está a unos 20 minutos a pie *It's 20 minutes on foot*
Está a unos 5 minutos en coche *It's 5 minutes by car*
Está a unos 800 metros de aquí *It's about 800 metres from here*
Está al final de la Calle Ortega y Gasset *It's at the end of the Calle Ortega y Gasset*
Está en el centro de la ciudad *It's in the town centre*
Por favor ¿dónde está la salida de urgencia? *Excuse me, where is the emergency exit?*
Siga por el pasillo hasta el letrero 'No fumadores' y tuerza a la derecha. La salida está al final del pasillo *You go along the corridor as far as the 'no smoking' notice and you turn to the right. The exit is at the end of the corridor*
Siga todo derecho *Go straight on*
Siga todo recto *Go straight on*
Tome la tercera calle a la derecha *Take the third street on the right*

C3 Weather

el calor *heat*
el chubasco *shower, downpour*
el claro *bright period*
el clima *climate*
el grado *degree*
el granizo *hail*
el hielo *ice*
la lluvia *rain*
el mar *sea*
la marea *tide*
el mejoramiento *improvement*
la neblina *mist*
la niebla *fog*
la nieve *snow*
la nube *cloud*
las precipitaciones *precipitation (usually of rain or snow)*
el pronóstico *weather forecast*
la puesta del sol *sunset*
el relámpago *lightning*
la salida del sol *sunrise*
el sol *sun*
la sombra *shadow*
la temperatura *temperature*
el temporal *storm*
el tiempo *weather*
la tormenta *storm*
el trueno *thunder*
el viento *wind*
la visibilidad *visibility*
estar harto/a de *to be fed up with*
gustar *to please*
habrá *there will be*
hacer buen tiempo, calor, frío *to be fine, warm, cold*
hay *there is*
helar (ie) *to freeze*
llover a cántaros *to pour with rain*
llover (ue) *to rain*
nevar (ie) *to snow*
ponerse frío *to become cold*
ponerse templado *to become mild*
pronosticar *to forecast*
ser de día *to be light*
soplar *to blow*
tronar (ue) *to thunder*
agradable *pleasant*
azul *blue*
caliente *hot*
cubierto *cloudy*
de nieve *snowy*
frío/a *cold, chilly*
fuerte *strong*
húmedo/a *damp*
ligero/a *light*
lluvioso/a *rainy*
máximo/a *maximum*

mínimo/a *minimum*
nublado/a *cloudy*
próximo/a *next*
raro/a *rare*
seco/a *dry*
sofocante *heavy*
soleado *sunny*
tempestuoso/a / tormentoso/a *stormy*
templado *mild*
triste *sad*
variable *variable*
a pesar de *in spite of*
a pleno sol *in full sunshine*
apenas *hardly, scarcely*
buen tiempo *fine*
en este caso *in this case*
hoy *today*
mejor *better*
raramente *rarely*
sin embargo *however*
Está lloviendo, nevando, helando, (etc.) *It's raining, snowing, freezing, (etc.)*
¿Qué tiempo hace? *What's the weather like?*

The weather forecast

la foto de satélite *satellite photo*
el parte meteorológico *weather bulletin*
la presión *pressure*
deshelar (ie) *to thaw, melt*
estallar *to burst*

C4 Shopping

los almacenes *department store*
la carnicería *butcher's shop*
el centro comercial *shopping centre*
la charcutería *pork butcher's shop, cold meats*
la churrería *'churro' shop*
la confitería *sweet shop*
la droguería *toiletries and hardware shop*
el estanco *tobacconist's shop*
la farmacia *chemist's shop*
la ferretería *hardware shop*
la frutería *grocer's shop*
el hipermercado *hypermarket*
la lechería *dairy*
la librería *bookshop*
el mercado *market*
la panadería *baker's shop*
la papelería *stationery shop*
la pastelería *cake shop*
la peluquería *hairdressing salon*
la perfumería *perfume shop*
la pescadería *fish shop*
la sección *department*
el supermercado *supermarket*
la tienda *(small) shop*
la tienda de comestibles *grocer's shop*
la tienda de ultramarinos *grocer's shop*
la verdulería *greengrocer's shop*
la zapatería *shoe shop*
el alimento *food*
el ascensor *lift*
el autoservicio *self-service*
el boli/bolígrafo *ball-point pen*
la botella *bottle*
el café *café, coffee*
la caja *cash desk, till*
el cambio *change, currency*
la cantidad *quantity*
la cosa *thing*
el/la dependiente/dependienta *sales assistant*
el deporte *sport*
el desodorante *deodorant*
el diario *(daily) newspaper*
el disco *record*
la docena *dozen, about twelve*
el escaparate *shop window*
la cerilla *match*
el gramo *gramme*
el juguete *toy*
el kilo *kilogramme*
el lápiz *pencil*
la lata *box, tin, can*
la libra *pound*
la liquidación *sale*
la lista *list*
el litro *litre*
el maquillaje *make-up*
el metro *metre*
la mitad *half*
el papel de escribir *writing paper*
el paquete *parcel*
el patrón *boss*
la película *film (for a camera)*
el perfume *perfume*
el piso *floor, storey*
la planta baja *ground floor*
la rebaja *reduction*
la reclamación *complaint*
el recuerdo *souvenir*
el regalo *present*
la revista *magazine*
el sobre *envelope*
el tarro *jar, pot*
el sótano *basement*
el tabaco *tobacco*
la tarjeta (de crédito) *(credit) card*
la (tarjeta) postal *post card*
el/la tendero/a *shopkeeper, market trader*
el tiempo libre *leisure*
la tienda *small shop*
el tipo *sort, kind*
el trozo *bit, piece, slice*
el/la vendedor/a *salesman*
abrir *to open*

agradecer *to thank*
cambiar *to exchange*
cerrar (ie) *to close*
comprar *to buy*
costar (ue) *to cost*
desear *to want*
estar situado/a *to be situated*
gustar *to like*
hacer la compra *to do the shopping*
ir a buscar *to go and get*
mostrar (ue) *to show*
ofrecer *to offer*
pagar *to pay (for)*
preferir (ie) *to prefer*
probar (ue) *to try (on)*
querer (ie) *to want (to)*
reclamar *to complain*
robar *to steal*
tener *to have*
tomar *to take*
vender *to sell*
barato/a *cheap*
caro/a *dear, expensive*
corto/a *short*
diferente *different*
justo/a *exact*
largo/a *long*
mucho/a/s *a lot, many*
otro/a *other*
pequeño/a *small*
varios/as *several*
a parte de . . . *apart from . . .*
a partir de *from*
de nada *don't mention it*
excepto *except*
gracias *thank you*
más (un poco más) *more (a little more)*
Quiero *I would like*
vale *that's all right*

In the shop

el abrigo *overcoat*
los alimentos *food*
los alimentos congelados *frozen food*
la alpargata *canvas sandal*
el anorak *anorak*
la aspirina *aspirin*
el banco *bank*
la bebida *drink*
el billete de mil pesetas *1000-peseta note*
la blusa *blouse*
la bota *boot*
las bragas *knickers*
el calcetín *sock*
la calidad *quality*
los calzoncillos *underpants*
la camisa *shirt*
el carrito *trolley*
la cazadora *blouson, bomber jacket*
el centímetro *centimetre*
la cereza *cherry*
la cesta *basket*
la chaqueta *jacket*
el cheque *cheque*
el/la cliente *customer*
el color *colour*
la corbata *tie*
el día de fiesta *public holiday*
el día festivo *public holiday*
el día laborable *weekday, working day*
el dinero *money*
el dulce *sweet*
la ensalada *lettuce, salad*
la escalera mecánica *escalator*
el estante *shelf, set of shelves*
la falda *skirt*
la fresa *strawberry*
la fruta *fruit*
la galleta *biscuit*
el gerente *manager*
el huevo *egg*
el impermeable *raincoat*
el jersey *pullover*
el ladrón *thief*
la lana *wool*
la leche *milk*
la lechuga *lettuce*
la libra *pound, 500 grammes*
la libra esterlina *pound sterling*
la librería *bookshop*
la lista *list*
la mantequilla *butter*
la medida *measure*
la mermelada *jam*
el metal *metal*
la moda *fashion*
el mostrador *counter*
la naranja *orange*
el nailon *nylon*
el número *size (shoes)*
el pantalón corto *shorts*
los pantalones *pair of trousers*
el panti *tights*
el pañuelo *handkerchief*
el paquete *packet, parcel*
el par (de) *pair (of)*
el paraguas *umbrella*
la peseta *peseta*
el pijama *pyjamas*
el plástico *plastic*
el precio *price*
la promoción *offer*
el queso *cheese*
la ropa *clothes*
la sandalia *sandal*
el sombrero *hat*
el surtido *choice*
la talla *size (clothes)*
el talonario (de cheques) *cheque book*
el tamaño *height, size*

el tomate *tomato*
el traje de baño *bathing costume*
los vaqueros *jeans*
el vestido *dress*
el yogur *yoghurt*
el zapato *shoe*
el zumo de fruta *fruit juice*
aceptar *to accept*
aconsejar *to advise*
ayudar *to help*
contar (ue) *to count*
deber *to owe*
devolver (ue) *to give back*
distribuir *to distribute*
hacer falta *to lack*
llevar *to carry, wear*
necesitar *to need*
no funcionar *not to work*
pedir (i) *to ask (for)*
pesar *to weigh*
probar (ue) *to try (on)*
robar *to steal*
ver escaparates *to window shop*
devolver (ue) *to bring back, return*
ancho/a *broad*
claro/a *light (in colour)*
desgarrado/a *torn*
entero/a *complete*
estrecho/a *narrow*
fresco/a *fresh*
gratuito/a *free (no charge)*
largo/a *long*
ligero/a *light*
maduro/a *ripe*
mismo/a *same*
normal *normal*
nuevo/a *new*
oscuro/a *dark (in colour)*
pesado/a *heavy*
rayado/a *striped*
algo *something*
bastante *enough, fairly*
cada uno/a *each one*
de *in (e.g.* de cuero – *in leather)*
de algodón *made of cotton*
de cuero *made of leather*
de día *by day*
de noche *by night*
debajo de *underneath*
demasiado *too, too much*
encima de *above*
exactamente *exactly*
gratis *free (no charge)*
incluido *included*
¿A quién le toca? *Whose turn is it now?*
¿Algo más? *Anything else?*
¿Cuánto vale este/esta . . . ? *What does this . . . cost?*
¿Cuánto valen los . . . ? *How much are the . . . ?*
¿Cuánto le debo? *How much do I owe you*
¿Cuánto/a/os/as? *how much, how many*
¿De dónde viene este/esta . . . ? *Where does this . . . come from?*
¿De qué clase? *What kind?*
¿Dónde puedo encontrar . . . ? *Where could I find some . . . ?*
¿Es todo? *Is that all?*
¿Estos/as? *These?*
¿Hay . . . ? *Are there any . . . ?*
¿Le están despachando? *Are you being served?*
¿Tiene algo más barato/a? *Have you anything cheaper?*
¿Puede envolverlo/la? *Could you wrap it for me?*
¿Puedo escoger los . . . ? *May I choose the . . . ?*
¿Qué desea (Vd.)? *What would you like?*
¿Cuáles son los mejores? *Which are the best?*
¿Qué tiene de . . . ? *What have you got in the way of . . . ?*
¿Tiene cambio? *Have you any change?*
¿Tiene . . . ? *Have you any . . . ?*
¿Vende Vd . . . ? *Do you sell . . . ?*
Aquí tiene el cambio *Here's your change*
Aquí tiene Vd. ¿Algo más? *There. Anything else?*
Cuesta 500 pesetas el kilo *It's 500 pesetas a kilo*
Me quedo con ellos *I'll take them*
No importa *It doesn't matter*
No me quedan *I haven't any left*
Normalmente tengo, pero no me quedan *Usually I have some, but I've none left*
Quiero media libra, por favor *I would like half a pound, please*
Quiero un trozo de . . . *I'd like a piece of . . .*
Quiero unos/as . . . y unos/as . . . *I would like some . . . and some . . .*
Se vende a peso *It's sold by weight*
Sí, por favor *Yes, please*
Sí, es todo *Yes, that will be all*
Sí, tengo más *Yes, I have some more*
Sí, claro *Yes, of course*
Sí/No *Yes/No*
Sólo tengo un billete de (mil) pesetas *I only have a (1000) peseta note*
Tengo estos/as . . . y estos/as . . . *I have these . . . and these . . .*
Un poco más grande, por favor *A little bigger, please*
Vale . . . *It's worth . . . , It costs . . .*
Viene de . . . *It comes from . . .*
Voy a pensarlo *I'll think about it*

C5 Services

Post Office

el buzón *letter box*
la carta *letter*
la carta certificada *recorded letter*
el/la cartero/a *postman/postwoman*
el correo *post, mail*
Correos *post office*
la dirección *address*

el extranjero *abroad, overseas*
el formulario, el impreso *form*
el giro postal *postal order*
la lista de Correos *post to be collected*
la lista de tarifas *price list*
la moneda *coin*
el paquete *parcel*
la recogida *postal collection*
el sello *stamp*
un sello de cuarenta y cinco pesetas *a 45 peseta stamp*
las señas *address*
el servicio de ventanilla *counter service*
la ventanilla *counter position*
cobrar un cheque/un giro *to cash a cheque/postal order*
contar (ue) *to count*
dirigirse a *to apply to*
equivocarse *to make a mistake*
hay que tener *you must have*
llamar *to call*
oír *to hear*
pagar por palabra *to pay by the word*
rellenar *to fill in*
repartir el correo *to deliver the post*
frágil *fragile*
libre *free*
ocupado/a *occupied*
urgente *urgent*
aquí *here*
por avión *by air mail*
¿Cuánto quiere mandar? *How much do you want to send?*
¿Cuánto vale mandar una carta a Inglaterra? *How much is a letter to England?*
¿Dónde hay un teléfono? *Where is there a telephone?*
¿Dónde puedo telefonear a Inglaterra? *Where can I telephone England from?*
¿Hay una cabina telefónica cerca de aquí? *Is there a phone box near here?*
¿Por avion? *By air?*
Aquél, en el mostrador *That one, on the counter*
Aquí tiene el dinero *Here's the money*
Aquí tiene. Ya está rellenado. Hay diecisiete palabras *There, it's complete. There are 17 words*
Bueno. Son . . . pesetas en total *Good. That will cost . . . pesetas altogether*
Claro. Es gratuito *Yes, of course. It's free*
Puede mandar un giro postal. Hay que rellenar este impreso *You could send a postal order. You have to fill in this coupon*
Puede consultaras en Correos. Están al lado de los locutorios *You can look at them here in the post office. They are next to the phone boxes*
Quiero mandar dinero. ¿Qué debo hacer? *I would like to send some money. What should I do?*
Quiero mandar esta carta *I would like to send this letter*
Quiero mandar un telegrama *I would like to send a telegram*
Rellena este formulario *Complete this form*
También quiero llamar por teléfono *I would also like to ring someone*
¿Dónde están las guías? *Where can I find the directories?*
También quiero mandar este paquete al extranjero *I would also like to send this package abroad*
Voy a pesarlo *I'll weigh it*
Ya está. He terminado *There, I have finished*
See also 'D5 Communication' for telephone calls

Bank or exchange office

el banco *bank*
el billete de mil pesetas *1000-peseta note*
la caja *cash desk, till*
el carnet de identidad *identity card*
el cheque *cheque*
el cheque de viajero *traveller's cheque*
la comisión *commission*
el dinero *money*
la libra esterlina *pound sterling*
la mitad *half*
la moneda *coin*
la moneda suelta *change*
el número de cuenta *account number*
el pasaporte *passport*
la tarjeta de banco *banker's card*
la tarjeta de crédito *credit card*
el cambio *rate of exchange*
la ventanilla *counter window*
la ventanilla de cambio *exchange counter*
aceptar, admitir *to accept*
cambiar *to change*
cobrar una comisión *to take a commission*
firmar *to sign*
pasar a la caja *to go on to the cash desk*
valer *to be worth*
vale *is valid*
por ciento *per cent*
¿A cuánto está la libra esterlina? *What is the pound worth?*
Aquí tiene *There*
Aquí tiene el dinero. ¡Que lo pase bien! *Here's your money. Have a good stay!*
Deme sus cheques de viajero y la documentación *Give me your travellers' cheques and some proof of identity*
El cambio es . . . pesetas. Aquí tiene el impreso. Puede pasar a la caja. *The rate of exchange is . . . pesetas. Here's your ticket. You can go to the cash desk now*
Firme aquí, por favor *Sign here, please*
Hay una comisión del tres por ciento en los cheques de viajero *There is a commission of 3 per cent on travellers' cheques*
Quiero cambiar unas libras esterlinas/unos cheques de viajero, por favor *I would like to change some pounds/traveller's cheques, please*

Sí, claro. ¿Billetes o cheques de viajero? *Of course. Banknotes or traveller's cheques?*
Sí, claro *Of course*
Un pasaporte, ¿vale? *Is a passport all right?*

Lost property office

el arreglo *regulation, settlement*
la bicicleta *bicycle*
el bolsillo *pocket*
el bolso *handbag*
la cámara cinematográfica *cine camera*
la cartera *wallet*
el ciclomotor *motor-assisted bicycle*
el cinturón *belt*
el color *colour*
el consulado *consulate*
el daño *damage*
la descripción *description*
el flash *flash gun (photography)*
la forma *form, shape*
el formulario, el impreso *form*
el ladrón *burglar, thief*
la llave *key*
la maleta *suitcase*
la máquina fotográfica *camera*
la marca *make, brand name*
los medios *means*
la mochila *rucksack*
el monedero *purse*
el nombre *name*
la oficina de objetos perdidos *lost property office*
el pañuelo *handkerchief*
el paraguas *umbrella*
la recompensa *reward*
el reloj *watch*
el robo *theft*
el talonario (de cheques) *cheque book*
el tamaño *size, height*
acordarse (ue) de *to remember*
acusar *to accuse*
asombrar, extrañar *to astonish*
buscar *to look for*
conseguir (i) *to manage*
darse cuenta de (que) *to realize (that)*
deber *to owe*
dejar *to let, leave*
desaparecer *to disappear*
describir *to describe*
descubrir *to discover*
devolver (ue) *to give back*
dudar *to doubt*
encontrar (ue) *to find*
engañar *to mislead*
extraviar *to mislay*
forzar (ue) *to break in to*
firmar *to sign*
guardar *to keep*
marcar *to mark*
olvidar(se) *to forget*
parecerse a *to look like, resemble*
pedir (i) prestado *to borrow*
perder (ie) *to lose*
perdonar *to forgive*
pertenecer a *to belong to*
reconocer *to recognize*
rellenar *to fill, fill in*
saber *to know (a fact)*
ancho/a *broad*
cierto/a *certain*
claro/a *light (colour)*
contento/a *pleased*
corto/a *short*
cuadrado/a *square*
debajo de *underneath*
decepcionado/a *disappointed*
delgado/a *thin*
diferente *different*
enfadado/a *angry*
estrecho/a *narrow*
feliz *happy, lucky*
fenomenal *great*
flamante *brand new*
furioso/a *furious*
imposible *impossible*
largo/a *long*
lleno/a *full*
nuevo/a *new*
oscuro/a *dark (colour)*
pequeño/a *small*
posible *possible*
rectangular *rectangular*
redondo/a *round*
seguro/a *sure*
sólido/a *solid*
vacío/a *empty*
viejo/a *old*
como *as, like*
con éxito *with success*
dentro *inside*
en vía de *in the process of*
encima de *above*
es necesario *it is necessary*
Eso no sirve para nada *That's no use*
No tengo suerte *I've no luck*
se trata de *it's a question of, it's about*
un tipo de, una clase de *a kind of*
ya que *since*
Perdí mi cartera *I've lost my wallet*
¿Puede describírmelo? *Can you describe it to me?*

Having things repaired or cleaned

el agujero *hole*
la avería *breakdown*
la batería *battery (of car)*
el botón *button*
la crítica *criticism, complaint*
el dueño del garaje *garage owner*
el electricista *electrician*
el embrague *clutch*
el estado *state, condition*
el fontanero *plumber*
el freno *brake*

la fuga *leak*
el garaje *garage*
la inundación *flood*
la linterna *torch*
el lavado automático *car wash, launderette*
la lavadora *washing machine*
la limpieza en seco *dry cleaning*
la marca *make, brand*
el mecánico *mechanic*
el motor *engine*
la pieza de recambio *spare part*
la pila *battery (small)*
el radiador *radiator*
la reclamación *complaint*
las reparaciones *the repair*
la rueda de repuesto *spare wheel*
el ruido *noise*
la seguridad *security*
la (tienda de) reparación de calzado *shoe repairer's shop*
las velocidades *gears*
aceptar, admitir *to accept*
aceptar devoluciones *to take back goods*
agradecer *to thank*
arreglar *to fix*
cambiar *to exchange*
criticar *to criticize*
dejar caer *to drop*
fiarse de *to trust*
funcionar *to work, function*
garantizar *to guarantee*
lavar *to wash*
limpiar en seco *to dry clean*
llevar a limpiar *to have cleaned*
llevar a reparar *to have repaired*
negarse a *to refuse*
probar (ue) *to prove*
prometer *to promise*
proponer *to propose*
reclamar, quejarse (de) *to complain (about)*
reembolsar *to reimburse*
regresar *to come back*
reparar *to repair*
romper *to break, to tear*
sugerir (ie) *to suggest*
sustituir *to replace*
verificar *to check*
amable *kind*
capaz *capable*
listo/a *ready*
pinchado *punctured*
raro/a *odd, strange*
recibido *received*
a pesar de *in spite of*
¿Cuánto tiempo? *How long?*
en este caso *in this case*
naturalmente *of course*
No funciona *out of order, broken down*
No vale la pena *it's not worth it*

C6 Getting around

Public transport

Trains

el andén, la vía *platform*
el AVE *high speed train*
el billete *ticket*
el billete sencillo *single ticket*
el billete de ida y vuelta *return ticket*
el cambio de horario *timetable change*
la cantina *buffet*
el coche-cama *couchette, sleeper*
el coche-comedor *dining car*
la consigna *left luggage office*
la correspondencia *connection*
el departamento *compartment*
el destino *destination*
la estación *station*
el expreso *night express*
el ferrocarril *railway*
el horario *timetable*
la lista de precios *price list*
la llegada *arrival*
la maleta *suitcase*
el metro *underground (railway)*
el mozo *porter*
la parada *stop*
la parada de taxis *taxi rank*
la plaza reservada *reservation*
la primera clase *first class*
la puerta *door*
la rebaja *reduction*
la RENFE *Spanish railways*
la sala de espera *waiting room*
la salida *departure, exit*
la segunda clase *second class*
el TALGO *intercity luxury train*
la taquilla *ticket office*
el TER *inter-city express*
el tranvía *stopping train*
el transporte (público) *(public) transport*
el tren *train*
el/la turista *tourist*
la vía *track*
el viajero *traveller, passenger*
anunciar *to announce*
bajar de *to get out of (a vehicle)*
cambiar *to change*
coger un tren *to catch a train*
consultar *to consult*
durar *to last*
durar tres horas *to take three hours*
esperar *to wait for*
hacer transbordo *to change trains*
indicar *to show, indicate*
instalarse *to settle*
llevar *to wear, carry*
parar(se) *to stop*

perder (ie) *to miss*
picar *to date, punch (ticket)*
reducir la velocidad *to slow down*
revisar *to check*
subir a *to get into (a vehicle)*
tomar el tren *to take the train*
viajar *to travel, move*
ocupado/a *occupied*
próximo/a *next*
siguiente *next, following*
último/a *last*
con destino a *going to*
de fumadores *smoking*
no fumadores *non-smoking*
procedente de *coming from*
suplemento *extra*
¿A qué hora llega el tren? *At what time does the train arrive?*
¿A qué hora sale el próximo tren para Madrid? ¿Y el siguiente? *At what time is the next train for Madrid? And the one after that?*
¿A qué hora sale el tren? *At what time does the train leave?*
¡Buen viaje! *Have a good trip!*
¿De dónde sale el tren para Salamanca? *Where does the Salamanca train leave from?*
¿De ida sólo, o de ida y vuelta? *Single or return?*
¿De primera o segunda clase? *Are you going first or second class?*
¿Dónde puedo dejar mi equipaje? *Where can I leave my luggage?*
¿Es un tranvía o un TER? *Is it a slow or a fast train?*
¿Sale de aquí el tren para Salamanca? *Is this where the Salamanca train leaves from?*
¿Dónde está el coche-comedor? *Where is the dining car?*
¿Quiere reservar? *Do you want to reserve a seat?*
Allí está el horario de salidas y llegadas *Departure and arrival times are posted over there*
Coche once, asiento cinco *Coach 11, seat 5*
La sala de espera está al otro lado *The waiting room is on the other side*
No, éstos son los trenes de cercanías *No, these are the suburban trains*
Puede dejarlo en la consigna, o en la consigna automática *You can put it in the left luggage office or use the automatic luggage locker*
Quiero un billete para Madrid, por favor *I'd like a ticket for Madrid, please*

Buses

el autobús *bus*
el autocar *coach, long distance bus*
el billete *ticket*
el bonobús *ticket for ten journeys*
el coche de línea *coach*
la estación de autobuses *bus station*
la línea *line, route*
el número *number*
la parada *stop*

Ships and hovercraft

el aerodeslizador *hovercraft*
el barco *boat*
el ferry *ferry*
el puerto *port*
el transbordador (de coches) *car ferry*
la travesía *crossing*
desembarcar *to disembark*
embarcar *to embark*

Aeroplanes

el avión *aeroplane*
el cinturón de seguridad *safety belt*
el vuelo *flight*
aterrizar *to land*
despegar *to take off*
volar (ue) *to fly*

Going through Customs

la aduana *customs*
el/la aduanero/a *customs official*
la frontera *frontier, border*
el pasaporte *passport*
Abra las maletas, por favor *Open your cases, please*
No tengo nada que declarar *I have nothing to declare*
Tengo unos cigarillos y alcohol que declarar *I have some cigarettes and some alcohol to declare*
¿Tiene Vd. algo que declarar? *Have you anything to declare?*
See also C5 Lost property office

Private transport

General

la acera *pavement*
el aparcamiento *car park*
la área de descanso *picnic area*
el atasco, el embotellamiento *traffic jam*
la autoescuela *driving school*
la bici(cleta) *bicycle*
la calzada *roadway*
el camión *lorry*
la camioneta *van*
el carnet de conducir *driving licence*
la carretera nacional *major road*
la carta verde *green card*
el casco *helmet*
el ciclomotor *motorized bicycle*
el código de la circulación *highway code*
el conductor *driver*
la curva *turn, bend*

el desvío *diversion*
el disco de aparcamiento *parking disc*
el garaje *garage*
la hora punta *rush hour*
el mapa de carreteras *road map*
la matrícula *numberplate*
el mecánico *mechanic*
la moto *motorbike*
la multa *fine*
las obras *road works*
los papeles, la documentación *papers*
el peaje *toll*
el peatón *pedestrian*
la póliza de seguros *insurance policy*
la preferencia *right of way*
el seguro *insurance*
la velocidad *speed, gear*
la zona azul *blue zone (parking)*
adelantar *to overtake*
alquilar *to hire*
andar *to walk*
aparcar *to park*
conducir *to drive*
frenar *to brake*
ir en bicicleta *to go by bicycle*
ir en coche *to go by car*
ir a pie *to go on foot*
reducir la velocidad *to slow down*
regresar *to return*
torcer (ue) *to turn*
automático/a *automatic*
obligatorio *obligatory, compulsory*
a pie *on foot*
preferencia a la derecha *priority from the right*
¡Cuidado! *look out!*
Está prohibido aparcar aquí *It is forbidden to park here*
Hay que frenar antes de la curva *You have to brake before the bend*

The car

el asiento *seat*
el automóvil *car*
la avería *breakdown*
la batería *battery*
el cinturón de seguridad *safety belt*
el coche *car*
el espejo *driving mirror*
el faro *headlight*
el freno *brake*
el limpiaparabrisas *windscreen wiper*
la llave del coche *car key*
el maletero *boot*
el motor *engine*
el neumático *tyre*
el parabrisas *windscreen*
la parte delantera *the front*
la parte trasera *the back*
el pinchazo *puncture*
la puerta *door*
el volante *steering wheel*
acelerar *to accelerate*
apagar *to put out lights, switch off engine*
arrancar *to start*
averiarse *to break down*
bajar del coche *to get out of the car*
cambiar de velocidad *to change gear*
conducir *to drive*
encender (ie) las luces *to put on lights*
funcionar *to function, work*
parar(se) *to stop*
quedarse sin gasolina *run out of petrol*
reparar *to repair*
subir al coche *to get into the car*
El motor no funciona *The engine doesn't work*

At the service station

el aceite *oil*
el agua (*feminine*) *water*
el aire *air*
el dos tiempos *two-stroke*
el empleado de la gasolinera *petrol pump attendant*
el gas-oil *diesel*
la gasolina *petrol*
la gasolina sin plomo *unleaded petrol*
el humo *smoke*
el lavado automático *carwash*
el litro *litre*
los servicios *toilets*
comprobar (ue) el aceite *to check the oil level*
comprobar (ue) el agua *to check the water level*
comprobar (ue) la presión *to check tyre pressure*
normal *2-star petrol*
súper *4-star petrol*
Es autoservicio aquí *It's self-service here*
Necesito aceite *I need oil*
¿Puede lavarme el parabrisas, por favor? *Can you wash the windscreen, please?*
¿Quiere comprobar el agua, por favor? *Would you check the water level, please*
Quiero también comprar un mapa de carreteras *I would also like to buy a road map*

Accidents

el accidente *accident*
la ambulancia *ambulance*
el choque *collision*
la clínica *clinic*
el/la médico/a *doctor*
la marca de coche *make of car*
acercarse a *to approach*
aplastar *to crush*
arriesgar *to risk*
ayudar *to help*
chocar contra *to bump*
matar *to kill*
suicidarse *to commit suicide*

herido/a *injured*
peligroso/a *dangerous*
See also A3 Health and fitness

D1 Further education and training

Mi madre es dentista *My mother is a dentist*
Mi padre es mecánico *My father is a mechanic*
Pienso hacer la carrera universitaria *I intend to take a degree*
Quiero ser . . . *I would like to be . . .*
Quiero trabajar . . . *I would like to work . . .*
. . . al aire libre *. . . in the open air*
. . . con animales *. . . with animals*
. . . con niños *. . . with children*
. . . con ordenadores *. . . with computers*
. . . en un colegio *. . . in a school*
. . . en un hospital *. . . in a hospital*
. . . en un hotel *. . . in a hotel*
. . . en una fábrica *. . . in a factory*
. . . en una oficina *. . . in an office*
. . . en una tienda *. . . in a shop*
Quiero ir a trabajar al extranjero *I would like to work abroad*
Quisiera ser veterinario/a *I would like to be a vet*
Si no, no tendré trabajo *Otherwise I shall be unemployed*
Voy a estudiar una carrera universitaria *I am going to study at university*
Voy a pasar el bachillerato *I will take 'bachillerato' (A Levels)*
See also A1 School

D2 Careers and employment

Occupations

el/la abogado/a *lawyer*
el/la actor/actriz *actor/actress*
la administración *administration*
agricultor *farmer, farm worker*
el albañil *bricklayer*
el ama de casa (*feminine*) *housewife*
la azafata *air hostess*
el/la arquitecto/a *architect*
el bombero *fireman*
el/la cajero/a *cashier*
el/la camarero/a *waiter/waitress*
el/la cantante *singer*
el/la carnicero/a *butcher*
el carpintero *carpenter*
el/la cartero/a *postman/postwoman*
el/la científico/a *scientist*
el/la cirujano/a *surgeon*
el/la cobrador/a *bus conductor/conductress*
el/la cocinero/a *cook*
el/la comerciante *trader*
el constructor *builder*
el/la contable *accountant*
el chófer *driver*
la criada *housemaid*
el cura *priest*
el/la decorador/a *decorator*
el/la dentista *dentist*
el/la dependiente/dependienta *shop assistant*
el/la deportista *sportsman/woman*
el/la director/a *director, headteacher, manager*
el/la diseñador/a *designer*
el/la electricista *electrician*
el/la empleado/a *employee, clerk*
el/la empleado/a de banco *bank clerk*
el empleo *occupation*
el encargado *person in charge, foreman*
el/la enfermero/a *nurse*
el/la escritor/a *writer*
la estrella *film star*
el/la estudiante *student*
el/la fabricante *manufacturer*
el fontanero *plumber*
el/la funcionario/a *civil servant*
el/la fotógrafo/a *photographer*
el/la gerente *manager*
el granjero *farmer*
el hombre de negocios *businessman*
la industria *industry*
el/la ingeniero/a *engineer*
el/la jardinero/a *gardener*
el/la jefe *boss*
el juez *judge*
el lechero *milkman*
el/la maestro/a *(primary school) teacher*
el/la maquinista *machinist, engine driver*
el marinero *sailor*
el/la mecanógrafo/a *typist*
el minero *miner*
la mujer de negocios *businesswoman*
el/la músico *musician*
el/la obrero/a *worker*
el oficio *job*
el/la organizador/a *organiser*
el/la panadero/a *baker*
el/la pastelero/a *pastrycook*
el patrón (de restaurante) *(restaurant) owner*
el/la peluquero/a *hairdresser*
el/la periodista *journalist*
el pescador *fisherman*
el/la piloto *pilot*
el/la pintor/a *painter/decorator*
el/la policía *policeman, policewoman*
el/la portero/a *porter, doorkeeper*
la profesión *profession*
el/la profesor/a *teacher*
el/la programador/a *programmer*
el puesto de trabajo *job, post, position*
el/la recepcionista *receptionist*
el/la repartidor/a de periódicos *paper boy/girl*
el/la representante *representative*
el/la secretario/a *secretary*

el soldado *soldier*
el/la taquimeca(nógrafo/a) *shorthand typist*
el/la técnico/a *technician*
el/la telefonista *telephonist*
el/la tendero/a *shopkeeper*
el trabajo *job*
el/la vendedor/a *salesperson, market trader*
el/la verdulero/a *greengrocer*
el/la veterinario/a *veterinary surgeon*
en el paro *unemployed*

Places of work

la agencia de viajes *travel agency*
el Ayuntamiento *Town Hall*
el banco *bank*
el colegio *secondary school*
la compañía de seguros *insurance company*
la escuela *primary school*
la fábrica *factory*
la granja *farm*
el laboratorio *laboratory*
la oficina *office*
la tienda *shop*

D3 Travel to work and school

la distancia *distance*
la estación *station*
el medio de transporte *means of transport*
el transporte *transport*
andar *to walk*
cruzar *to cross*
darse prisa *to hurry*
durar *to last*
entrar *to enter*
estar de regreso *to be back*
llegar a las nueve *to arrive at 9 o'clock*
perder (ie) *to miss (bus, etc.)*
ponerse en marcha, en camino *to set out*
preferir (ie) *to prefer*
quedar *to remain*
regresar *to return*
tomar el tren *to go by train*
tardar veinte minutos *to take 20 minutes*
utilizar *to use*
viajar en tren *to go by train*
a pie *on foot*
con retraso *late*
en autobús *by bus*
en bicicleta *by bicycle*
en ciclomotor *by motorized bicycle*
en coche de línea *by coach*
en metro *by tube*
en mi casa *at my home, at my house*
en tren *by train*
por adelantado *in advance*
puntual *on time*

Me deja delante del colegio *She drops me outside school*
Mi madre me lleva en coche *My mother takes me in the car*
Mi padre me lleva en coche por la tarde *My father drives me in the evening*
Prefiero llegar temprano *I prefer arriving early*
Regreso a eso de las cinco *I am back home at about 5 o'clock*
Salgo de casa a eso de las ocho *I leave home at about 8 o'clock*
Tardo veinte minutos en llegar al colegio *It takes me 20 minutes to get to school*

See also C6 Getting around

D4 Advertising and publicity

el buen acabado *(good) finish*
la agencia de publicidad *advertising agency*
el anuncio clasificado *classified advertisement*
el anuncio publicitario *advertisement*
el anuncio de trabajo *job advertisement*
el armario empotrado *built-in wardrobe*
la calefacción *heating*
la campaña publicitaria *publicity campaign*
el cartel *poster*
la cartelera *advertising hoarding*
la climatización *air conditioning*
el consumidor *consumer*
el currículo *curriculum vitae*
la entrada *deposit, down payment*
la entrevista *interview*
la hoja de solicitud *application form*
el eslogan *slogan*
la financiación *finance (loan)*
la grifería monomando *mixer taps*
la hipoteca *mortgage*
el intermedio *commercial break*
el jardín comunitario *communal garden*
la muestra gratuita *free sample*
el obsequio *free gift*
la oferta *offer*
el piso piloto *show flat*
las rebajas *price cuts, sale*
la recomendación *testimonial*
la referencia *reference*
el solicitante *applicant*
la solicitud *application*
la titulación *qualifications*
las ventanas *double glazing*
la zona residencial *residential area*
de superlujo *very luxurious*
disponible *available*
equipado/a *equipped*
excelente *excellent*
garantizado/a *guaranteed*
nuevo/a *new*

A buen precio *Good value*
Aproveche(n) *Take advantage of*
Compre *Buy*
Desde *From (price)*
Envíe este cupón *Send this coupon*
Es fenomenal *It's terrific*
Gran surtido *Large selection/Wide range*
Gran liquidación *Clearance sale*
Grandes rebajas *Big reductions*
Infórmate sin compromiso *Enquire without obligation*
¡Novedad! *New!*
el 15 por ciento de descuento *15% discount*
Se busca *Wanted*
Se vende *For sale*
sensacional *Sensational*
Sin interés *Interest free*
Solicite *Send for/Ask for*

D5 Communication

el auricular *receiver*
la cabina telefónica *telephone box*
el cambio *change*
la conferencia *long distance call*
la extensión *extension*
la guía telefónica *telephone directory*
la llamada telefónica *telephone call*
la línea *line*
el locutorio *telephone booth*
las monedas de _____ pesetas _____ *peseta coins*
el número *number*
el número de teléfono *telephone number*
la ranura *slot*
la tarjeta telefónica *phone card*
el/la telefonista *operator*
el telegrama *telegram*
el tono de llamada *ringing tone*
el tono (de marcar) *dialling tone*
colgar (ue) *to put the receiver down*
descolgar (ue) *to pick up (the receiver)*
devolver (ue) una llamada *to return a call*
marcar *to dial*
telefonear *to telephone*
volver (ue) a llamar *to call again*
ocupado *busy, engaged*
a cobro revertido *reversed charges*
al aparato *speaking, on the phone*
en nombre de *on behalf of*
Bueno, marque el 00 y espere el tono *Well, dial 00 and wait for the tone*
Dígale que . . . *Tell him/her that . . .*
Dígame *Hello (answering telephone)*
Está comunicando *The line is engaged*
Luego, marque el 44 para Gran Bretaña, seguido del número que quiere, sin olvidar el prefijo de la región, pero sin el cero *Then, you dial the code for Great Britain, 44. then the number you wish, not forgetting the local code omitting the zero*
Mañana (por la mañana) *Tomorrow (morning)*
No cuelgue(s) *Don't ring off*
No funciona *Out of order*
Puede ponerse en contacto por . . . *You can contact me by . . .*
. . . correo electrónico *. . . E-mail*
. . . fax *. . . fax*
. . . teléfono *. . . telephone*
Quiero una conferencia a cobro revertido *I'd like to make a reversed charge call*
Quiero una tarjeta telefónica, por favor *I'd like a phone card, please*
Se ha equivocado de número *You have dialled the wrong number*
Se oye muy mal *The line is bad*
Siento mucho molestarle *I'm sorry to have troubled you*
Soy yo *That's me/speaking*
Un momento *Wait a moment please*
Un momento, voy a apuntarlo *Just a moment, I'll write that down*
Voy a ponerle *I'll put you through (to him/her)*
Vuelvo a llamar más tarde *I'll call back later*
¿A qué hora? *At what time?*
¿Cómo se escribe? *How do you spell that?*
¿De parte de quién? *Who's calling?*
¿Cómo? *Sorry?*
¿Puede repetir? *Could you repeat that?*
¿Puedo dejar un recado? *Can I leave a message?*
¿Quiere dejar un recado? *Would you like to leave a message?*
¿Quiere volver a llamar? *Would you like to ring again?*

E1 Life in other countries/communities

el aceite *oil*
el almuerzo *lunch*
el bocadillo *sandwich (Spanish bread)*
la cena *dinner, evening meal*
la corrida *bullfight*
el desayuno *breakfast*
la Guardia Civil *Civil Guard (national police force)*
el kilo *kilogram*
la lata *box, tin*
la merienda *tea*
el paquete *packet*
la paella *paella*
la peseta *peseta*
el pimiento *pepper*
la plaza de toros *bullring*
la sal *salt*
la siesta *siesta, afternoon rest*
las tapas *small snacks taken with a drink*
la tortilla (española) *(Spanish) omelette*
el trozo *slice, piece*
los toros *bullfighting*
asar *to roast*

asar a la parrilla *to grill on a barbecue*
batir *to beat*
cortar *to cut, chop*
freír *to fry*
hervir *to boil*
mezclar *to mix*
pelar *to peel*
un tipo de *a kind of*
¿De qué es? *What is it made of?*
¿Qué es exactamente el/la . . . ? *What is . . . exactly?*
See also A4 Food and Drink

E2 Tourism

la duración *length (of time), duration*
la excursión *excursion, trip*
el folleto *leaflet*
el horario *timetable*
la lista de hoteles/campings *list of hotels/campsites*
la lista de precios *price list*
la oficina de turismo *tourist office*
el plano de la ciudad *town plan*
el precio *price*
la salida *departure*
ir de vacaciones *to go on holiday*
en barco *by boat*
en coche de línea *by coach*
Deme un folleto, por favor *Give me a brochure, please*
El año que viene voy a los Estados Unidos *Next year I'm going to the United States*
Era . . . *It was . . .*
. . . impresionante *. . . impressive*
. . . interesante *. . . interesting*
. . . tranquilo/a *. . . restful*
. . . aburrido/a *. . . boring*
. . . fatal *. . . terrible*
. . . horrible *. . . awful*
. . . feo/a *. . . ugly*
. . . maravilloso/a *. . . marvellous*
. . . sucio/a *. . . dirty*
. . . limpio/a *. . . clean*
. . . moderno/a *. . . modern*
Fui con mi familia *I went with my family*
Fuimos a Turquía *We went to Turkey*
Fuimos de excursión a pie en la sierra *We went walking in the mountains*
Hacía mucho calor *It was very hot*
Hicimos excursiones en barco *We took boat trips*
Me gusta mucho broncearme en la playa *I like sunbathing at the beach*
Me hospedaré con amigos *I'll stay with friends*
Pasamos quince días allí *We spent a fortnight there*
Prefiero las vacaciones activas *I prefer active holidays*
Viajaré en avión *I'll go by plane*
Visitamos los monumentos históricos *We visited historic monuments*
Voy a hacer camping *I'll go camping*
¿Adónde fuiste de vacaciones? *Where did you go on holiday?*
¿Con quién fuiste? *Who did you go with?*
¿Cuánto tiempo estuviste allí? *How long did you go for?*
¿Qué hiciste allí? *What did you do while you were there?*
¿Qué tiempo hizo? *What was the weather like there?*
See also B5 Holidays

E3 Accommodation

Hotel

el ascensor *lift*
el baño *bath*
el cuarto de baño *bathroom*
la ducha *shower*
la entrada *entrance*
la escalera *staircase*
el hotel *hotel*
la llave *key*
el piso *floor, storey*
la planta baja *ground floor*
la puerta de entrada *front door*
la recepción *reception*
el restaurante *restaurant*
la salida *exit*
la salida de urgencia *emergency exit*
los servicios *toilets*
el sótano *basement*
el teléfono *telephone*
la televisión *TV*
la vista *view*
bastante barato/a *not expensive*
cómodo/a *comfortable*
de lujo *luxurious*
moderno/a *modern*
no demasiado caro/a *not too expensive*
pequeño/a *small*
privado/a *private*
ruidoso/a *noisy*
sólido/a *solid*

Use of the hotel

el camarero *waiter*
el cheque *cheque*
la criada, camarera *maid*
la señal *deposit*
el desayuno *breakfast*
el incendio *fire*
la maleta *suitcase*
la media pensión *half-board*
el patrón *manager*
la pensión *board, guest house*

la pensión completa *full board*
la percha *coat-hanger*
el precio máximo *maximum price*
el precio mínimo *minimum price*
el/la recepcionista *receptionist*
el suplemento *extra, addition*
aparcar *to park*
apreciar *to appreciate*
despertar(se) (ie) *to wake up*
empujar/EMPUJAD *to push/PUSH*
encontrar (ue) *to find*
llamar por teléfono *to telephone*
molestar *to disturb*
pulsar/PULSE *to press/PRESS*
reemplazar *to replace*
regresar *to return*
reservar *to reserve*
tirar/TIRAD *to pull/PULL*
disponible *available*
incluido/a *inclusive*
ocupado/a *occupied*
otro/a *other*
satisfecho/a *satisfied*
con *with*
Aquí tiene la llave. Habitación número veintidós *Here is your key. Room number 22*
El hotel está completo *The hotel is full*
El precio de la habitación es 4000 pesetas, servicio e IVA incluidos *It's 4000 pesetas for the room, service and VAT included*
Me quedo con ellos/as *I'll take them*
Hay que rellenar el formulario antes *Before that you must fill in the form*
Hay un aparcamiento detrás del hotel *There is a car park at the back*
Lo siento, pero no me conviene *I'm afraid that doesn't suit me*
No, lo siento, pero todo está ocupado *No, I'm afraid not, we are full*
No importa, me quedo con la habitación *Never mind, I'll take the room*
Quiero reservar una habitación para tres noches *I'd like to reserve a room for 3 nights*
Quiero una habitación con vista a la playa *I'd like a room looking on to the beach*
Se sirve el desayuno a partir de las ocho hasta las diez *Breakfast is served from 8.00 to 10.00 a.m.*
Su pasaporte, por favor *Your passport, please*
Una habitación grande con dos camas de matrimonio, ¿vale ? *A big room with two double beds, is that all right for you?*
¿Cuánto cuestan? *How much do they cost?*
¿Está incluido el desayuno? *Is breakfast included?*
¿Hay algo menos caro? *Have you anything cheaper?*
¿Hay una habitación con cuarto de baño? *Have you a room with a bathroom?*
¿Para cuántas personas y para cuánto tiempo? *For how many people and for how long?*
¿Puedo subir el equipaje ahora? *May I take my luggage up now?*
¿Quedan habitaciones libres? *Have you any free rooms left?*

Reservation problems

Estoy muy decepcionado/a *I am very disappointed*
Reservé por teléfono *I made reservations by phone*
¿A nombre de quién? *What name?*
¿Está Vd. seguro/a? *Are you sure?*
¿Es eso? *Is that it?*
¿Qué voy a hacer? *What shall I do?*

Asking for extras

Falta una almohada *A pillow is missing*
Necesito una toalla de baño, por favor *May I have a bath towel please?*
Quiero unas perchas, por favor *I'd like some coat-hangers, please*
Se la traigo en seguida *We'll bring one straight away*

Complaining

El lavabo está atascado *The wash-basin is blocked*
Gotea el grifo del agua fría *The cold water tap is dripping*
La ducha no funciona *The shower doesn't work*
La lámpara no funciona *The lamp does not work*
No hay jabón/No tenemos jabón *There is no soap*
No hay papel higiénico *There is no toilet paper*
Quiero otra habitación *I would like another room*
Vamos a ocuparnos de eso inmediatamente *We'll deal with that straight away*

Youth hostel

el agua caliente (*feminine*) *hot water*
el albergue juvenil *youth hostel*
la bienvenida *welcome*
la cocina *kitchen*
el comedor *dining room*
la comida *food, meal*
el cubo de la basura *dustbin*
el despacho *office*
el dormitorio *dormitory*
la estancia *stay*
el inconveniente *drawback*
la lista de precios/ tarifas *price list*
la manta *blanket*
la noche *night*
el par de sábanas *pair of sheets*
la persona responsable *the organizer, leader*

la ropa *linen*
el saco de dormir *sleeping bag*
la sala de juegos *games room*
el silencio *silence*
la tarjeta *card*
el carné *member's card*
la ventaja *advantage, facility*
el/la visitante *visitor*
abrir *to open*
agradecer *to thank*
alquilar *to hire*
arreglar *to tidy*
ayudar *to help*
barrer *to sweep*
cerrar (ie) *to close*
guardar *to keep, put away*
organizar *to organize*
pagar *to pay*
completo/a *full*
excepto *except*
prohibido/a *forbidden*
todo el año *all year round*

Camping

el agua no potable (*feminine*) *non-drinking water*
la botella de gas *gas cylinder*
la cama de campaña *camp bed*
el camping *campsite*
el/la campista *camper*
la caravana *caravan*
el carnet de camping *camping card*
las cerillas *matches*
la electricidad *electricity*
el enchufe *power point*
el equipo de camping *camping equipment*
el fregadero *washing up sink*
la hoguera *camp-fire, bonfire*
el hornillo de gas *gas cooker*
la lavadora *washing machine*
la lavandería *launderette*
la linterna *torch*
la ropa para lavar *washing* (*clothes*)
los servicios *toilet block*
el suplemento *extra payment*
el tazón *bowl*
el terreno *site, pitch*
la tienda *tent*
el vehículo *vehicle*
acampar *to camp*
armar la tienda *to put up the tent*
buscar *to look for*
cocinar *to cook*
costar (ue) *to cost*
hacer camping *to go camping*
indicar *to indicate, show*
lavar(se) *to wash oneself*
plegar (ie) *to fold*
vigilar *to supervise*
municipal *municipal, council-run*
sencillo/a *simple*
para llevarse *to take away*
El agua es potable *The water is drinkable*
Hay un guardián toda la noche *There is a warden all night*
Necesitamos un sacacorchos y unas pilas *We need a corkscrew and some batteries*
¿El camping está cerrado de noche? *Is the camp closed at night?*
¿El camping está iluminado de noche? *Is the camp lit up at night?*
¿Está a la sombra? *Is it in the shade?*
¿Está prohibido hacer fuego en el camping? *Is it forbidden to light a fire in the camp?*
¿Para cuántas personas? *For how many people?*
¿Queda sitio para una caravana? *Have you room left for a caravan?*
¿Se puede encender una barbacoa? *Is it allowed to light a barbecue?*

Holiday home in Spain

el alquiler de bicicletas *cycle hire*
el granero *barn*
el grupo de edificios *group of buildings*
la reclamación *complaint, claim*
la vendimia *grape picking*
la viña, el viñedo *vineyard*
el viticultor *vine cultivator*
amueblar *to furnish, equip*
cultivar *to cultivate*
devolver (ue) *to give back*
esperar *to wait* (*for*)
mejorar *to improve*
pedir (i) *to ask* (*for*)
presentarse *to introduce oneself*
querer (ie) ver *to want to see*
recoger fruta *to pick fruit*
independiente *independent*
libre *free*
ocupado/a *busy*
provisional, temporáneo *temporary*
cama y desayuno *guest room, B+B*
en buenas condiciones *in good condition*
en el mes de *in the month of*
en malas condiciones *in bad condition*
en otra parte *elsewhere*
fuera de temporada *out of season*
For holiday activities, see B2 Free time and social activities

E4 The wider world

Spanish-speaking and other countries
With countries, words in brackets are optional, and are more widely used in Latin America.

	COUNTRY		*ADJECTIVE*	*INHABITANTS*
	Países hispanohablantes			
(la)	Argentina	*Argentina*	argentino/a	un(a) argentino/a
	Bolivia (*f*)	*Bolivia*	boliviano/a	un(a) boliviano/a
	Chile (*m*)	*Chile*	chileno/a	un(a) chileno/a
	Colombia (*f*)	*Colombia*	colombiano/a	un(a) colombiano/a
	Costa Rica (*f*)	*Costa Rica*	costarricense	un(a) costarricense
	Cuba (*f*)	*Cuba*	cubano/a	un(a) cubano/a
(el)	Ecuador	*Ecuador*	ecuatoriano/a	un(a) ecuatoriano/a
	Guatemala (*f*)	*Guatemala*	guatemalteco	un(a) guatemalteco/a
	Honduras (*f*)	*Honduras*	hondureño/a	un(a) hondureño/a
	Méjico (*m*)	*Mexico*	mejicano/a	un(a) mejicano/a
	Nicaragua (*f*)	*Nicaragua*	nicaragüense	un(a) nicaragüense
	Panamá (*m*)	*Panama*	panameño/a	un(a) panameño/a
(el)	Paraguay	*Paraguay*	paraguayo/a	un(a) paraguayo/a
(el)	Perú	*Peru*	peruano/a	un(a) peruano/a
la	República Dominicana	*Dominican Republic*	dominicano/a	un(a) dominicano/a
el	Salvador	*El Salvador*	salvadoreño/a	un(a) salvadoreño/a
(el)	Uruguay	*Uruguay*	uruguayo/a	un(a) uruguayo/a
	Venezuela (*f*)	*Venezuela*	venezolano/a	un(a) venezolano/a
	Países europeos			
	Alemania (*f*)	*Germany*	alemán/alemana	un(a) alemán/alemana
	Bélgica (*f*)	*Belgium*	belga	un(a) belga
	Dinamarca (*f*)	*Denmark*	danés/danesa	un(a) danés/esa
	España (*f*)	*Spain*	español/a	un(a) español/a
	Europa (*f*)	*Europe*	europeo/a	un(a) europeo/a
	Francia (*f*)	*France*	francés/francesa	un(a) francés/esa
(la)	Gran Bretaña	*Great Britain*	británico/a	un(a) británico/a
	Grecia (*f*)	*Greece*	griego/a	un(a) griego/a
	Holanda (*f*)	*Holland*	holandés/holandesa	un(a) holandés/esa
	Inglaterra (*f*)	*England*	inglés/inglesa	un(a) inglés/esa
	Italia (*f*)	*Italy*	italiano/italiana	un(a) italiano/a
	Luxemburgo (*m*)	*Luxembourg*	luxemburgués/esa	un(a)luxemburgués/esa
los	Países Bajos	*Netherlands*	neerlandés/esa	un(a) neerlandés/esa
	Portugal (*m*)	*Portugal*	portugués/esa	un(a) portugués/esa
el	Reino Unido	*UK*	británico/a	un(a) británico/a
	Rusia (*f*)	*Russia*	ruso/a	un(a) ruso/a
	Suiza (*f*)	*Switzerland*	suizo/a	un(a) suizo/a
	Other countries			
	Australia (*f*)	*Australia*	australiano/a	un(a) australiano/a
	América (*f*)	*America*	americano/a	un(a) americano/a
(el)	Brasil	*Brazil*	brasileño/a	un(a) brasileño
(el)	Canadá	*Canada*	canadiense	un(a) canadiense
	China (*f*)	*China*	chino/a	un(a) chino/a
	Escocia (*f*)	*Scotland*	escocés/esa	un(a) escocés/esa
los	Estados Unidos	*USA*	americano/a	un(a) americano/a
(el)	(país de) Gales (*m*)	*Wales*	galés/esa	un(a) galés/esa
la	India	*India*	indio/a	un(a) indio/a
(la)	Irlanda del Norte	*Northern Ireland*	irlandés/esa	un(a) irlandés/esa
el	Japón	*Japan*	japonés/esa	un(a) japonés/esa

People and environment

el/la adolescente *adolescent*
el adulto *adult*
la alimentación *food, nutrition*
las armas *armaments, arms*
la caza *hunting*
la caza furtiva *poaching*
los/las chavales/las *kids*
la chica *girl*
el chico *boy*
la contaminación *pollution*
la despoblación forestal *deforestation*
el desarrollo *development*
la enfermedad *disease*
la especie *species*
el/la extranjero/a *foreigner*
la gente *people*
la guerra *war*
el habitat *habitat*
el hambre (*feminine*) *hunger, famine*
el hombre *man*
el/la joven *young man*
la lluvia ácida *acid rain*
el marido *husband*
el medio ambiente *environment*
la mujer *woman, wife*
el país de origen *country of origin*
la pobreza *poverty*
la polución *pollution*
el recalentamiento global *global warming*
la riqueza *wealth*
la señora *lady*
la sequía *drought*
el SIDA *AIDS*
el/la soltero/a *bachelor/spinster*
el Tercer Mundo *Third World*
la viuda *widow*
el viudo *widower*
la vivisección *vivisection*
(estar) prometido/a (*to be*) *engaged*
amenazado/a *threatened*
casado/a *married*
divorciado/a *divorced*
femenino/a *feminine*
masculino/a *masculine*
nuclear *nuclear*
separado/a *separated*
a causa de *because of*
Caballeros *Gentlemen*
Señoras *Ladies*
Soy inglés/esa *I am English*
Soy de nacionalidad inglesa *I am British*
¿De dónde viene(s)? *Where do you come from?*
¿Dónde naciste/nació? *Where were you born?*

E5 Current affairs

el acontecimiento *event*
el alcalde/la alcaldesa *mayor*
el artículo *article*
el asunto *case*
la aviación *air force*
la ayuda *aid, help*
la bomba *bomb*
la Comisión Europea *European Commission*
la crisis *crisis*
la democracia *democracy*
el desastre *disaster*
el desempleo *unemployment*
la dictadura *dictatorship*
el/la diputado/a *MP*
el discurso *speech*
la elección *election*
el ejército *army*
el empresario, patrón *employer*
la energía *energy*
la época *period of time*
la frontera *frontier*
el gobierno *government*
la guerra *war*
el hambre (*feminine*) *hunger, famine*
la huelga *strike*
el impuesto *tax*
la inmigración *immigration*
el/la inmigrante *immigrant*
la invasión *invasion*
la investigación *enquiry*
el IVA *VAT*
la manifestación *demonstration*
la marina *navy*
el/la ministro/a *minister*
el ministerio *ministry*
las Naciones Unidas *the United Nations*
el nivel de vida *standard of living*
las noticias *news*
la obra benéfica *charity*
la operación *operation*
la OTAN *NATO*
el parlamento *parliament*
el paro *unemployment*
la paz *peace*
la pobreza *poverty*
la policía *police*
la política *policy*
la pregunta *question*
la prensa *the press*
el/la presidente/presidenta *president*
el presupuesto *budget*
el/la primer(a) ministro/a *prime minister*
el problema *problem*
el rey *king*
la reina *queen*
la seguridad social *social security*
el sindicato *trade union*

la solución *solution*
el telediario *TV news*
el título *title*
el tratado *treaty*
las tropas *troops*
la Unión Europea *the European Union*
la violencia *violence*
admirar *to admire*
aumentar *to increase, augment*
declarar *to declare*
defender (ie) *to defend, forbid*
disminuir *to diminish*
mejorar *to improve*
ocurrir *to happen*
persuadir *to persuade*
prometer *to promise*
protestar *to protest*
suceder *to happen*
tener lugar *to take place*
grave *serious*
importante *important*
probable *probable*
reciente *recent*
social *social*

Examination rubrics

Your examining board has published a list of key words and expressions used in its examination rubrics (instructions to candidates). If you have a copy of that list, check it carefully to make sure you would understand those instructions if you found them in an actual examination paper. Alternatively, study the following list, which is based on rubrics from all the boards. In any case, almost all the boards will occasionally have to use expressions from outside their published lists, so it will be helpful if you understand all those given here.

General

Ahora te toca a tí *Now it's your turn*
Añade *Add*
Busca la palabra, la frase, los errores *Find the word, sentence, errors*
Copia (la letra/el número/el nombre/la palabra/la frase) correcto/a *Copy the correct (letter/number/name/word/sentence)*
Completa el cuadro (la tabla), la frase siguiente, la lista, la descripción, el formulario (la ficha) *Complete the table, the following sentence, the list, the description, the form*
Corrige (los errores, las palabras subrayadas) *Correct the errors, the underlined words*
¿Cuál/Cuáles? *Which?*
¿Cuáles de las explicaciones corresponden a . . . ? *Which of the explanations corresponds to . . . ?*
¿Cuáles son las diferencias entre . . . ? *What are the differences between . . . ?*
Da la información pedida *Give the requested information*
Decide cuál del/de los/de la/de las . . . *Decide which of the . . .*
Ejemplo *Example*
Empareja/Relaciona con . . . *Pair up . . .*
En cada casilla, pon el número del párrafo, de la frase, de la pregunta, de la palabra que corresponde a . . . *In each box write the number of the paragraph, the sentence, the question, the word corresponding to . . .*
Escoge/Elige la descripción que corresponde mejor *Choose the best description*
Escribe (el número, la letra, una lista, las palabras que faltan) *Write (the number, the letter, a list, the missing words)*
Haz un círculo en . . . *Circle . . .*
Incluye . . . *Include . . .*
Identifica . . . *Identify . . .*
Indica (con una equis (✗) una marca o señal (✓) en la(s) casilla(s) correcta(s), en el plano) *Indicate with a cross (✗) symbol or a tick (✓) in the correct box(es), on the map*
Indica sí o no/las diferencias *Indicate yes or no/the differences*
No necesitas todas las letras/los números *You will not need all the letters/numbers*
Ordena . . . *Order . . .*
Pon (en orden)/Coloca (en el orden correcto) *Put (in the correct order)*
Pon una cruz (✗) al lado de la palabra/la frase/el dibujo/número/correcto(a) *Put a cross (✗) next to the correct word/sentence/drawing/number*
Por ejemplo *For example*
Rellena la ficha (el formulario) la casilla/los detalles/los espacios (los blancos) *Fill in the form/the box/the details/the blanks*
Según la información . . . *According to the information . . .*
Subraya (la frase/la palabra) (correcta/falsa) *Underline the (correct/false)(sentence/word)*
Tacha (la palabra/la frase, etc.) falsa *Delete the wrong (word/sentence, etc.)*
Verdad/Mentira/No se sabe/Verdadero/Falso *True/False/Not known*

Listening

Contesta por escrito *Write your answer*
Escucha (atentamente la cinta/la conversación/el anuncio/el diálogo) *Listen (carefully to the tape/the conversation/the advertisement/the dialogue)*
Estás oyendo . . . *You are listening to . . .*
Numera (los diálogos siguientes) *Number (the following dialogues)*
Vas a oír la conversación dos veces *You will hear the conversation twice*
Vas a oír un mensaje/un programa/un reportaje en la radio/una entrevista entre dos personas *You*

are going to hear a message/a programme/a report on the radio/an interview between two people
(**Some Listening rubrics may overlap with Reading**)

Speaking

Comenta *Comment*
Compara *Compare*
Contesta (a las preguntas del examinador/la examinadora) *Answer (the examiner's questions)*
Cuenta *Tell*
Da la información siguiente *Give the following information*
Da las gracias *Say thank you*
Da tu opinión sobre . . . *Give your opinion on . . .*
Decide (cómo) *Decide (how)*
Di por qué/cómo . . . *Say why/how . . .*
Explica *Explain*
Habla de . . . *Talk about . . .*
Haz el papel de . . . *Take the role of . . .*
Haz preguntas *Ask some questions*
Haz un resumen *Give a summary*
Haz una entrevista *Conduct an interview*
Imagina *Imagine*
Justifica tu opinión *Justify your opinion*
Menciona *Mention*
No te olvides *Don't forget*
Pide *Ask (for)*
Pregunta *Ask*
Prepara una presentación oral sobre . . . *Prepare an oral presentation on . . .*
Preséntate *Introduce yourself*
Saluda al examinador/a la examinadora *Greet the examiner*
Sugiere *Suggest*
Termina la conversación *End the conversation*
Toma notas/apuntes sobre . . . *Take notes on . . .*
Utiliza los símbolos siguientes para hacer un diálogo *Use the following symbols to create a dialogue*

Reading

Apunta *Jot down*
Busca al intruso *Find the odd one out*
Cada una de estas frases/estos párrafos contiene un error *Each of these sentences/paragraphs contains an error*
Contesta a las preguntas *Answer the questions*
¿Dónde puedes leer estas frases? *Where can you read these sentences?*
Haz una lista (de las ventajas/ inconvenientes) *Make a list (of the advantages/disadvantages)*
He aquí una lista/alguna información/ una postal/una carta/unos anuncios/un texto/un extracto de un periódico/una revista, etc. *Here is a list/some information/a post card/a letter/some adverts/a text/ an extract from a newspaper/magazine, etc.*
Lee atentamente el texto, la noticia, la carta *Read the text, the notice, the letter, carefully*
Menciona los detalles/datos *Mention the details*
Pon el número del párrafo/de la frase/de la pregunta/ de la palabra que corresponde a . . . *Write the number of the paragraph/sentence/question/word corresponding to . . .*
¿Son verdaderas o falsas las siguientes afirmaciones? Si son falsas escribe la versión correcta *Are these sentences true or false? If false, write the correct version*
Tacha *Delete*

Writing

Cambia los detalles *Change the details*
Compara *Compare*
Completa los detalles en español *Complete the details in Spanish*
Contesta a las preguntas *Answer the questions*
Cuenta/Relata tus impresiones/lo que has hecho/dicho/oído *Describe your impressions/what you have done/said/heard*
Da tu opinión sobre . . . *Give your opinion on . . .*
Describe *Describe*
Escoge el tema 1 ó 2 *Select topic 1 or 2*
Escribe unas 100 palabras (más o menos) *Write around 100 words*
Escribe unas notas/una descripción/un resumen/una carta (contestando a las preguntas)/una postal/una respuesta *Write some notes/a description/a summary/a letter (answering the questions asked)/a postcard/an answer*
Explica *Explain*
Haz un resumen *Make a summary*
Haz una comparación *Make a comparison*
Imagina *Imagine*
Incluye *Include*
Justifica tu opinión *Justify your opinion*
Lee este artículo en el periódico y escribe una carta para dar tu opinión *Read this article in the newspaper and write a letter to give your opinion*
Pon en orden *Put in order*
Prepara un programa *Prepare a schedule*
No te olvides *Do not forget*

Chapter 4

Listening

GETTING STARTED

A **Listening** test is a compulsory part of GCSE Spanish and it is clear that many students tend to worry about it. This chapter aims to ensure that you understand what the test is about and what it requires of you. It also contains some advice on how you can become more confident and more capable in listening. Finally, it provides examples of the questions that have been set by the different examining boards.

The cassette that can be bought with this book contains the recordings for the questions and allows you, if you wish, to practise answering the questions just as you would in the examination. It helps you to become familiar with the speed and way of speaking that are normal in the GCSE. The transcripts of all the recordings are included towards the end of the chapter, which will enable you to check carefully the words you have heard. If you have not bought the cassette, you could get a friend or relative who speaks Spanish to read the transcripts aloud to allow you to attempt the questions.

There is no substitute for practice in listening, so do make time to use the material in this chapter.

TOPIC	STUDY	REVISION 1	REVISION 2
The place			
The recordings			
The nature of the questions			
Answering the questions			
Improving your listening skills			
G, F, E tasks			
D, C tasks			
B, A, A* tasks			
Examination questions			
Student's answers with examiner's comments			
Practice questions			
Answers to practice questions			
Transcripts of the recordings			

WHAT YOU NEED TO KNOW

The place

Since the Listening tests of all the examining boards involve cassette recordings, it is normal for schools and colleges to arrange for the examination to take place in a comparatively small room, so that you are able to hear clearly. Often a language laboratory is used. It is unlikely that your test will take place in the sort of large hall or gym where most other examinations are taken. So make sure you know where you are supposed to be. If you are using a language laboratory and there are a large number of candidates, you may well find that you have to take the examination in groups, with strict supervision of those who have yet to take the examination or who have just taken it. It is most important that you follow any special instructions about supervision and reporting times, so that your teachers can give the necessary assurances, not just that there was no contact between those who had already taken the test and those who had yet to take it, but that such contact would have been totally impossible.

The recordings

- The material you hear in the examination is recorded by native speakers of Spanish, so that you hear genuine Spanish pronunciation and accent.
- It may include, where appropriate, a limited amount of background noise, such as you would hear in the real-life setting.
- It is material that was specifically intended to be heard (i.e. it cannot consist of reading aloud from a text originally intended for silent reading, such as a newspaper or novel).
- Each item is heard at least twice.

The nature of the questions

- You will be tested only on your understanding of the material. (You will not be required to make any significant use of other skills, such as making calculations.)
- The tests are designed to ensure that they do not place undue emphasis on memory. (This is the main reason why items are kept short.)
- You write your answers on the question paper in the spaces provided.
- Answers (whether in Spanish or in English) are marked for the information given, not for quality of language.

A variety of different test-types are used. Up to 20 per cent of the questions will be in English, to be answered in English. All other questions are in Spanish and must be answered either with Spanish words or with ticks, crosses, figures or letters. The sort of questions you can expect to find in the papers are:

- Questions in English.
- Questions in Spanish.
- True/false questions.
- Grids to be completed (with figures, words, ticks or letters).
- Multiple-choice questions.
- Multiple-choice sentence completions.
- Spanish sentences with gaps to be filled.

In the **Foundation Tier** there is extensive use of **pictures** (mainly line drawings), which have to be matched to the words of the recordings. There is rather less use of pictures in **Higher Tier** papers.

You are allowed to write at any time and there will be pauses at suitable points in the recordings to give you time to write your answers.

You need to make sure that you know your **key question** words well:

¿Qué ... ? *What ... ?*
¿Quién/Quiénes ... ? *Who ... ?*
¿De quién ... ? *Whose ... ?*
¿Dónde ... ? *Where ... ?*
¿Adónde ... ? *Where ... to?*
¿Cuándo ... ? *When ... ?*
¿A qué hora ... ? *At what time ... ?*
¿Cuánto ... ? *How much ... ?*

¿Cuántos/as ... ? *How many ... ?*
¿Cómo ... ? *How ... ?*
¿Cómo es / son ... ? *What is it / are they like?*
¿Por qué ... ? *Why ... ?*
¿Para qué ... ? *For what purpose ... ?*

These questions suggest some areas of vocabulary that you would be well advised to make sure you know.

- **What?** Almost anything! Check out particularly school subjects and extra-curricular activities, shopping, food and drink and free time activities.
- **Who?** Family and friends, jobs; descriptions (physical appearance, size, age, etc.).
- **Where?** Position, location of places and buildings (*delante de la iglesia, enfrente de Correos,* etc.), landmarks, countries, distances and directions (*tome la primera calle a la derecha, cruce la plaza* etc.).
- **When?** Time of day by 12- and 24-hour clock, days, weeks, months, years, dates, frequency, expressions of time (today, yesterday etc.), seasons, important holidays (e.g. Christmas, New Year), beginning, middle, end.
- **How much?** Quantity, numbers (Remember that, because the Spanish peseta is normally valued somewhere in the region of 200 or more to the pound, prices in Spain involve some quite high numbers: 10 000 pesetas is roughly the equivalent of £50).
- **How many?** Numbers.
- **How?** Expressions of speed, ways of doing things, means of transport, tools and implements, directions.
- **What ... like?** Descriptions of people, buildings, towns and villages, school subjects etc.
- **Why?** Reasons.

Two other common types of question involve checking whether you can understand:

1. Spoken questions in Spanish (e.g. you are in a restaurant in Valencia and have just ordered a meal when the waiter asks you: *¿Qué quiere beber?* What does he want to know?).
2. Spoken instructions in Spanish (e.g. You are buying an article in a store in Madrid when the shop assistant says: *Por favor, pague en caja.* What is she telling you to do?).

Answering the questions

- **Remember that you do not have to understand every word** – only the ones relevant to the question.
- **Make use of the opportunity to read the questions before you hear the recording** so that you can target your listening specifically on the points being asked.
- **If you are confident of your answer, write it straight down in the space for it.** There is no real merit in making notes simply to copy them later – that is merely a waste of time. The real value of notes is probably restricted to noting a Spanish word or phrase in the hope of working out later what it means (or, for NEAB and WJEC, looking it up in the dictionary in the last few minutes of the examination.)
- **Read the question carefully** and make sure that what you write actually answers it! If you hear the speaker say, for example, *Mi hermana tiene el pelo largo y moreno*, and the question is 'What colour is her sister's hair?', for goodness' sake don't write 'Long' as the answer. This may seem obvious but many candidates make precisely that sort of mistake.
- **Remember to answer English questions in English and answer Spanish questions in Spanish.** Answers in the wrong language will almost certainly score no marks.
- **Keep your answers as short as possible** (but make sure you do give all the necessary information). Whole sentences are not required. If the speaker says: *Me gustaría ir a la discoteca* and the question is *¿Adónde quiere ir?*, you certainly do not need to write: *Dice que quiere ir a la discoteca.* If you do that you will waste a lot of time and may well miss the next point that you were supposed to listen for. All that is required in this case is: *discoteca.*
- **Check how many marks are awarded for the question.** (This is usually shown in brackets at the end of the question.) The number of marks will give you a good indication of the number of items of information that are required. If you are asked what

someone will be wearing and the allocation is 4 marks, you may find that he says only that he will be wearing a blue shirt and grey trousers. In this case it will be quite clear that the colours are important and carry one mark each. On the other hand, if the allocation is only 2 marks you would still be well advised to include them, because it could be that each item of clothing scores a mark only if the correct colour is given. Sometimes there are four possible answers and only two marks. In those cases both marks will almost certainly be given for any two correct answers.

- **Always give an answer.** Even if you have no idea, make an informed guess, based on what you have understood from the recording and the question itself. You never know, you might be right! In multiple-choice questions and true/false questions your chances of guessing the correct answer are particularly good.
- **Don't go in for 'blanket bombing' of the target area.** If you are asked what colour the car was, pick one colour if you have to guess. Listing every colour you can think of will not be very helpful. The examining boards have their own rules for marking such answers. They are likely either to mark the answer wrong straightaway or to mark only the first colour you have mentioned.
- If you are taking NEAB or WJEC examinations, you will be able to use the **dictionary** to check the meanings of words in the questions before you hear the recordings. You will also have a few minutes at the end when you can check a few words you have heard, if necessary. You must not open your dictionary while the recording is being played. (The other boards do not allow dictionaries in listening examinations.)

Remember that the questions about specific detail are normally in the order in which the information occurs in the recording. Questions asking you to identify the important points, themes, attitudes or emotions or to draw conclusions or identify relationships will normally come at the end of the section, since you will need to hear the whole recording before you can answer them.

Improving your listening skills

In Chapter 1 we looked at some ways of practising listening. The essential message was that there are several sources of listening material available and that you should use them. **The more Spanish you hear the better.**

Many students do worry about Listening and tend to feel it is the one skill in which they have no control over what happens. They can to some extent control what they say in the Speaking test and what they write in the Writing test. In both Reading and Writing they can go back and review what they have done. In Listening they hear each item twice, at whatever speed, and that is the end of the matter.

In the examination that is indeed true but, in practising for the examination, you can have far more control. You will certainly need some practice under the sort of conditions that apply in the examination, so, if you have bought the cassette that is available with this book, you will no doubt wish to keep at least some of the recordings for examination practice. If, however, you have real difficulty with listening, you could use some of the recordings and any other listening material as outlined below. The first aim must be to ensure you achieve some success in listening.

- Do not restrict yourself to hearing each item twice.
- Before you read the questions (if you are using test material), just listen to the recording and note down any words you recognize. If at first you don't recognize very many, listen again, as many times as you need to, in order to have a reasonable number of the words written down.
- Next, listen again and see how much of what is being said you actually understand. If the answer is 'not much', try it again.
- Only when you are confident you can understand a fair amount ought you to look at the questions. Then play the recording (or parts of it) as many times as you need in order to answer the questions.
- If, in the end, you have to admit defeat, look at the answer and check the transcript to make sure you can identify the key words.
- Finally, play the recording to make sure you can now recognize the key words when you hear them. If you can't, listen again, if necessary with the transcript in front of you.

In this way, you will ensure that you have an excellent chance of understanding the same expressions next time you hear them. You will also find that, since you have geared yourself to end on a note of success, you will achieve that success slightly more easily next time you practise. If the first time you listen to a recording you find you have to listen twelve times, you should find that the number of hearings you require gradually decreases with recordings you listen to in later practice sessions. Obviously, you must not expect to understand as much of broadcast material as you would of GCSE recordings. But, even with quite difficult material, word-recognition practice is well worthwhile. (If you are having to rely on a friend reading the transcripts to you, it is a good idea to make clear before you begin that you may be asking for things to be repeated several times!)

Regular practice of listening will bring considerable improvement – provided you go about it in a positive way, with the emphasis on what you can do.

One final point: don't forget that you do **not** have to understand every word. In developing your skills, concentrate first on what you do understand and then on what is needed to answer the questions. In examinations and examination practice concentrate on what you need in order to answer the questions. Ignore the irrelevant words you don't need.

G, F, E tasks

The types of spoken material you will hear are:

1. Announcements (e.g. in shops, stations and campsites).
2. Spoken instructions.
3. Requests.
4. Broadcast news items, weather forecasts and traffic reports.
5. Telephone messages.
6. Conversations, interviews and discussions.

- Each item is quite short. Even the 'longer' items are comparatively short and often they are broken into sections the second time you hear them.
- The speakers speak clearly and at below normal Spanish speed.
- The vocabulary tested is almost always from the **Core Vocabulary** list published by the board, though other words which are not tested may come from outside the list.
- You are expected to demonstrate understanding of the main points and some details. (You will not be required to summarize or draw conclusions.)

D, C tasks

For questions targeted at this level, the recordings are generally longer and cover a wider range of vocabulary, but care is taken to ensure that they do not place too much emphasis on memory, and for that reason the longer recordings tend to be split into sections. In some cases you will hear the whole recording first, then each section again with a pause between sections. In other cases the recording is split into sections the first time you hear it, with each section heard twice before you move on to the next. The different examining boards tend to have their own preferences about which pattern to use.

What are the other specific features of D and C level recordings?

- The speakers speak faster (and therefore tend to sound more natural).
- They include reference to past and future events – so you will need to recognize past and future tenses.
- They are drawn from a variety of topics which include familiar language in unfamiliar contexts.
- There is a variety of 'registers' (the different ways in which people speak, according to the place they are in and who they are talking to). The most frequently tested are the registers used:
  - on radio and television;
  - in the home;
  - in more formal situations;
  - by sixteen-year-olds in Spain.

Quite often the recordings will include the natural hesitations, repetitions and re-wording that are features of people's normal everyday speech. (Think how often people you know say things like 'um', 'er', 'what I mean is ... '.) Apart from making the speakers sound more natural, these features of speech, when they occur, can, in fact, be very helpful to you as you listen. Repetition and re-wording are obviously helpful and the hesitations give you more time to note down points you have just heard.

The types of spoken material you are likely to hear are:

1. Announcements.
2. Conversations.
3. Discussions and arguments.
4. Requests and instructions.
5. Telephone calls.
6. Broadcast news items, weather forecasts and traffic reports.
7. Sustained single-voice items (such as tour guides and longer recorded telephone messages).

In addition to identifying and noting main points and extracting details, questions at this level require an ability to recognize points of view being expressed.

B, A, A* tasks

At this level, in addition to demonstrating understanding of main points and specific details and identifying points of view, you are expected to be able to:

- Identify the attitudes, emotions and ideas of the speakers.
- Draw conclusions from what you hear.
- Identify the relationship between ideas expressed.

These skills imply an ability to select what is relevant and disregard what is irrelevant, when listening to the recordings.

It is obviously a good idea to make sure you know the vocabulary of emotions and attitudes (e.g. *triste, alegre, enfadado, le gusta*) but you must bear in mind that a genuine 'Attitudes and Emotions' question does not, in fact, depend so directly on that vocabulary. If you are asked to identify the emotion of someone who says *Estoy muy contento*, you are really answering a question that tests a specific detail of vocabulary. You may well be asked to identify the emotion expressed in words such as *¡Qué bien! Creí que no te iba a ver*. In this case the word for 'happy' (or possibly 'relieved') has not been said but the emotion has been expressed without it.

EXAMINATION QUESTIONS

You are recommended to try the questions yourself before looking at the Students' Answers with Examiner's Comments, which are on pages 78–80. Transcripts of the recordings are included towards the end of the chapter, on pages 91–95, so that you can check the wording later.

G, F, E, tasks

At this level, the tests normally begin with a series of short recordings, with a single question on each. Later there are likely to be some recordings linked to two or three questions. Finally there could be some longer recordings linked to rather more questions. Sometimes, though not always, the short recordings have links with each other, so that they follow through different stages of a particular incident.

Find Recording 1 on the cassette, then attempt the questions before looking at the student's answers. Remember to read the question carefully. It may include clues to help you.

Recording 1

Read the questions below then play Recording 1 (or listen to your friend read the transcript on page 91).

Questions 1–5

To your great surprise a Spanish friend of yours has just arrived in England and he telephones you to let you know of his arrival.

1 Where does your friend say that he is?

.... (*1*)

2 You ask him where he intends to stay while he is in England. Why should you already know?

.... (*1*)

3 So you ask him again where he is going to stay. In what sort of accommodation is he going to stay?

.... (*1*)

4 You ask him what he is going to do during his stay. What sort of work will he be doing?

.... (*1*)

5 Finally, you want to know when you will be able to meet him. What does he suggest that you do straightaway?

.... (*1*)

(SEG 1990)

Recording 2 Estás oyendo la radio. Decide en cada caso si hablan de:

A	Un crimen.	E	El tiempo.
B	Un accidente de tráfico.	F	Un desastre.
C	Un deporte.	G	Una muerte.
D	Publicidad.		

Escribe una letra en cada casilla.

Ejemplo G

Ahora escucha los reportajes.

Reportaje 1	☐	(*1*)
Reportaje 2	☐	(*1*)
Reportaje 3	☐	(*1*)
Reportaje 4	☐	(*1*)
Reportaje 5	☐	(*1*)

(*Total: 5 marks*)

(MEG)

D, C tasks

Recording 3 Vitoria

Your mother mistakenly thinks Vitoria is a person. You explain it is a town in Spain and answer her questions about it.

(a) In which part of Spain is Vitoria?

.... (*1*)

(b) Which is the most important industry?

.... (*1*)

(c) What is Vitoria like?

.... (*1*)

(d) In which month are the main festivals?

.... (*1*)

(NEAB)

Recording 4 Escucha primero lo que dice Pablo y escribe sus preferencias respecto a sus asignaturas de colegio, sus ambiciones y sus pasatiempos. Después escucha lo que dice Marisa.

Como ejemplo ya está escrito lo que prefieren como deportes. Ahora escribe las otras preferencias **en español.**

Pablo habla primero.

Pablo
Asignatura preferida ....(1)
Ambición ....(1)
Pasatiempo preferido ....(1)
Deporte preferido *el fútbol*

Ahora habla Marisa.

Marisa
Asignatura preferida ....(1)
Ambición ....(1)
Pasatiempo preferido ....(1)
Deporte preferido *nadar*

(WJEC)

B, A, A* tasks

Recording 5

Read the questions below then play Recording 5 (or listen to your friend read the transcript on page 91).

You are on an exchange in Spain and you hear a series of conversations over two days between your partner Teresa and her friend, Rosa.

Listen to their conversations and for each one select from List 1 below, the **topic** which best fits the conversation and write it in the space provided.

(e.g. The conversation is about **a family illness**.) You will not need to use every word in the list.

Also listen to the conversations and for each one select from List 2 below, the word that best describes the speaker's **attitude**.

(e.g. The speaker is **happy**.) You will not need to use every word in the list. You will hear each conversation twice. Now look through the questions.

List 1 – Topics	**List 2 – Attitudes**
An unexpected journey	happy
A request for help	grateful
A break in routine	worried
A family illness	insistent
A new friend	unsympathetic
An unwillingness to be involved	apologetic
Trouble with parents	jealous

Conversation 1

Rosa is talking to Teresa.

1 Here, Rosa is talking about .... (1)
2 She is .... (1)

Conversation 2

Teresa replies to what Rosa has said.

3 Here, Teresa is talking about .... (1)
4 She is .... (1)

Conversation 3

Rosa replies to what Teresa has said.

5 Here, Rosa is talking about .... (1)
6 She is .... (1)

Conversation 4

The following day, Teresa again talks to Rosa.

7 Here, Teresa is talking about .... (1)
8 She is .... (1)

Conversation 5

Rosa replies to what Teresa has said.

9 Here, Teresa is talking about .... (*1*)
10 She is .... (*1*)

STUDENTS' ANSWERS WITH EXAMINER'S COMMENTS

Recording 1

Student's answers

1 *Manchester.*
2 *He has written it in his letter.*
3 *Youth Hostel.*
4 *In an office in the city.*
5 *Go to the airport straight away.*

Examiner's comments

1 Not enough information. The answer is 'Manchester airport'.
2 Good answer. Could have been shorter, e.g. 'He told me in a letter'.
3 Excellent answer.
4 Good answer. You didn't actually need to add 'in the city'.
5 Good answer, but you certainly don't need to write 'straight away' – that was in the question.

Recording 2

Student's answers

Reportaje 1 *A*
Reportaje 2 *C*
Reportaje 3 *E*
Reportaje 4 *F*
Reportaje 5 *B*

Examiner's comments

Reportaje 1: Good. You obviously recognized the significance of *armados* and *robaron.*
Reportaje 2: Good. You clearly understood at least some of *estadio, baloncesto* and *equipo.*
Reportaje 3: Good.
Reportaje 4: No. One broken arm (*el brazo roto*) is an accident, but hardly a disaster. The correct answer is B.
Reportaje 5: No. *Tráfico* is clearly relevant here, but not *accidente.* This is advertising the car (*publicidad*). The correct answer is D.

D, C tasks

Recording 3

Student's answers

(a) *It is in the North, 60 kilometres from Bilbao.*
(b) *The ladelana industry is important.*
(c) *There are a lot of animals in Victoria.*
(d) *The main festivals are in August.*

Examiner's comments

(a) You are right about it being in the North of Spain and should get your mark for that, even though you have made the very common mistake of confusing *setenta* (70) with *sesenta* (60).
(b) You obviously cannot expect a mark for this meaningless answer. If you have no idea of the

answer, you should always make a guess that at least makes sense. *La de lana* = 'that of wool' (i.e. the industry of wool: the woollen industry).

(c) No. *Animada* means 'lively'. It has nothing to do with animals. Incidentally, you have made a mistake in copying *Vitoria* from the question.

(d) No problem here. You have correctly identified *agosto* as August.

One general point: your answers are longer than they need be. 'North; wool; lively; August,' would score all four marks.

Recording 4

Student's answers

Pablo

Asignatura: *Idiomas*
Ambición: *Quiero ser policía*
Pasatiempo: *El baloncesto*

Marisa

Asignatura: *La biología*
Ambición: *Quisiera profesora*
Pasatiempo: *Me gusta escuchar musica*

Examiner's comments

Pablo

Asignatura: Fine, or you could have been more precise and said *el inglés*.

Ambición: You will probably get your mark, even though, by copying words directly from the text, you have said that it is *your* ambition to be a policeman. As an answer to the question, a Spaniard would know what you meant.

Pasatiempo: No. This is another sport. You should have said *coleccionar (tarjetas) postales.*

Marisa

Asignatura: Fine.

Ambición: The key word here is *profesora*, so you will get your mark, though if you use *Quisiera*, you really need to include *ser*.

Pasatiempo: Again you have copied directly from the text, so you have said this is what *you* like doing, but you will probably get a mark.

B, A, A* tasks

Recording 5

Student's answers

1 Here, Rosa is talking about *a family illness* (1)
2 She is *worried* (1)
3 Here, Teresa is talking about *unwillingness to be involved* (1)
4 She is *unsympathetic* (1)
5 Here, Rosa is talking about *a request for help* (1)
6 She is *apologetic* (1)
7 Here, Teresa is talking about *a break in routine* (1)
8 She is *apologetic* (1)
9 Here, Rosa is talking about *a new friend* (1)
10 She is *jealous* (1)

Examiner's comments

1 Presumably you have jumped to a conclusion about why Jaime has not been in touch but he is not in the family and there is no evidence he is ill. We just do not know yet why he is not following the routine. The correct answer is: A break in routine.

2, 3, 4 and 5 are fine.

6 People often do apologise when asking for help but listen carefully – Rosa doesn't. But she does repeat herself (*Llámale*) and she does emphasize her past help for Teresa. The answer is: A request for help.

7 This is unfortunate. In a sense it is true but you were supposed to use this answer for Q.1! If

you had been right on Q.1 you might have given the right answer here. This question is about going to France at short notice (an unexpected journey).

8 Good – but it is just as well on this occasion that you didn't reject 'apologetic' because you had already used it! (Normally you should expect to use each answer once only.)

9 Good.

10 Wrong. You may think Teresa could be jealous that Rosa is going out with Alejandro but you were asked about the attitude of Rosa (the speaker). The correct answer is: Happy.

PRACTICE QUESTIONS

Suggested answers to these questions are on pages 89–91.

G, F, E tasks

Recording 6 En el restaurante

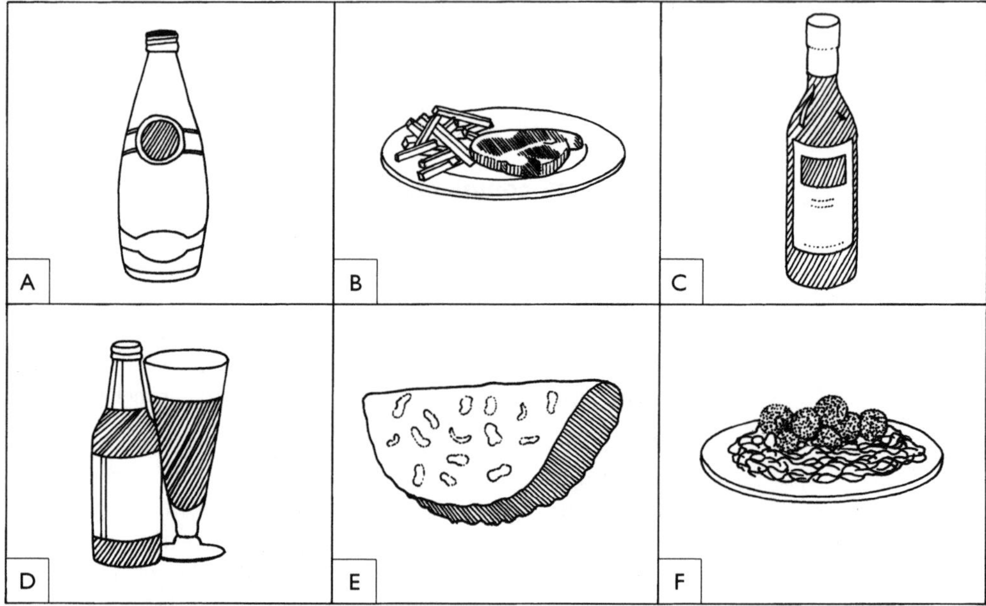

¿Qué van a tomar? En cada casilla, pon la letra adecuada.

Ejemplo: [A]

(a) ☐

(b) ☐

(c) ☐

(d) ☐

(4)
(Edexcel)

Recording 7 Escucha el anuncio en un supermercado.
Indica en la tabla la cantidad y el precio de los artículos.

Por ejemplo:

Manzanas	2 kilos	220 pesetas
ARTICULO	CANTIDAD	PRECIO

Naranjas		
Azúcar		
Guisantes		
Sardinas		
Chorizo		

(10)
(NICCEA)

Recording 8 En una cuidad en España quieres ir a la estación de autobuses y preguntas a una señora por dónde tienes que ir. La flecha → indica donde estás.

(a) Pon una X para mostrar la situación de la estación de autobuses. (2)

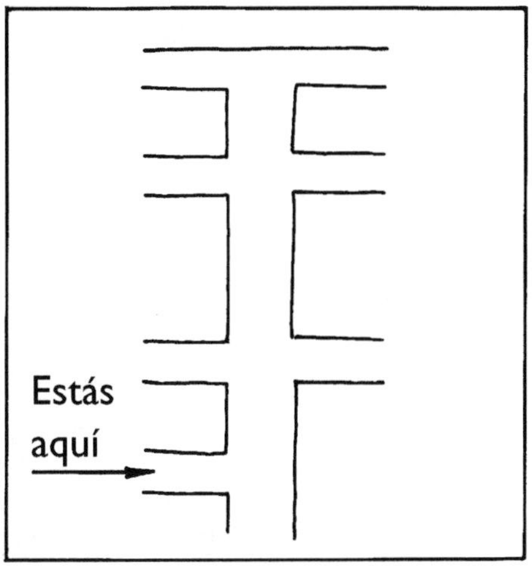

Estás aquí

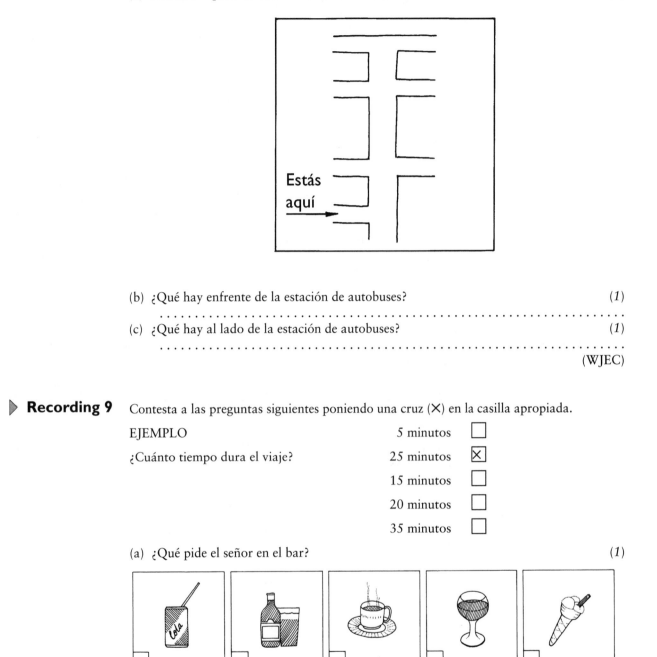

(b) ¿Qué hay enfrente de la estación de autobuses? (*1*)

. . . .

(c) ¿Qué hay al lado de la estación de autobuses? (*1*)

. . . .

(WJEC)

Recording 9 Contesta a las preguntas siguientes poniendo una cruz (X) en la casilla apropiada.

EJEMPLO

¿Cuánto tiempo dura el viaje?

5 minutos	☐
25 minutos	☒
15 minutos	☐
20 minutos	☐
35 minutos	☐

(a) ¿Qué pide el señor en el bar? (*1*)

Cola

(b) ¿Qué clase de transporte es el más cómodo según esta señora? (*1*)

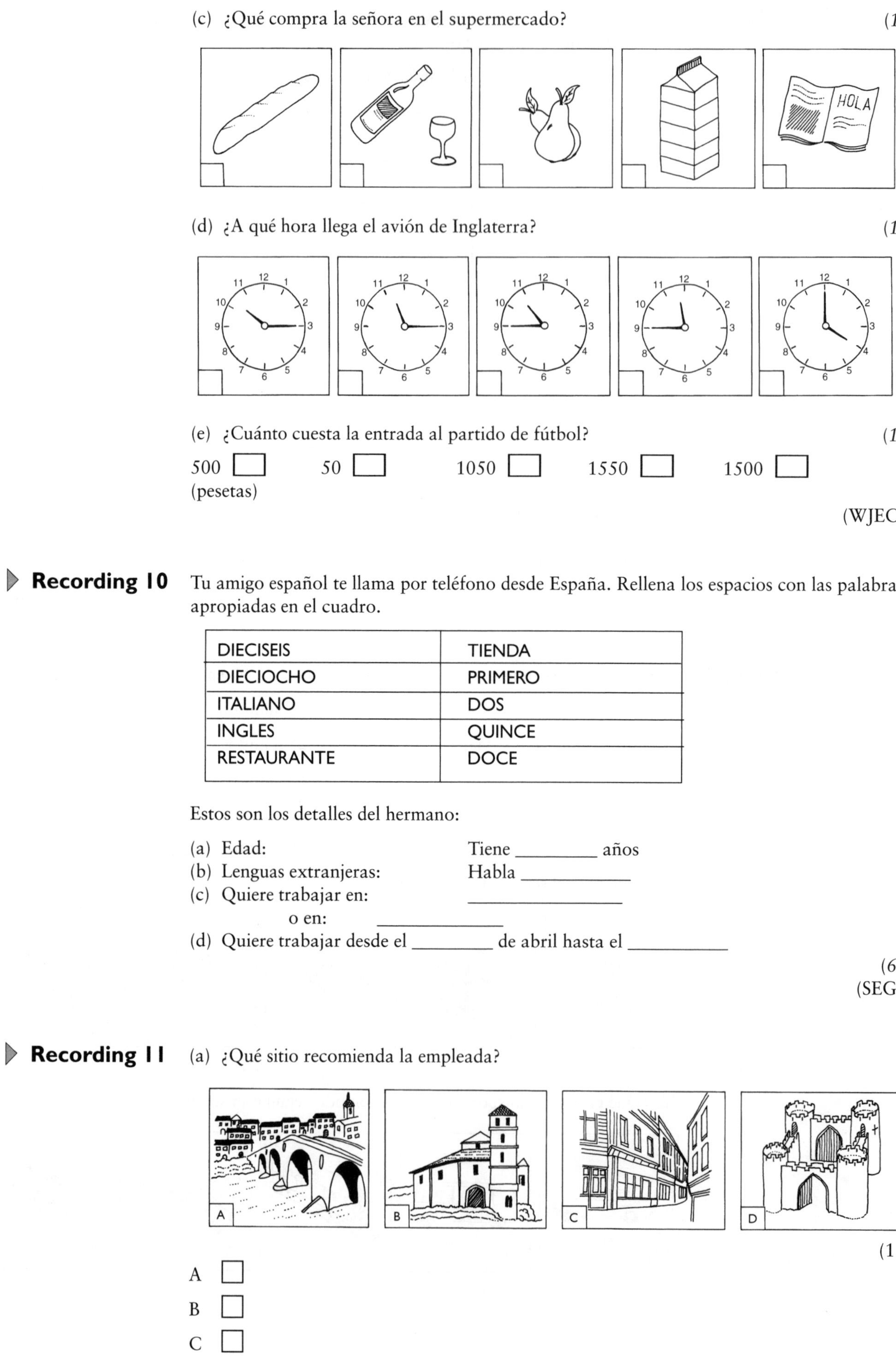

(c) ¿Qué compra la señora en el supermercado? *(1)*

(d) ¿A qué hora llega el avión de Inglaterra? *(1)*

(e) ¿Cuánto cuesta la entrada al partido de fútbol? *(1)*

500 ☐ 50 ☐ 1050 ☐ 1550 ☐ 1500 ☐
(pesetas)

(WJEC)

Recording 10 Tu amigo español te llama por teléfono desde España. Rellena los espacios con las palabras apropiadas en el cuadro.

DIECISEIS	TIENDA
DIECIOCHO	PRIMERO
ITALIANO	DOS
INGLES	QUINCE
RESTAURANTE	DOCE

Estos son los detalles del hermano:

(a) Edad: Tiene ________ años
(b) Lenguas extranjeras: Habla ___________
(c) Quiere trabajar en: ________________
o en: ______________
(d) Quiere trabajar desde el ________ de abril hasta el __________

(6)
(SEG)

Recording 11 (a) ¿Qué sitio recomienda la empleada?

(1)

A ☐
B ☐
C ☐
D ☐

(b) En unos grandes almacenes.
¿Dónde están las camisetas?

A Planta baja B Primera planta
C Tercera planta D Quinta planta

A ☐
B ☐
C ☐
D ☐

(c) En la estación.
¿A qué hora sale el tren?

A 10.00 B 12.00
C 20.00 D 02.00

A ☐
B ☐
C ☐
D ☐

(d) Transportes.
¿Cómo va Elena al colegio?

A B C D

A ☐
B ☐
C ☐
D ☐

(*1*)

(e) Planes para mañana.
¿Adónde van a ir?

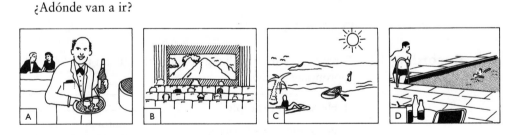

A B C D

A ☐
B ☐
C ☐
D ☐

(*1*)
(NEAB)

Recording 12 Ahora vas a oír una serie de ocho observaciones o diálogos cortos.
Escucha las observaciones y contesta a las preguntas **en español.**

Ejemplo.

Estás en una tienda muy, muy grande, El Corte Inglés, con unos amigos. Buscáis el restaurante.

Un hombre dice donde está.

¿Dónde exactamente está el restaurante?

En el primer piso

Ahora, escucha las observaciones.
Entras en el restaurante. El camarero quiere saber algo.

(a) ¿Qué quiere saber?

.... *(1)*

(b) ¿Dónde está la mesa?

.... *(1)*

(c) ¿Qué va a traer el camarero?

.... *(1)*

(d) ¿Qué recomienda el camarero?

.... *(1)*

Una amiga habla con el camarero.

(e) ¿Qué hay en la tortilla?

.... *(1)*

La amiga habla con el camarero otra vez.

(f) ¿Qué quiere Mercedes de primero?

.... *(1)*

José quiere algo.

(g) ¿Qué quiere José?

.... *(1)*

(h) ¿Qué quiere José ahora?

.... *(1)*

(Total: 8 marks)
(MEG)

D, C tasks

Recording 13 Three Spaniards are talking about school. Put a tick (✓) in the correct space to indicate the appropriate person.

Here is an example.

Who goes home for lunch?

The answer is Reyes.

Antonio	Paco	Reyes

Now read questions (a)–(e).

Now listen to the exercise.

	Antonio	Paco	Reyes	
(a) Who likes going to school?				*(1)*
(b) Who does not like French?				*(1)*
(c) Who does not attend all his/her classes?				*(1)*
(d) Who says that they like their holidays?				*(1)*
(e) Who does not like English lessons?				*(1)*

(Total: 5 marks)
(MEG)

Recording 14 *Vamos de compras*

Llena el espacio con una palabra de la lista.

Ejemplo: Hoy el ..queso.......... de la Vaca Blanca es más barato.

(a) Moda 2000 vende artículos de moda para los ....
Moda 2000 ofrece una gran variedad de .... (2)

(b) El Palacio del Juguete vende .... eléctricas.
El Palacio del Juguete vende juguetes y bicicletas en .... tiendas. (2)

(c) Se puede comprar muebles a precios muy .... en Bazar de los Muebles.
El Bazar de los Muebles tiene una gran variedad de .... (2)

queso	comida	doce
ropa	camas	caros
coches	baratos	jóvenes
motos	dos	mujeres

(*Total: 6 marks*)
(Edexcel)

Recording 15

Estás en una tienda de ultramarinos cuando oyes esta conversación entre un cliente y la tendera.

Debes indicar si el cliente compra el artículo (✓) o no (✗). También debes indicar la cantidad que compra o la razón por la que no compra el artículo.

Ejemplo.

	Compra (✓) o no (✗)	Cantidad que compra o razón por la que no compra el artículo
	✗	No hay

Ahora mira los artículos.

Ahora escucha el ejercicio.

	Compra (✓) o no (✗)	Cantidad que compra o razón por la que no compra el artículo

	Compra (✓) o no (✗)	Cantidad que compra o razón por la que no compra el artículo

(10)
(MEG)

B, A, A* tasks

Recording 16 Un padre describe una excursión con su hijo.
Contesta las preguntas **en inglés**.

Sección 1

(a) Why did Pedro and his father wear a heavy jacket and boots?
.... *(1)*

Sección 2

(b) What was especially suitable about the place where they stopped?
.... *(1)*

(c) What were the only visible signs of movement?
.... *(1)*

Sección 3

(d) Was it the father or the son who fell asleep?
.... *(1)*

(e) What opinion does the father express about eating?
.... *(1)*

(Total: 5 marks)
(NICCEA)

Recording 17 Escucha el reportaje siguiente sobre una huelga de alumnos en un colegio español. Contesta a las preguntas que siguen. Hay 2 secciones.

Sección 1

(a) ¿Por qué se declararon en huelga los alumnos?

.... (*1*)

(b) ¿Qué pensaban los padres de lo que hacían sus hijos? – pon una cruz (x) en la casilla al lado de la frase apropiada. (*1*)

(i) ☐ Estaban enfadados con sus hijos.

(ii) ☐ Estaban tristes a causa de lo que hacían sus hijos.

(iii) ☐ Apoyaban lo que hacían sus hijos.

(iv) ☐ Pensaban que sus hijos deberían volver en seguida al colegio.

(v) ☐ Pensaban que el director, Julio García, debería asistir a un curso en la capital.

Seccíon 2

(c) Completa las frases siguientes.

(i) La profesora no había asistido al colegio porque ....

.... (*1*)

(ii) El profesor no había asistido al colegio porque ....

.... (*1*)

(d) Para asegurar a los chicos y sus padres que la situación había sido resuelta, el portavoz del Ministerio de Educación dijo que ....

....

(2)

(e) ¿Cuál fue la actitud del Ministerio de Educación? (*1*)
Pon una cruz (X) en la casilla apropiada:

☐ distraída

☐ comprensiva

☐ indiferente

☐ enojada

☐ triste

(WJEC)

Recording 18

El carácter

Pon una X en la casilla correcta.

(a) Pablo es una persona ambiciosa. A ☐

Pablo es una persona que quiere divertirse mucho. B ☐

Pablo es una persona sensible. C ☐

Pablo es una persona valiente. D ☐

(b) Inma es una persona ambiciosa. A ☐

Inma es una persona que quiere divertirse mucho. B ☐

Inma es una persona sensible. C ☐

Inma es una persona valiente. D ☐

(c) Carmen es una persona ambiciosa. A ☐

Carmen es una persona que quiere divertirse mucho. B ☐

Carmen es una persona sensible. C ☐

Carmen es una persona valiente. D ☐

(3)

(NEAB)

Recording 19 De vacaciones en España, oyes una serie de conversaciones entre tu amigo, José Luis, sus padres y su amigo Rafael.

Debes escoger en la Lista A el tema de la conversación y en la Lista B la actitud de la persona que habla.

Mira las listas.

Ejemplo.

La madre de José Luis habla de ..planes para un viaje..............................

Su actitud es que ..tiene ganas de ver cosas nuevas..............................

Ahora el ejercicio.

Lista A	Lista B
una amistad aprobada	quiere ayudar
un regalo	no se puede decidir
una solución posible	tiene ganas de ver cosas nuevas
una enfermedad en la familia	no aprueba
planes para un viaje	tiene celos
la importancia de los estudios	siente orgullo
una decisión	siente agradecimiento

Conversación 1

La madre de José Luis habla de ....

Su actitud es que ....

[*Pausa*]

Conversación 2

José Luis habla de ....

Su actitud es que ....

[*Pausa*]

Conversación 3

La madre de José Luis habla de ....

Su actitud es que ....

[*Pausa*]

Conversación 4

Rafael habla de ....

Su actitud es que ....

[*Pausa*]

Conversación 5

La madre de José Luis habla de ....

Su actitud es que ....

[*Pausa*]

(*8*)
(MEG)

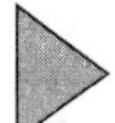

ANSWERS TO PRACTICE QUESTIONS

G, F, E tasks

Recording 6 (Answers)

(a) D
(b) E
(c) C
(d) B

Recording 7 (Answers)

Naranjas:	1 kilo	50 pesetas
Azúcar:	1 paquete	120 pesetas
Guisantes:	400 gramos	90 pesetas
Sardinas:	1 lata	95 pesetas
Chorizo:	125 gramos	110 pesetas

Recording 8 (Answers)

(a)

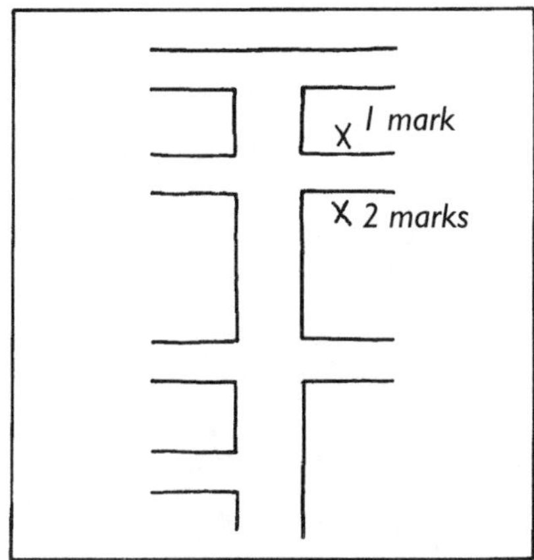

(b) Banco (de Bilbao)
(c) Supermercado

Recording 9 (Answers)

(a) C
(b) C
(c) C
(d) C
(e) E

Recording 10 (Answers)

(a) dieciocho
(b) inglés
(c) restaurante
tienda
(d) primero
quince

Recording 11 (Answers)

(a) D
(b) B
(c) A
(d) B
(e) A

Recording 12 (Answers)

The wording is not critical, as long as the correct idea is expressed.

(a) ¿Mesa para cuántos?
(b) Cerca de la ventana
(c) El menú
(d) Mariscos
(e) Champiñones
(f) Sopa
(g) (Más) patatas
(h) Volver a casa

D, C tasks

Recording 13 (Answers)

(a) Paco
(b) Antonio
(c) Antonio
(d) Reyes
(e) Paco

Recording 14 (Answers)

(a) jóvenes
ropa
(b) motos
dos
(c) baratos
camas

Recording 15 (Answers)

Compra – Medio kilo
No compra – No queda OR No hay
No compra – Es (demasiado) caro OR El precio
Compra – 2 paquetes
No compra – A su mujer no le gusta

B, A, A* tasks

Recording 16 (Answers)

(a) They were going fishing
(b) Good (place) for trout
(c) Birds
(d) Father
(e) He likes fish (a lot)

Recording 17 (Answers)

(a) Para protestar por la ausencia de dos profesores.
(b) (iii)
(c) (i) Había asistido a un curso.
(ii) Estaba enfermo.
(d) La profesora volvería al día siguiente.
La ausencia del profesor había sido cubierta.
(e) Comprensiva

Recording 18 (Answers)

(a) B
(b) A
(c) C

Recording 19 (Answers)

1. un regalo
siente agradecimiento
2. una decisión
no se puede decidir
3. la importancia de los estudios
no aprueba

4. una solución
   quiere ayudar
5. una amistad aprobada
   siente orgullo

TRANSCRIPTS OF THE RECORDINGS

Recording 1 (Transcript)

1. Hola. Te telefoneo para decirte que ya estoy en el aeropuerto de Manchester.
2. Pues, ¿no has recibido mi carta?
3. Voy a hospedarme en un albergue de jóvenes cerca de tu casa.
4. Voy a pasar un mes trabajando en una oficina en el centro de la ciudad.
5. Pues, si vienes al aeropuerto, nos vamos a encontrar muy pronto.

Recording 2 (Transcript)

Reportaje 1 Esta mañana dos hombres armados con pistolas entraron en el Banco de España en el centro de la ciudad y robaron quinientas mil pesetas. Se escaparon en un Ford Sierra.

Reportaje 2 Esta tarde en el estadio municipal hubo un partido de baloncesto entre un equipo inglés y el equipo local. Muchos espectadores vieron ganar sin mucha dificultad al equipo español.

Reportaje 3 Mañana lunes hará sol con altas temperaturas por toda España. Por la costa habrá vientos fuertes. Pasado mañana va a llover durante todo el día.

Reportaje 4 A las cinco de la tarde un coche chocó con un camión en la Calle Mayor. El conductor del coche fue llevado al hospital. Tiene el brazo roto. El conductor del camión no resultó herido.

Reportaje 5 Señoras, señores, vengan a ver el coche del año, el nuevo modelo 405. Es un coche de lujo a un precio atractivo, Vd. puede ser dueño del coche del año.

Recording 3 (Transcript)

Vitoria es la capital del País Vasco. Está en el norte de España a unos setenta kilómetros de Bilbao. La industria más importante es la de lana. Me gusta vivir allí porque es una ciudad animada y hay tantas posibilidades para deportes. Las fiestas de la Virgen Blanca en agosto son muy conocidas. Durante estas fiestas todo el mundo se divierte.

Recording 4 (Transcript)

Pablo

A mí no me gustan las ciencias. Prefiero los idiomas, sobre todo el inglés. Me interesa porque tengo un amigo galés que vive en Tenby. Al terminar mis estudios quiero ser policía aunque primero tendré que aprobar los exámenes.

En mi tiempo libre me gusta coleccionar tarjetas postales; ya tengo unas doscientas de varios países del mundo.

Mi deporte preferido es el fútbol pero también juego al baloncesto.

Marisa

En el instituto estudio ocho asignaturas. Prefiero la biología porque me interesan mucho los animales. Quisiera ser profesora de biología en un colegio o instituto en España. Cuando no tengo demasiados deberes me gusta escuchar música. Mi grupo favorito es Mecano.

No me gusta mucho el deporte pero sí que me gusta nadar, sobre todo en el mar durante las vacaciones de verano.

Recording 5 (Transcript)

Conversation 1 Bueno, Teresa, me parece que las cosas no van bien. Ya sabes que llevo tres meses saliendo con Jaime. Me llamaba cada noche y los viernes y los sábados salíamos a los bares, a un cine, cualquier cosa. Pero el fin de semana pasado no llamó y no salimos. Esta semana no ha llamado, ni una vez. Estoy muy preocupada.

Conversation 2 Oye, Rosa, lo de tu novio ... Mira, yo tengo mis propios problemas con mis estudios y todo. No me aburras. ¿Qué puedo hacer yo? Siempre es igual contigo y tus

chicos. Siempre hay drama. Siempre hay algo. Déjame en paz ¿quieres?
Conversation 3 Pero, Teresa, tienes que ayudarme. Tienes que hacer algo. ¿No te ayudé yo con tu problema con Enrique? Ya nos conocemos mucho tiempo, amiga. Me debes muchos favores. Ya sabes que conoces a un amigo de Jaime. Conoces a Francisco ¿no? Llámale a ver si él sabe lo que ha pasado, por favor, Teresa. Llámale.
Conversation 4 Hola, Rosa. Esto ... lo que ocurrió ayer ... lo que dije, lo siento mucho. Mira, llamé al amigo de Jaime ayer para preguntar qué le pasaba. Jaime se ha ido a Francia. Su tío iba a Francia de negocios. En el último momento invitó a Jaime a ir con él. Jaime no tuvo tiempo para llamar a nadie. ¡Qué tonta soy! ¿Me perdonas, Rosa?
Conversation 5 Teresa, escucha, una gran noticia. Anoche fui a la discoteca en la calle Mayor ... «La Mariposa» ¿sabes? Y ¿sabes quién estaba allí? Pues, Alejandro. Tú lo conoces: el hermano de Conchita. Pues, cuando entré, me invitó a bailar. Bailamos juntos toda la tarde y esta tarde vamos a un restaurante. ¿Qué dices, Teresa?

Recording 6 (Transcript)

En el restaurante

Ejemplo: Tráigame una botella de agua mineral con gas.

Pregunta (a) Una cerveza, por favor.
Pregunta (b) Yo, pues quiero una tortilla francesa.
Pregunta (c) Para beber, tráigame una botella de vino tinto.
Pregunta (d) Para mí, un bistec con patatas fritas.

Recording 7 (Transcript)

Buenos días a todas. ¿Por qué no os aprovecháis de las ofertas especiales que tenemos hoy?

Naranjas, un kilo, cincuenta pesetas.
Azúcar, el paquete, ciento veinte pesetas.
Guisantes, cuatrocientos gramos, noventa pesetas.
Sardinas, la lata, noventa y cinco pesetas.
Chorizo, ciento veinticinco gramos, ciento diez pesetas.

Recording 8 (Transcript)

(*Señora*)
Pues al final de esta calle tuerce a la izquierda y toma la segunda calle a la derecha. La estación de autobuses está a mano derecha.

Enfrente está el Banco de Bilbao y al lado se encuentra el supermercado 'Consum' que es muy grande y moderno.

Recording 9 (Transcript)

Ejemplo

Sí, señorita es un viaje de 25 minutos.

(a) Tráigame un café con leche – Sí, señor, en seguida – un café con leche.
(b) Siempre prefiero viajar en tren porque es más cómodo.
(c) Póngame un kilo de peras.
(d) Señoras y sres. el vuelo número 274 de Manchester llegará a las once menos cuarto.
(e) Lo siento señor pero la entrada más barata vale 1500 pesetas – es un partido muy importante ¿comprende?

Recording 10 (Transcript)

Hola, ¿qué tal? Quisiera saber si puedes encontrar un trabajo para mi hermano. Ya sabes que tiene dieciocho años y habla muy bien inglés. Quiere trabajar en un restaurante o en una tienda desde el uno de abril hasta el quince ...

Recording 11 (Transcript)

(a) M ¿Que hay de interés aquí?
F Pues, aquí hay de todo. ¿Le interesa la historia?
M Ah, sí, mucho.
F Pues tiene Vd. que visitar el castillo que data del siglo doce.

(b) Señoras y señores. Grandes rebajas hoy en la sección de ropa en la primera planta. 25% de descuento en todos los artículos en la sección de ropa en la primera planta.
(c) Atención. El Talgo con destino a Madrid sale a las 10.00. Faltan dos minutos para que efectúe su salida, vía 1.
(d) F1 Dime, Paca, ¿cómo vas al colegio?
F2 Pues como vivo cerca suelo ir en bici, pero cuando llueve mi madre me lleva en coche. Y tú, Elena, ¿qué haces?
F1 Pues, yo voy en autobús todos los días.
(e) M Parece que mañana hará sol. ¿Por qué no vamos a pasar el día en la playa?
F ¿Has olvidado? Paco nos ha invitado a comer en un restaurante para celebrar su cumpleaños.
M Ah, sí, tienes razón. Tendremos que ir a la playa otro día.

Recording 12 (Transcript)

Ejemplo.
Estás en una tienda muy, muy grande, El Corte Inglés, con unos amigos. Buscáis el restaurante. Un hombre dice dónde está.

¿Dónde exactamenta está el restaurante?

[*Setting: large store*]

¿El restaurante?
M2: En el primer piso.
(a) M1: Buenos días. ¿Queréis una mesa para cuántas personas?
(b) M1: Hay una mesa aquí cerca de la ventana.
(c) M1: Un momento. Voy a quitar esta botella de la mesa y voy a traer el menú.
(d) M1: Sí, sí. Tenemos mariscos y son muy buenos. Pescado no tenemos.
(e) F1: Pedro quiere tortilla de champiñones y una ensalada de tomate.
(f) F1: Mercedes quiere pollo. Pero para empezar quiere sopa.
(g) M2: No, no, no pidas la cuenta. Tengo hambre todavía. Pide más patatas.
(h) M2: Ya es muy tarde. Quiero volver a casa.

Recording 13 (Transcript)

Example
[*Setting: school yard noise*]
M1: Me llamo Antonio.
Siempre me quedo en el colegio para comer.
M2: Me llamo Paco.
No vuelvo nunca a casa para comer.
F1: Me llamo Reyes.
Me gusta volver a casa para comer y echar una siesta.
The answer is Reyes.
M1: Me llamo Antonio.
No me gusta el colegio. Siempre llego tarde y a veces si me aburro me marcho del colegio antes del final de las clases.
Mi asignatura favorita es el inglés: la profesora es muy simpática.
Pero no voy nunca a las clases de francés porque la profesora es muy severa.
M2: Me llamo Paco.
Los fines de semana me aburro porque no tengo clases en el colegio.
[*pause*]
Me aburro también durante las vacaciones. Siempre voy a mis clases.
[*pause*]
Me gustan casi todas mis asignaturas sobre todo el francés. La profesora de inglés es poco simpática.
F1: Me llamo Reyes.
El colegio es para mí un aburrimiento.
[*pause*]
Todos mis profesores son buenos y no tengo problemas con ninguno.
[*pause*]
Sin embargo el trabajo es duro y espero las vacaciones con mucha impaciencia.

Recording 14 (Transcript)

Vamos de compras

Ejemplo: Compre queso de la Vaca Blanca con el 50% de descuento. Hoy solamente.

Pregunta (a) ¡Jóvenes! ¡El mundo de la ropa te espera en Moda 2000! Camisas, camisetas, vaqueros, faldas – ¡toda la última moda en Moda 2000!

Pregunta (b) Compren sus regalos en el Palacio del Juguete: motos eléctricas, bicicletas, muñecas. Todo en nuestros dos locales: Plaza de Castilla y Calle Mayor.

Pregunta (c) ¿Estrena piso? Le invitamos a nuestra fantástica exposición de muebles a precios baratos: mesas, sofás, camas de todo tipo – lo tenemos todo. Bazar de los Muebles.

Recording 15 (Transcript)

Ejemplo:
F1: Hola. ¿Qué quieres?
M1: Buenos días. Un litro de leche por favor.
F1: Leche no hay. Lo siento.
M2: Ahora escucha el ejercicio.
F1: Hola. ¿Qué quieres?
M1: ¿Tienes queso?
F1: Sí, ¿cuánto quieres?
M1: Medio kilo, por favor. ¿Tienes jamón?
F1: Normalmente sí pero hoy ya no queda.
M1: ¿Tienes aceite?
F1: Tenemos este aceite excepcional. Es de marca superior y es bastante caro.
M1: ¿Cuánto es?
F1: Ochocientas pesetas.
M1: No gracias, buscaré algo más barato en otro sitio. ¿Tienes café?
F1: Tenemos un café excelente. Es de Colombia.
M1: Dame dos paquetes. ¿Tienes mermelada?
F1: Sí. Tenemos mermelada de melocotón. Es la única que tenemos.
M1: No gracias. A mi mujer no le gusta la mermelada de melocotón.
F1: ¿Algo más? Pues son mil doscientas pesetas.
M1: Gracias. Adiós.

Recording 16 (Transcript)

Sección 1

Un día de primavera yo fui a la sierra con Pedro. Pusimos las cañas de pescar en el coche, y, por supuesto, llevábamos una chaqueta gruesa y botas.

Sección 2

Al llegar a un buen sitio para las truchas montamos las cañas y esperamos. Durante media hora no pasó nada. Se veían sólo los pájaros que volaban por encima de los árboles.

Sección 3

De repente mi hijo me despertó. Tiré de la caña y allí había un pez. Era una hermosa trucha grande. La metí en mi mochila. ¡Me gusta mucho el pescado!

Recording 17 (Transcript)

Sección 1

Los alumnos del Colegio Nacional Francisco Faton en el barrio de Vallecas, se declararon en huelga ayer para protestar por la ausencia de dos profesores.

Acompañados de sus padres, los alumnos se concentraron ante las puertas del colegio y explicaron su decisión de no volver a clase mientras los dos profesores no vuelvan a su trabajo.

Sección 2

Según el director del colegio, Julio García, una profesora había tenido que asistir a un curso en la capital y el profesor estaba enfermo y su médico le había dicho que tenía que guardar cama durante dos semanas por los menos.

Un portavoz de la Delegación Provincial del Ministerio de Educación declaró que la profesora volvería al día siguiente y que la ausencia del profesor había sido cubierta. Dijo también que aunque sentía mucho las ausencias, es esencial que los alumnos vuelvan inmediatamente a sus clases.

Recording 18 (Transcript)

M: Oye, Inma, ¿viste el nuevo culebrón ayer?

F1: Claro que no. No tengo tiempo para perder en cosas así. Tengo mucho que hacer para los exámenes. Si los apruebo podré estudiar medicina en la universidad.

M: Y tú, Carmen, ¿no eres tan trabajadora, no?

F2: Así es. Sí lo vi, pero me pareció ridículo. Me gustó más el documental más tarde en la segunda.

M: Ah, sí. ¿Por qué?

F2: Como ya sabes, me interesan los problemas del tercer mundo y este documental trataba de las dificultades de los indios del Brasil frente al progreso.

M: ¡Ay! ¡Sois tan serias! Tú, Inma, con los estudios y tú, Carmen, con tus preocupaciones por los desafortunados. La vida es para vivir. Lo que me gusta es pasarlo bien.

Recording 19 (Transcript)

F1: **Ejemplo.**
Habla la madre de José Luis.
[*Setting: meal time – chinking of cutlery, etc.*]

F2: Oye, si el amigo inglés de José Luis nos invita, ¿por qué no vamos a Inglaterra? Nunca he estado allí. Quiero saber todo lo que hay que saber sobre la cultura inglesa, quiero visitar todos los sitios de interés, quiero conocer a los ingleses. Sería un viaje inolvidable.

F1: Ahora escucha el ejercicio.

F1: Conversación 1. Habla la madre de José Luis.

F2: Pero ¿cómo sabías que me gustan tanto las joyas y sobre todo el oro? ¿De verdad es para mí? Fenomenal. Debe ser de parte de tus padres, ¿no? Voy a escribirles para decirles cuánto me ha encantado.

F1: Conversación 2. Habla José Luis.

M2: Mira Rafael. Si no le hablo, si no salgo con ella, sabes qué pasará, ¿no? Va a salir con otro. Y luego habré perdido la oportunidad. Lo que dices es la verdad. Mis padres van a enfadarse como tengo tantos deberes, pero tengo que hacer algo. Ahora no sé qué hacer.

F1: Conversación 3. Habla la madre de José Luis.

F2: José Luis, no puede ser. ¿No te acuerdas de lo que te ha dicho tu padre? Ya sabes que tienes que levantarte muy de mañana para ir al colegio. Y tienes tanto que hacer para tus exámenes. Aún eres muy joven para esto, José Luis. Tienes que estudiar, José Luis.

F1: Conversación 4. Habla Rafael.

M2: Bueno, me parece que tienes problemas, José Luis, pero quizás no son tan grandes. Escucha. Te voy a proponer una cosa. Si tus padres conocieran a esta chica, a lo mejor les encantaría. ¿Por qué no la invitas a tu casa? Puedes decir a tus padres que ella va a ayudarte con tu inglés. Así que puedes estar con ella y tus padres estarán contentos a la vez.

F1: Conversación 5. Habla la madre de José Luis.

F2: Oye, ¿sabes una cosa? En lo de anoche, la visita de aquella chica. Me siento tan orgullosa de tener un hijo como José Luis. Hicieron tanto trabajo anoche. Saben estudiar y divertirse a la vez. Y cuando José Luis hablaba tanto inglés, di gracias a Dios por tener un hijo así.

A STEP FURTHER

See if you can **identify any particular weaknesses** in your listening. Many people have difficulty with numbers, prices, times and days of the week. For others the key question words are a problem. Instructions can also cause trouble. Whatever you find is a weakness in your listening, you can **enlist the help of a friend** to say things to you in Spanish including those particular expressions. The more practice you can be given the sooner you will remedy the weakness. Why not get someone to record a series of your problem expressions for you on a cassette, so that you can practise listening to them on your own?

In order to deal effectively with Higher Tier questions about **attitudes and emotions**, it is a good idea to make a list of several different attitudes and emotions. Then note down next to each the Spanish word that describes it (e.g. *simpático, tranquilo, trabajador, contento, triste*). Next, you should think of the sort of sentences that might be used in Spanish by someone displaying each of those attitudes and emotions – but take care *not* to use the specific word you listed before. For example, you might write down 'worried' and then the Spanish word *preocupado*. You then need to write a sentence, or possibly two, such as *¡Ay! ¡Qué problema! Yo no sé lo que va a pasar.*

Chapter

5

Speaking

GETTING STARTED

Everybody has to take a **Speaking** test. This is hardly surprising since one of the primary aims of learning a language is to be able to speak to people. The Speaking test carries the same weight as other papers. So it is worth doing it well.

Candidates who gain good marks in Foundation Speaking will be able to cope with straightforward situations likely to be met by a visitor to a Spanish-speaking country. They will also be able to answer simple questions about themselves and their lives and interests. They will pronounce Spanish words well enough to be understood by a 'sympathetic' Spanish speaker – one who is prepared to make some effort, where necessary, to understand.

The examining boards, although there are minor differences, have very similar Speaking tests.

- The test will be done between March and June at a time to be decided by your school or college.
- It will be conducted by your own teacher.
- It will be recorded on cassette so that the examining board can check the way it was conducted and whether it was marked to the correct standard.
- Your teacher may mark the examination, or the recording may be sent away for someone else to mark.
- It will last between eight and fifteen minutes.
- It will consist of role-plays and conversation.
- You will have between eight and fifteen minutes to prepare the role-play tasks, usually while the previous candidate is being tested.

TOPIC	STUDY	REVISION 1	REVISION 2
Role-plays			
Topics and settings			
Coping with problems			
Approaching the role-plays			
G, F, E tasks			
D, C tasks			
B, A, A* tasks			
Practice role-plays			
Possible answers to practice role-plays			
Conversation			
Topics covered			
Preparing for the test			
Grades G, F, E			
Grades D–A*			
Practice questions			
Sample answers			
Presentations			

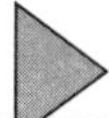

ROLE-PLAYS – WHAT YOU NEED TO KNOW

The role-plays will require you to take the initiative, so be prepared to talk! You will need to be able to do things such as the following:

- **Buy items**, e.g. in a shop, café or restaurant.
- **Ask for information**, e.g. in a tourist office.
- **Give information**, e.g. reporting lost property.
- **Make bookings**, e.g. for journeys or accommodation.
- **Make arrangements**, e.g. over the telephone.

You will perform the role-plays with your teacher, who will be asked to take the part of a helpful native-speaker of Spanish. This means that **if what you say is not clear, your teacher can give you another opportunity**, just as a Spanish-speaker would, by saying something like *¿Cómo?* or *No entiendo*. It can also mean that if you accidentally convey the wrong meaning, your teacher can express surprise, which may give you **the chance to correct yourself**. For example, if you ask in the restaurant for *una mesa para doce* when you were supposed to ask for a table for two, your teacher could exclaim *¡Para doce!* and, with any luck, you will realize your mistake and correct it. Such a correction is acceptable, since it is what would happen in real life. Of course, this does mean that **you have to listen** to what your teacher says and not simply move on to the next task on the card! Remember also that your teacher is playing the role of someone who does not understand English, so you cannot ask for the Spanish for certain English words!

You will have to do **two role-plays** (except for SEG, when you will have only one, having already done two elements of spoken coursework). At least one of the role-plays (and almost certainly both at Higher Tier) will have some **element of unpredictability**, usually requiring you to respond to one or more questions that are not marked on the role-play card. This means that you have to try to anticipate what the problems may be. You must be prepared to listen carefully to what the examiner says and then to think and react as quickly as you can.

You will be required to arrive at the room for the examination ten to fifteen minutes before your test actually begins, to allow for your preparation time. **Make sure you do not have to rush** at the last minute; it is important to be as calm as you can be in the circumstances. You will be given the role-play cards on which you will be tested.

- **Preparation time**: you have some eight to fifteen minutes to prepare yourself to carry out the instructions on the cards.
- **Situation and general instructions**: the setting of the scene and any general instructions will be given on the card in English (except for NICCEA, which sets the scene briefly in Spanish).
- **Details of the tasks**: details of what you have to do are given by means of **pictures** or by **instructions or questions in Spanish** or by a mixture of the two. (NICCEA gives any instructions at this point in English.)
- **Dictionary**: you will have a dictionary available to help with your preparation.
- **No written notes**: you will not be allowed to make notes while you are preparing but you will still have the cards with you during the examination and can refer to them whenever you like.

You are not required to use perfect Spanish. **The main point is to make yourself understood** (though there are some marks for quality of language on role-plays set to test performance for higher grades). That means you need to speak as clearly as you can, to pronounce the words as well as you can, so that the other person can understand. At all stages your teacher will attempt to be as helpful as possible, to allow you to show exactly what you can do. If there are things on the cards that you find difficult, try to work out some way of dealing with them. Above all, do not sit in silence when you come to them in the actual test, leaving your teacher to wonder if you are about to speak. **Keep the conversation going,** even if the best you can do is to say something you know is wrong, such as asking for wine because you have forgotten the Spanish for beer. At least you will avoid an embarrassing silence, which would only make you feel more uncomfortable and undermine your confidence.

Be positive from the start.

Topics and settings

Some topics and settings lend themselves more readily to role-plays than others, so the most common situations you are likely to meet in this section of the examination are listed below.

- School.
- Visiting a Spanish-speaking family.
- Dealing with illnesses, injuries and dental problems.
- Accidents and emergencies.
- Cafés and restaurants.
- Places of entertainment.
- Meeting new people.
- Making arrangements to meet.
- Asking the way.
- Shopping.
- Banks, post offices, customs and tourist offices.
- Repairs and complaints.
- Trains, buses, taxis and airports.
- Garages and petrol stations.
- Reporting lost property.
- Using the telephone.
- Hotels, youth hostels and campsites.

Please remember that this list only represents the most likely situations to be covered. It is not an exhaustive list and you should be prepared to deal with other possibilities.

Coping with problems

The fact that you have a dictionary to help with your preparation of the role-plays means that, in theory at least, individual words should not be a problem. But do be careful how you use the dictionary! Remember the advice given in Chapter 3 and make sure you know whether the word you are choosing is a noun, verb or adjective, etc.

In the examination you may find you have forgotten one of the words you looked up, or you may well find that one of the questions you are asked (the 'unpredictable' element we mentioned earlier) is one you have not anticipated and prepared the vocabulary for. In this case, think how you can get round it. One of the following strategies may be useful.

- **Do you know the opposite expression?** If you have to ask if a place is far and you cannot remember *lejos*, why not ask *¿Está cerca?* You would certainly get the information you needed, so you should get your mark. If you cannot remember the Spanish for 'to change trains', ask if the train is direct.
- **Can you explain what you mean without the key word?** This involves a definition or description. If you cannot remember the word *hombro* and have to explain to the doctor or chemist that you have a pain in your shoulder, you could try saying *Me duele donde el brazo se une al cuerpo* or . . . *entre el brazo y el cuerpo*. (In real life, of course, you would point to your shoulder and say *Me duele aquí* but at GCSE you have to show you can communicate with words, not by pointing.)

  If you have to buy carrots and cannot remember *zanahoria*, you could ask for *la legumbre larga y delgada que es color naranja*.
- **Can you explain the function of the item?** If you have to ask for a knife and cannot remember *cuchillo*, you could ask for *algo para cortar el pan* (or *algo para cortar la carne*).

It is a good idea to practise these techniques. You can do this on your own but it can work even better with a friend. If your friend can understand what you mean, there is every chance a Spanish person (or your teacher) would!

Approaching the role-plays

So how should you go about preparing for and tackling the role-plays?

As always, a methodical approach will pay dividends. A thorough preparation of the material likely to be covered in the role-plays is essential.

1. Make sure you know just what topics are on the syllabus.
2. Check the likely settings and the language tasks and make sure you can cope with the Spanish you will need to use and understand. Cross-check with Chapter 3 and any details provided by your teacher and your examining board.
3. Study as many role-play situations as you can. You can practise with a friend and you can test yourself. Use your checklists.
4. Try making up your own role-play situations and then try them out with a friend. This can be fun as well as being useful practice. You could try being a 'difficult' shop assistant, hotel receptionist, etc.

When studying the role-play card, the following points should be helpful:

- Check what the crucial elements in each task are and work out what you are going to say. Remember that there are usually many different ways of saying the same thing.
- Try and work out what the examiner might say, and the possible 'twists' in the dialogue. In most cases these will, in fact, be reasonably predictable. (How many different questions is a hotel receptionist really likely to ask when you are booking a room? You can work out almost all of them in advance.) Again the more practice you get, the more predictable they will become.
- Don't panic! There may well be something that at first you don't understand but which, when you look at it more carefully, is not really important. Equip yourself with a series of useful phrases to ask the examiner to repeat something, to ask him or her to say something more slowly, to explain that you didn't quite catch what s/he said. As long as you can do this in Spanish, you will not lose marks. But remember, the examiner is playing the part of a Spanish-speaker with no knowledge of English.
- If you have any doubts whether the plan you are adopting in order to carry out one of the tasks will actually work, have a 'fall-back' plan to use if the examiner says something like *¿Cómo? No entiendo.*

G, F, E tasks

Now that you are more confident about what to expect, it is time to look at the role-plays in detail, and how best to prepare for them.

The first thing you need to do is to **study the card carefully** and to work out exactly what the tasks are and what you have to say. Let's look at an example.

En el restaurante

You are in a restaurant in Spain. Your teacher will play the part of the waiter/waitress and will start the conversation.

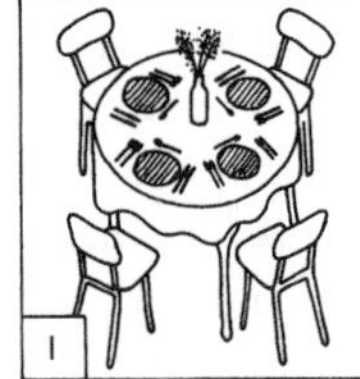

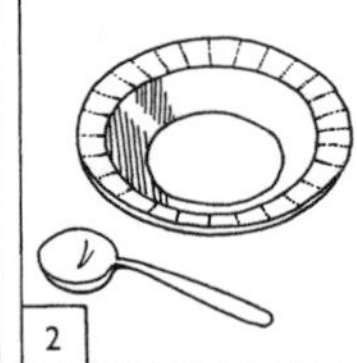

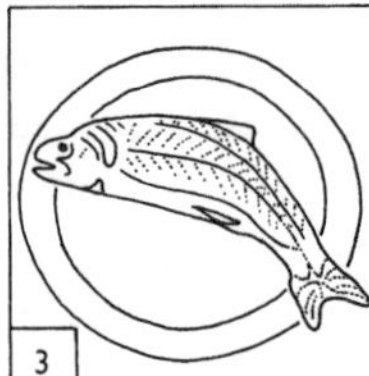

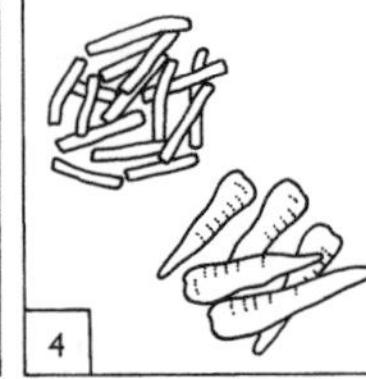

(MEG)

The first thing, then, is to work out exactly what you have to say. You do **not** have to describe the pictures on the card. Although you will be speaking to the waiter/waitress and will be asking for and ordering things, you will almost certainly not use the words for 'ask', 'order', 'say', 'tell', 'waiter' or 'waitress'. You do not need to use long-winded British expressions of courtesy, such as 'I should be grateful if you would bring me . . .' Spanish courtesies are much more brief and concise than that. You need to identify the key words you will use in communicating each request. If you were performing the role-play in English you would say something like:

1. A table for four, please.
2. Soup, please.
3. Fish, please.
4. With chips and carrots, please.
5. A bottle of wine, please.

So what you will say in Spanish will be something like this:

1. Por favor una mesa para cuatro.
2. Sopa, por favor.
3. Pescado, por favor.
4. Con patatas fritas y zanahorias.
5. Una botella de vino.

Remember that there are many different ways of saying the same thing and it does not matter which you use as long as you get your message across.

Now you try the following situation for yourself.

En el hotel

You are in a hotel and wish to book a room. The examiner will play the part of the receptionist. You speak first.

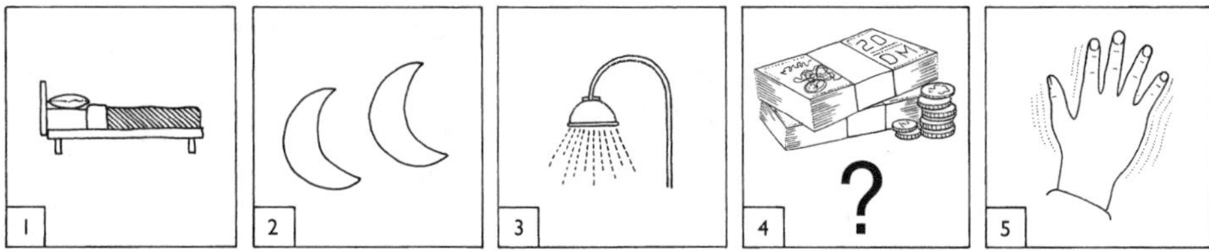

You will soon get used to the symbols used. Remember that a question mark means you have to ask a question.

If you were performing this role-play in English, you would say something like:

1. Good evening. Could I have a (bed) room, please.
2. For two nights.
3. With a shower.
4. How much is it?
5. Thank you. Good-bye.

Here is an example of how it could be done in Spanish:

1. Buenas tardes. Una habitación, por favor.
2. Para dos noches.
3. Con ducha.
4. ¿Cuánto es?
5. Gracias. Adiós.

If you used the word *cama*, instead of *habitación*, your intention would be clear and you would get the room (or the mark, in the case of the examination). You could use the word *Quiero*, but it is not essential. In some situations what your teacher says may give you the clue to what you have to say next. It may contain a key word you were unsure about. For example, if you were to forget the word *noches* and asked simply for *una habitación*, the logical thing would be for the receptionist to ask you *¿Para cuántas noches?* So it will pay to listen carefully to what your teacher says. Again, don't panic if there is something you do not understand or hear clearly. Ask for it to be said again, e.g. *¿Cómo?*

The next section will provide a number of different role-plays for you to work through. Get as much practice as you can. Perhaps you can work with a friend or someone at home. Make up your own role-plays and test each other. Whatever interesting ideas you come up with, the easier you will find it to make progress.

D, C tasks

At this level most of the boards use more words and fewer pictures on their cards. There will also almost certainly be one 'unpredictable' task, shown on the card with the words *Contesta a la pregunta* (for NICCEA *Answer the question*) or, for Edexcel, with an exclamation mark (!). The task is 'unpredictable' only in the sense that you are not told on the card exactly what you will have to answer, so you will have to listen carefully to what your teacher asks. But in fact you can usually work out two or three likely questions that you could be asked in the situation. So prepare for those – you will probably be right!

Hablando con el médico/la médica

Your English friend who speaks only English falls ill while you are in Spain. Your teacher will play the part of the doctor.

1. Explica por qué habéis venido a la consulta y por qué tu amigo/a no le habla.
2. Dile dos síntomas que tiene tu amigo/a.
3. Contesta a la pregunta.
4. Di en qué hotel estáis y dónde está.
5. Cuando receta unas pastillas, haz una pregunta sobre el tratamiento.

(MEG)

It is worth considering first of all what the *pregunta* might be. Logic suggests that it will not be about another symptom, since you have already mentioned two which your teacher could not predict. The most likely question is how long your friend has been ill or what (s)he has eaten. In fact it is *Y ¿cuándo empezó esto?* Further consideration of the role-play shows that you have a considerable degree of choice in deciding what to say. You decide what the symptoms are, what hotel you are in, where it is and what question to ask about the treatment. Make sure you choose things you can say! You could say something like:

1. Mi amiga está enferma y no habla español.
2. Tiene fiebre y dolor de cabeza.
3. Empezó ayer.
4. Estamos en el Hotel Colón, que está en la calle de San Francisco.
5. ¿Cuántas tiene que tomar cada día?

B, A, A* tasks

The final role-play of the Higher Tier is likely to require you to say rather more, though the amount will depend to some extent on the style of role-play set by your examining board. Again, the questions you are likely to be asked will be very largely predictable from the information given on the card.

Tus vacaciones en España

The notes and pictures below give an outline of your holidays in Spain last year. Tell the examiner what happened. You need not mention every detail but cover all the main events. Be prepared to respond to questions or comments from the Examiner.

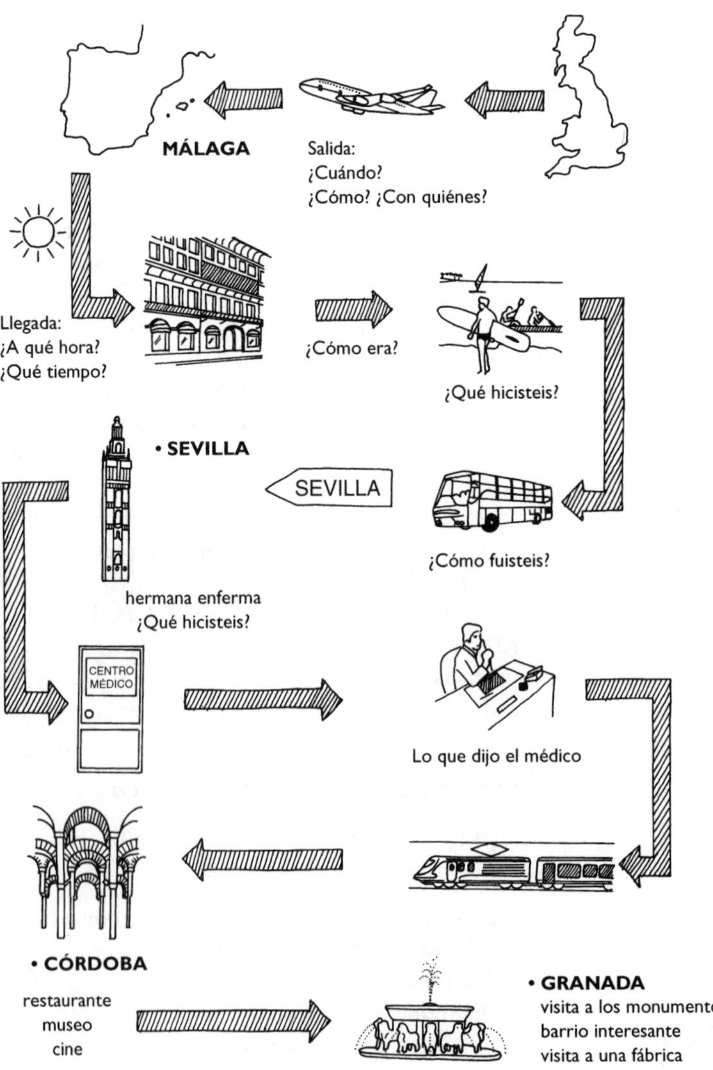

(MEG)

A conversation on this task might begin something like this:

Examiner: De modo que fuiste a España de vacaciones, ¿no?

Candidate: Sí, fui a España con mi familia. Salimos un miércoles por la mañana y viajamos en avión, directamente a Málaga.

Examiner: ¿Sí? Y ¿a qué hora llegasteis?

Candidate: Llegamos a las dos de la tarde y fuimos directamente al hotel. Era muy grande y moderno. Me gustó mucho, porque estaba al lado del mar y tenía una playa reservada a sus clientes. Cuando llegamos, hacía mucho calor y salimos a la playa. Nos bañamos y tomamos el sol.

Examiner: ¿Os quedasteis en Málaga todo el tiempo?

Candidate: No. Dos días después fuimos a Sevilla en autocar.

Examiner: Y ¿tuvisteis algún problema?

Candidate: Sí. En Sevilla mi hermana se puso enferma y tuvimos que llevarla al centro médico . . .

PRACTICE ROLE-PLAYS

G, F, E tasks

The following role-play exercises give you an idea of the sort of tasks that could be set at this level for different situations. After the role-plays there are suggested ways of dealing with them. There are also comments intended to help you to tackle other similar ones with confidence. Of course, in between each of your tasks your teacher will have to say something, but you will not know what that is until you hear it, so it cannot affect your preparation. Your teacher will also introduce the situation in Spanish, briefly summarizing what you have already found out from the printed English introduction on the card.

Role-play 1 *En la oficina de turismo*

You are in a tourist office in Spain. Your teacher will play the part of the tourist office employee and will start the conversation.

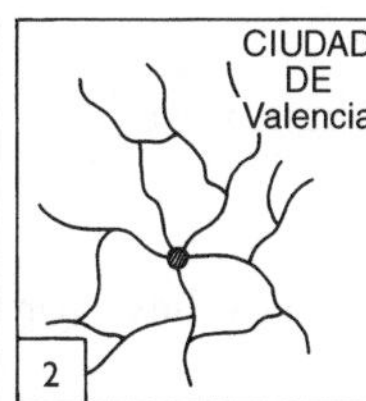

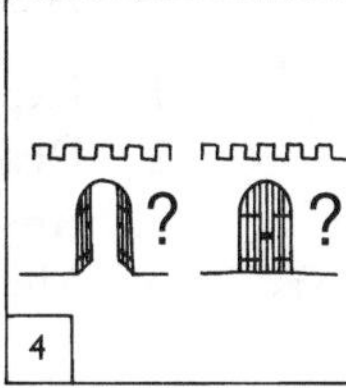

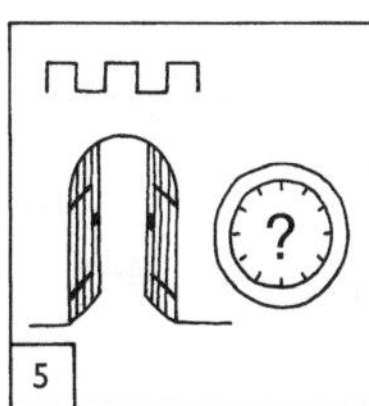

(MEG)

Role-play 2 *Comprando regalos*

You are buying presents and need to buy two items. Remember to greet the shopkeeper and end the conversation politely.

(Edexcel)

Role-play 3 *En la estación*

You are in Málaga railway station. You want a second class return ticket to Sevilla. You need to find out how much the ticket costs and when the train leaves.

Your teacher will play the part of the ticket clerk and will speak first.

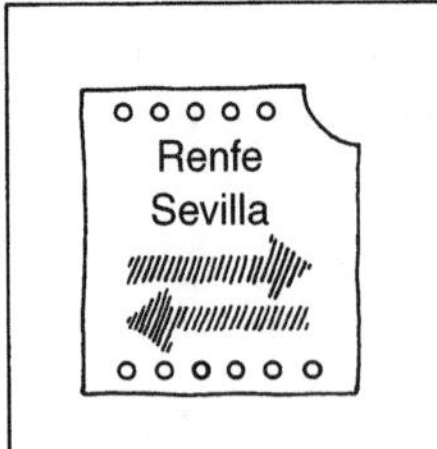

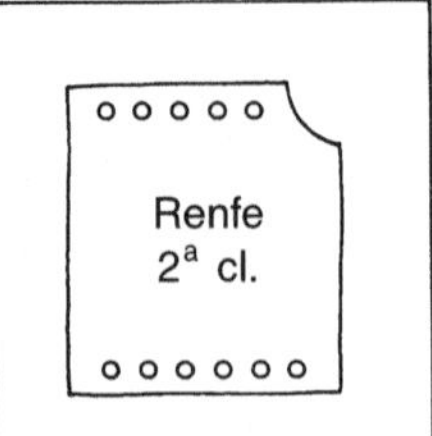

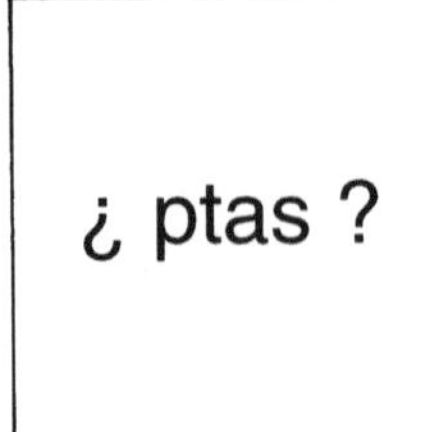

(NEAB)

Role-play 4 *En la estación de servicio*

You are in a service-station in Spain. Your teacher will play the part of the attendant and will start the conversation.

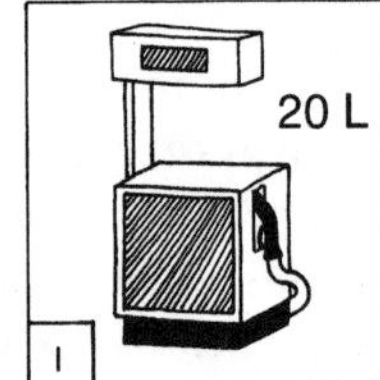

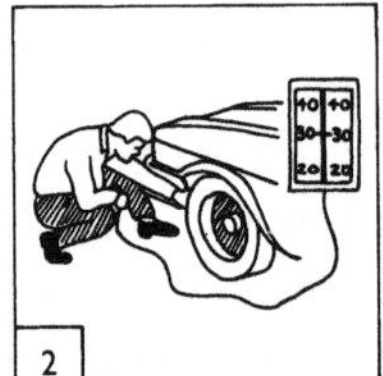

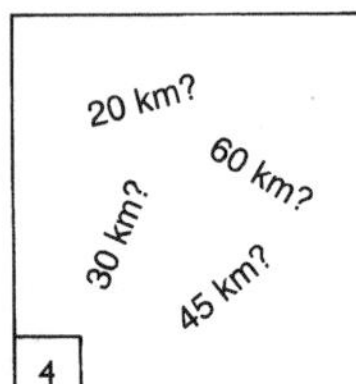

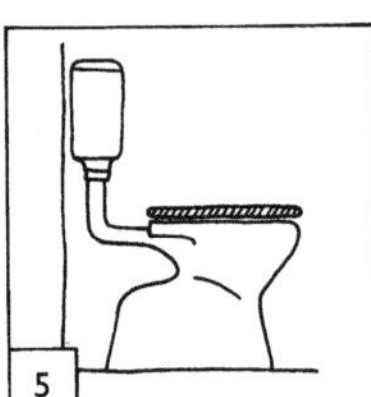

(MEG)

D, C tasks

Role-play 5 *En casa de un(a) amigo/a español(a)*

Candidate

1. Explain that you have a light meal.
2. Describe what you have.
3. Answer the question.
4. Mention a couple of items you have for tea.

Teacher Input
Hablas con un(a) amigo(a) español(a) sobre las comidas en Irlanda del Norte.

Yo soy el(la) amigo(a). Yo empiezo.

1. ¿Qué tomas a mediodía en Irlanda del Norte?
2. ¿Por ejemplo?
3. ¿Y para beber?
4. ¿Qué tomas para la cena?
5. Muy bien.

(NICCEA)

Role-play 6 *¿Adónde vamos?*

You are staying with your Spanish penfriend, discussing where you want to go today and what time you will go out. Remember to reply to your penfriend's questions. The examiner will begin the conversation.

(Edexcel)

Role-play 7 *En casa de tu amigo/a*

It is your first night staying with your penfriend. Before going to bed, you want to find out about breakfast time and to have a shower or bath. Remember to reply to your penfriend's questions. The examiner will begin the conversation.

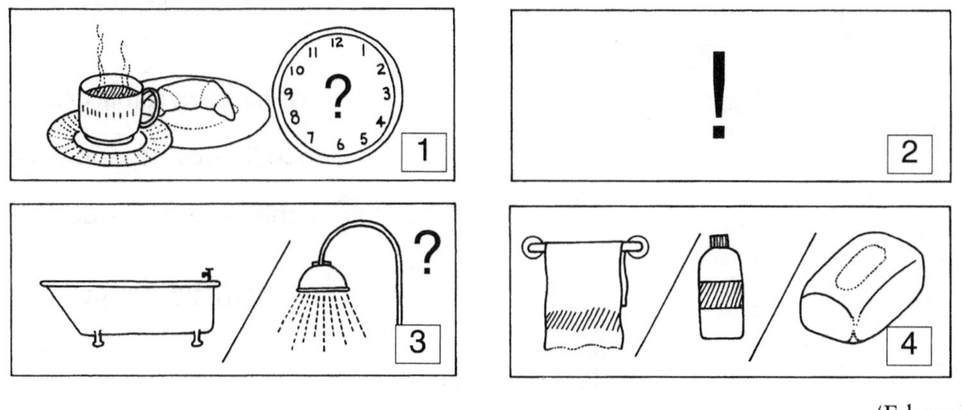

(Edexcel)

Role-play 8 *En la comisaría*

You are in a Spanish city and your suitcase is stolen. You go to the police station. Your teacher will play the part of the policeman/woman.

1. Explica que te han robado la maleta y cuándo ocurrió.
2. Dile dónde estabas y qué hacías cuando ocurrió el robo.
3. Haz una descripción del ladrón.
4. Contesta a la pregunta del/de la policía.
5. Explica dónde estás alojado/a y hasta cuándo.

(MEG)

B, A, A* tasks

Role-play 9 *En un restaurante español*

Candidate
Your are in a Spanish reataurant with a friend. You order the first course of a meal. Then you ask the waiter/waitress what they would recommend for the main course. You decide to take what is suggested. Finally you must order suitable drinks.

Teacher Input
Estás en un restaurante español con un(a) amigo(a).
Yo soy el (la) camarero(a). Yo empiezo.
¿Qué quieren, señores?
Muy bien.
Pues, una paella es algo típico de esta región.
Vale. ¿Qué quieren beber?
Muy bien.

(NICCEA)

Role-play 10 *Buscando trabajo*

You see this advert for summer jobs at the Camping Vistamar and decide to ring up to give details about yourself and to find out more information. The examiner will begin the conversation.

CAMPING VISTAMAR

Temporada de verano de 1998

Necesitamos

camareros/camareras

dependientes/dependientas

chicos/chicas para guardería niños

Tfo. 72 33 44

- ¿Razón de la llamada?
- Detalles personales
- Horas de trabajo

Suggested teacher/examiner prompts and responses

(The following utterances are examples of how the role-play may be sustained. All prompts and responses given by the teacher/examiner will depend on what the candidate says. Teacher/examiner should try to ensure that the conversation which takes place is as natural as possible.)

¿Puede darme algunos detalles personales?
¿Su nombre, edad, lenguas habladas?
Vale. ¿Quiere mandarnos su currículum?

You must ask the following during the conversation.

¿Qué experiencia tiene de este tipo de trabajo?
¿Cuándo puede comenzar?

(Edexcel)

Role-play 11 *Una fiesta en casa*

The notes and pictures below give an outline of preparations for a party. Tell the examiner what happened. You need not mention every detail but cover all the main events. Be prepared to respond to questions or comments from the examiner.

SUPERMERCADO

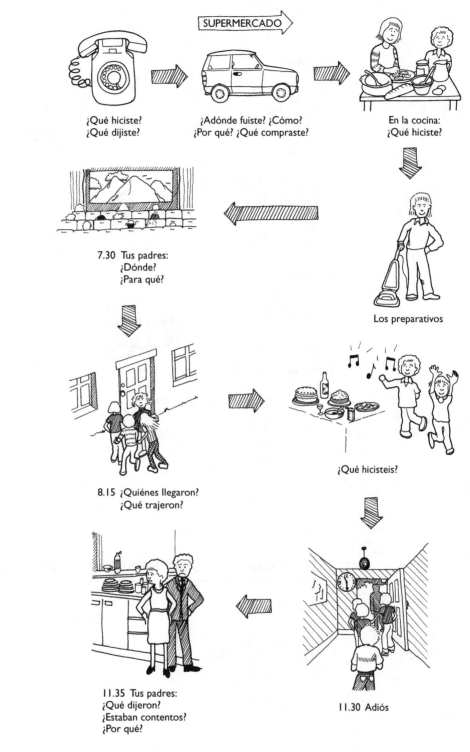

¿Qué hiciste?
¿Qué dijiste?

¿Adónde fuiste? ¿Cómo?
¿Por qué? ¿Qué compraste?

En la cocina:
¿Qué hiciste?

7.30 Tus padres:
¿Dónde?
¿Para qué?

Los preparativos

8.15 ¿Quiénes llegaron?
¿Qué trajeron?

¿Qué hicisteis?

11.35 Tus padres:
¿Qué dijeron?
¿Estaban contentos?
¿Por qué?

11.30 Adiós

(MEG)

Role-play 12 You are in Spain and have applied for a job in a shop for the summer. You are now being interviewed by the manager.

Tienes que dar la información siguiente:

¿Dónde?

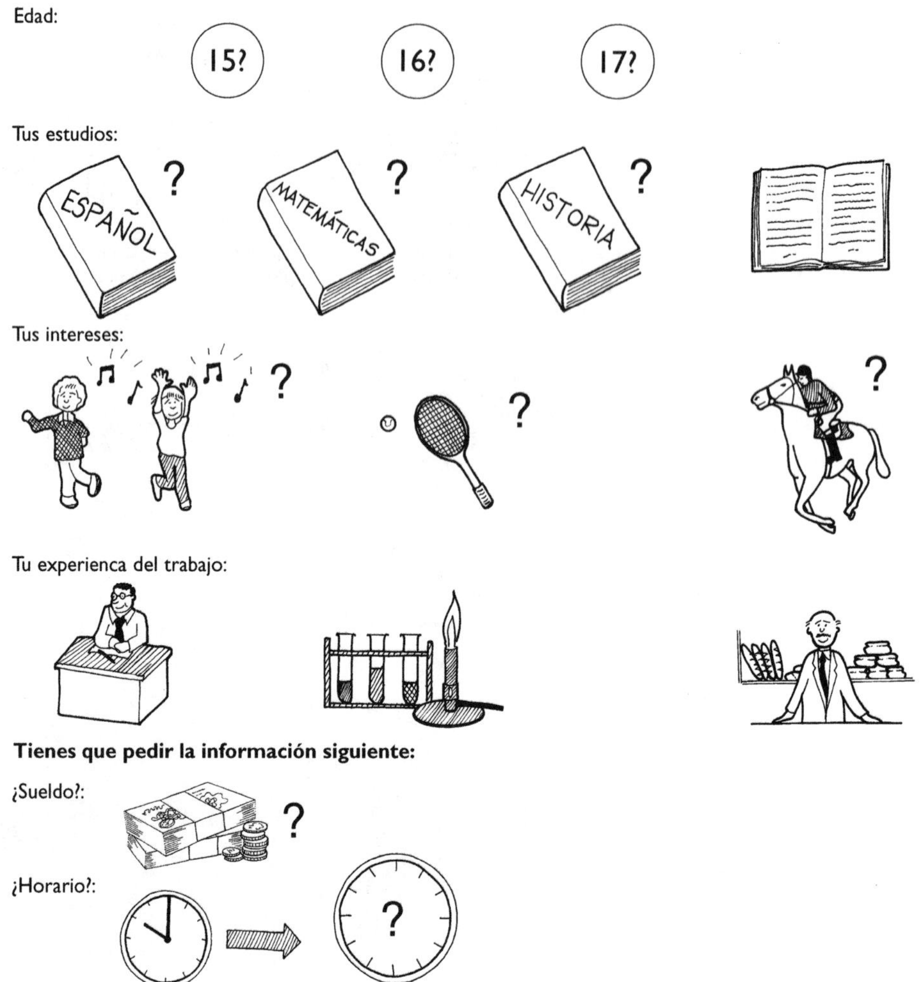

(SEG)

POSSIBLE ANSWERS TO PRACTICE ROLE-PLAYS

G, F, E tasks

Role-play 1 (Answer)

1. Una lista de hoteles, por favor.
2. Y un plano de la ciudad.
3. ¿Dónde está el castillo, por favor?
4. ¿El castillo está abierto?
5. ¿A qué hora se abre?

Notes:

1. *'Por favor'* is one of the most important expressions for you to know and use. It will work for any request.
2. If you asked for *'un mapa'*, you would be all right, though the correct word for a map of a town is *'plano'*.
3. Another frequently needed question: *'¿Dónde está . . . ?'*.
4. If you cannot remember *'abierto'*, you could use the opposite, *'cerrado'*, or ask *'¿Se puede entrar en el castillo ahora?'*.
5. *'¿A qué hora . . . ?'* is another key question. You could ask *'¿A qué hora se puede entrar?'*.

Role-play 2 (Answer)

1. Buenos días.
2. ¿Tienen plumas y camisetas?

3. ¿Cuánto valen?
4. Está bien. Me las quedo.
5. Adiós.

Notes:
1. *'Buenas tardes'* and *'Hola'* are other possibilities.
2. You must ask about any two of the pictured items. That should not be too much of a problem, since you have a dictionary available during the preparation period.
3. *'¿Cuánto cuestan?'* and *'¿Cuánto son?'* are alternatives and even here, for two items, *'¿Cuánto es?'* (asking how much you have to pay in total) would be valid.
4. Any answer that makes clear you will buy the items is valid.
5. There should not be any problem about this!

Role-play 3 (Answer)

1. Por favor, un billete de ida y vuelta para Sevilla.
2. De segunda clase.
3. ¿Cuánto es?
4. ¿A qué hora sale (el tren)?

Notes:
1. If you only ask for *'un billete'*, your teacher will no doubt ask *'¿Billete sencillo?' so* that you have the chance to clarify the point and score the full mark.
3. Another question you will regularly need in role-plays.
4. *'¿A qué hora es el tren?'* would also work.

Role-play 4 (Answer)

1. Por favor, veinte litros de gasolina.
2. ¿Quiere comprobar los neumáticos, por favor?
3. ¿Por dónde se va a Valencia?
4. ¿Está lejos?
5. ¿Hay servicios aquí?

Notes:
2. It is not clear whether you are to ask the attendant to check the tyres or say you want to do so. In such a situation, either interpretation of the picture will be accepted.
4. You could ask *'¿A qué distancia está Valencia?'* or *'¿Cuántos kilómetros hay de aquí a Valencia?'*.

D, C tasks

Role-play 5 (Answer)

1. Tomo una comida ligera.
2. Un sandwich de queso y tomate.
3. Bebo zumo de naranja.
4. Generalmente tomo una hamburguesa con patatas fritas.

Notes:
The 'unpredictable' question was fairly easy to anticipate. It was likely to be about what you drank, where you ate or at what time, so you could prepare for all of those.

Role-play 6 (Answer)

1. Me gustaría ir a la piscina.
2. No quiero ir a ver monumentos históricos.
3. *You could prepare answers to the following: what you would like to do afterwards; where you would like to eat. The first was, in fact, the question so you could answer:* Me gustaría ir a la cafetería.
4. A las diez y media.

Role-play 7 (Answer)

1. ¿A qué hora es el desayuno?
2. *This will almost certainly be about what you want to have for breakfast. Did you prepare for that?* Quiero tomar tostadas y café con leche.

3. ¿Puedo bañarme o ducharme?
4. Tengo una toalla, champú y jabón.

Role-play 8 (Answer)

1. Me han robado la maleta hace media hora.
2. Estaba en la plaza, tomando una Coca-cola.
3. El ladrón es alto y delgado y tiene el pelo rubio.
4. *This will probably be about the contents of the case or where the thief went. Did you prepare for those?* Contiene ropa y una máquina fotográfica. *Or* Salió de la plaza hacia la Catedral.

CONVERSATION – WHAT YOU NEED TO KNOW

For all the examining boards the format of this test is the same for both tiers. It involves conversation on **at least two topic areas.** For Edexcel, MEG and NEAB, candidates choose one topic and make a short presentation of it before moving on to discuss it with the examiner. This is followed by discussion of a further one or more topics from the syllabus. Some advice on preparation of topics for presentation follows later, but, in general, the conversation should be very similar on topics chosen by the candidate and those that arise on the day of the examination.

The marks awarded will again depend on your ability to **make yourself understood**, to communicate some meaning. Your teacher will be trying to help you by taking the role of a sympathetic native-speaker, and, if there is something he or she does not understand, then he or she will react just as if it were a real-life situation. For instance, in real life, if you met a Spanish teenager at a party and asked how old he or she was and you got the reply 'Sixty', you wouldn't just leave it there and go on to another question. You would probably express surprise (!) and say something like 'Sixty? I don't think that is what you mean!' The Spanish teenager would then have a chance to correct the previous answer, 'No, I mean sixteen'. As this is what happens in normal conversation, your teacher is allowed to help you in the same way.

The conversation is not a cross-examination! The idea is not to probe into your secrets, but simply to assess your ability to speak Spanish. The conversation will be **based on the material you have covered throughout your course.** The questions and topic areas covered will sample what you have been doing all along in your oral work in class and at home. Your teacher will not be trying to 'trick' you or catch you out and you are most unlikely to be asked a question that has not been asked on a number of occasions during the course. Given that you now know that every effort is made to help you, make sure you help yourself by being prepared to say something!

Try to **avoid one-word answers** such as *Sí* or *No* or just the name of your home town or village. You really cannot expect to score many marks for showing you can manage that! Always **look for the chance to give at least a whole sentence** as the answer. Ideally, the questions will not lend themselves to 'Yes ' or 'No' answers but often you have to be asked, for example, if you have any brothers or sisters before any further questions can be asked about them. If you are asked, *¿Tienes hermanos?*, rather than simply saying *Sí*, you should anticipate the next possible question by giving more information, saying something like *Sí, tengo un hermano y una hermana* or *Sí, tengo una hermana que se llama Tracy.* Even if you have no brothers or sisters, there are still ways of saying more than *No.* You could, for example, say *No, pero tengo un perro* or *No, pero tengo tres primos.*

It is also important to remember that **you are not on oath in the witness box!** Your teacher is out to assess how well you can speak Spanish – not how truthful you are! He or she will not come round to your house in the evening after the examination to check whether you really do have a dog like the one you have described. He or she is not going to rush off to check the school records to see if they confirm what you have said about any member of your family, so you are free to change the facts, if you need to, to match what you can say in Spanish.

Remember also that the aim is to **show how much you can say** in Spanish, **not** to avoid making actual mistakes by saying as little as possible. Don't see each question as something to be 'blocked' with great caution, but as an opportunity to show off what you can say. If you are going to change the facts about your family, it will always make far more sense to invent a brother or sister you don't actually have, so that you can say something about them in Spanish, rather than to deny the existence of a brother who does exist, which will only force your teacher to ask you something else, which could well prove a little more difficult.

Topics covered

The topic areas and vocabulary covered will be those listed in the syllabus and set out in Chapter 3 of this book. Again, just check the exact requirements for your examining board. In practice, though, some topics lend themselves more to conversation than others. You can talk quite a lot about holidays but it is quite difficult to have a realistic conversation about lost property (unless it has arisen naturally out of something you have said about your holidays).

The topics you are likely to be asked about will include:

- Your school or college.
- Your home life.
- Your daily routines.
- Food and drink.
- Yourself and your family.
- Your friends.
- Your free time, interests and hobbies.
- Your holidays.
- Your home town, village or area.
- Shopping.
- Travel and transport.
- Your future plans.
- The world of work.
- Life in other countries.

The conversation will cover two or more of these topics and will usually follow a fairly logical sequence. You are likely to be asked a number of questions on one topic area before going on to a different one.

Preparing for the test

Students quite often claim that it is not possible to revise or prepare for an oral examination, but that simply is not true.

Once you have checked the topic areas, you can **work out small groups of questions for each topic area** and make sure that you can answer them. The vocabulary and language tasks in Chapter 3 will help you to do so. Use the sample questions given later in this chapter.

If your teacher gives you a list of possible questions, use it. You cannot be told in advance which of the questions you will be asked, but at least you will have plenty of opportunity to prepare for a range of questions, some of which you will be asked.

Pick out areas of special interest to you. After all, if you are interested in something, you are likely to have something to say! You should then prepare these topics thoroughly. The conversation will not be very long, but string together a series of sentences so that you can talk confidently on each individual topic for more than a minute. In the examination you will not be allowed to give a pre-learnt talk but, certainly for the higher grades, you will be expected to volunteer ideas and information.

Next you should concentrate on the other possible themes that are perhaps of less interest to you. Remember, though, that you should **aim to be interesting in the examination**, so pretend, think of ways of conveying enthusiasm, e.g. by using particular items of vocabulary and idioms.

You are allowed to ask questions also, if you wish. For example, when talking about your holiday in Málaga, you could ask the examiner, *¿Conoce usted Málaga?* But do be careful. One, or at most two, questions will be enough. You don't want to spend your examination time listening to your teacher reminiscing happily about his or her holiday, only to find there is insufficient time for you to show what you can say!

When you are in the examination, if you are asked a question you do not understand, don't panic. **You can ask the teacher to repeat the question** – *¿Cómo?* – or re-phrase it – *No entiendo*. Make sure you have a few phrases 'up your sleeve' to help you out of such difficulties. Above all, **do not sit in silence** – it will only make you feel more embarrassed and uncomfortable. If all else fails, if you still do not understand after a question is repeated, think what it might mean and give an answer to that – you might actually be right!

Grades G, F, E

G, F, E candidates will find that their conversation usually consists of a series of questions which can be answered fairly briefly, but the fuller your answers, the more impressed the examiner will be and the fewer different questions you will have to answer in the time available.

Here are some examples of the kind of questions you can expect. A possible answer is given after some questions (with italics to show things you will need to adapt to suit your own life). In other cases the beginning of an answer is given, to set you off on a correctly constructed answer, with dots (. . . .) where you have to supply the rest of the answer.

Remember, though, that you are strongly advised to give longer answers, so really you should also look at the next section as well.

Your school or college

¿Cómo vienes al colegio por la mañana?	Vengo *a pie.*
¿A qué hora llegas?	Llego a las . . . .
¿A qué hora empiezan las clases?	Empiezan a las . . . .
¿Cuántas clases tienes por la mañana?	Hay *cuatro.*
¿Cuánto tiempo dura cada clase?	Dura *treinta y cinco* minutos.
¿Cuánto tiempo dura el recreo?	Dura *un cuarto de hora.*
¿Cuál es tu asignatura preferida?	Es *el español.*
¿Qué asignatura te gusta menos?	Me gusta menos . . . .
Para ti ¿cuál es la asignatura más difícil?	Es . . . .
¿Cuántos alumnos hay en el colegio?	Hay *unos mil* alumnos.
¿Cuántos profesores hay en el colegio?	Hay . . . .
¿Qué haces durante el recreo?	*Hablo con mis amigos.*
¿Qué haces a la hora de comer?	*Como y hablo con mis amigos.*
¿Qué deportes practicas en el colegio?	*Juego al . . . .*

Your home life

¿Dónde vives?	Vivo en . . . .
¿Cómo es tu casa?	Es *grande y moderna.*
¿Está cerca del centro de la ciudad?	Está a *tres* kilometros del centro.
¿Cuántas habitaciones hay en tu casa?	Hay . . . .
¿Qué hay en tu dormitorio?	Hay una cama, *una mesa, una silla y un armario.*
¿Dónde haces los deberes?	Los hago en *mi dormitorio.*
¿Qué hacéis en el salón?	Hablamos y *vemos la televisión.*
¿Tenéis un jardín?	*Sí. Es bastante grande. Hay flores y dos árboles.*
¿Qué se cultiva en el jardín?	Se cultivan *flores y árboles.*
¿Tienes animales en casa?	*Sí. Tenemos dos gatos y un pez rojo.*

Your daily routines

¿A qué hora te levantas normalmente?	Me levanto a las . . . .
¿Qué haces luego?	*Me lavo y me visto.*
¿Dónde desayunas?	*Desayuno en la cocina.* OR: *No desayuno.*
¿Con quién desayunas?	Desayuno con *mi hermana.*
¿Qué desayunas?	Desayuno *tostadas y té.*
¿A qué hora cenas?	Ceno a las . . . .
¿A qué hora te acuestas?	Me acuesto a las . . . .
¿A qué hora llegas al colegio?	Llego a las *nueve menos cuarto.*
¿Cuántas clases tienes cada día?	Tengo *ocho* clases.
¿Dónde haces tus deberes?	Los hago en *mi dormitorio.*

Food and drink

¿A qué hora desayunas?	Desayuno a las *ocho.*

¿Dónde desayunas?	Desayuno en *la cocina.*
¿A qué hora comes/cenas?	Como/ceno a las *ocho/siete.*
¿Qué te gusta comer?	Me gusta mucho *el pescado.*
¿Qué te gusta beber?	Me gustan *los zumos.*
¿Qué desayunaste hoy?	Tomé *tostadas con mermelada.*
¿Qué bebes con el desayuno?	Bebo *café con leche.*
¿Qué vas a cenar esta noche?	Tomaré *cordero con patatas fritas.*

Yourself and your family

¿Cuántos años tienes?	Tengo *dieciséis* años.
¿Cuándo es tu cumpleaños?	Es el *veinte de junio.*
¿En qué año naciste?	Nací en mil novecientos *ochenta y dos*
¿Dónde vives?	Vivo en . . . .
¿A qué distancia del colegio vives?	Vivo a *tres* kilómetros del colegio.
¿Qué cosas te gustan?	Me gustan . . . .
¿Cuántas personas hay en tu familia?	Hay *cuatro* personas en mi familia: *mis padres, mi hermana* y yo.
¿Quiénes son?	Son *mis padres, mi hermana* y yo.
¿Tienes hermanos?	*Sí, tengo una hermana.*
¿Cuántos años tiene?	Tiene *catorce* años.
¿Qué hace tu padre?	Trabaja en *un banco.*
¿Qué hace tu madre?	Es *secretaria.*

Your friends

¿Cómo se llama tu mejor amigo/a?	Se llama *Mark/Karen.*
¿Dónde vive?	Vive *a dos minutos de mi casa.*
¿Cuántos años tiene?	Tiene *dieciséis* años.
¿Cómo es?	Es alto/a y delgado/a.
¿Qué cosas le gustan?	Le gustan *los deportes y las discotecas.*
¿Qué le gusta comer?	Le gustan *las patatas fritas.*
¿Adónde vas con tus amigos?	Vamos a *las tiendas y las discotecas.*

Your free time, interests and hobbies

¿Qué te gusta hacer los sábados?	Me gusta *ir de compras con mis amigos/as.*
Si vas al cine ¿a qué hora tienes que volver a casa?	Tengo que volver a las . . . .
¿Cuáles son tus pasatiempos favoritos?	Son . . . .
¿Qué haces en tu tiempo libre?	Me gusta . . . .
¿Con quién juegas al . . .?	Juego al. . . con *mi hermano.*
¿Con quién vas al . . .?	Voy con . . . .
¿Dónde juegas al . . .?	Juego en. . . .
¿Dónde tocas *el piano*?	*Lo* toco en . . . .
¿Qué deportes practicas?	Juego al . . . .
¿Cuándo?	Juego *los sábados por la mañana.*
¿Con quién?	Juego con . . . .
¿Te gusta la música?	*Sí. Me gusta mucho la música pop.*

Your holidays

¿Adónde fuiste de vacaciones el verano pasado?	Fui a . . . .
¿Con quién?	Fui con . . . .
¿Cómo fuiste(is)?	Fui (fuimos) en *avión.*
¿Dónde os alojasteis?	Nos alojamos en *un hotel.*
¿Cuánto tiempo pasasteis allí?	Pasamos *quince días* allí.
¿Qué tiempo hizo?	*Hizo muy buen tiempo. Hizo sol.*
¿Qué hiciste allí?	*Me bañé y fui a la discoteca*
¿Visitaste algunos sitios interesantes?	*Sí, visité . . . .*

¿Qué te gustó más allí?	Me gustó más . . . .
¿Te gustaría volver allí?	*Sí. Me gustaría porque lo pasé muy bien.*
¿Has visitado España?	*Sí. Fui allí el verano pasado.* *No. Pero quiero ir un año.*
¿Adónde vas de vacaciones este verano?	Voy a . . . .
¿Has estado allí antes?	No. Es la primera vez. OR: Sí. Fui *hace dos años.*

Your home town, village or area

¿Dónde está tu casa?	Está en *las afueras de Leeds.*
¿Dónde está *Leeds*?	Está en *el norte de Inglaterra.*
¿Qué clase de pueblo o ciudad es?	Es *una ciudad industrial.*
¿Qué hay que hacer en *Leeds*?	Hay *cines, piscinas, discotecas y mucho más.*
¿Qué hay de interés en *Leeds*?	Hay . . . .
¿Cómo es *Leeds*?	Es *una gran ciudad industrial.*

Shopping

¿Cuándo vas de compras?	Voy *todos los sábados*
¿Adónde vas de compras?	Voy al centro de *Nottingham.*
¿Con quién te gusta ir de compras?	Me gusta ir con *mis amigos.*
¿Qué clase de tienda te gusta más?	Me gustan más *las tiendas de ropa/los grandes almacenes.*
¿Cuál es tu tienda preferida?	*Una tienda que se llama 'Tunes'.*
¿Qué venden allí?	Venden *discos.*
¿En qué gastas tu dinero?	Compro *ropa.*
Imagina que te han dado 50 libras. ¿En qué las vas a gastar?	*Voy a comprar una chaqueta.*
¿Qué compraste la última vez que fuiste de compras?	Compré *tres discos y un libro.*
¿Qué regalo comprarás para el cumpleaños de tu hermano/madre?	Compraré . . . .

Travel and transport

¿Cómo vienes al colegio por la mañana?	Vengo *en autobús.*
¿Con quién vienes al colegio?	Vengo con *mis amigos.*
¿Tenéis un coche?	*Sí, tenemos un Ford viejo.*
¿Qué medio de transporte te gusta más?	Prefiero *el avión.*
¿Por qué te gusta?	Porque *es muy rápido.*
Si haces vas de excursión, ¿adónde te gusta ir?	Me gusta ir *a la sierra.*
¿Qué países has visitado?	He visitado *Francia y España.* OR: Nunca he ido al extranjero.
¿Cuál es el último viaje largo que hiciste?	Fui a *España el año pasado.*
¿Cómo viajaste?	Fui en *avión.*
¿Cuánto tiempo duró el viaje?	Duró *dos horas.*

Your future plans

¿Qué vas a hacer el año que viene?	Voy a estudiar *el español* . . . . OR: Voy a trabajar *en un banco.*
¿Qué estudios quieres hacer?	Quiero estudiar *historia en la universidad.*
Al final de tus estudios, ¿qué quieres hacer?	Quiero *ser dentista.*
¿Por qué quieres ser *dentista*?	*Me parece muy interesante.*
¿Has trabajado con *un dentista*?	*Sí, trabajé con mi tío en agosto.*

The world of work

¿Qué hace tu padre/tu madre?	Es *empleado/a de banco.* OR: *No tiene trabajo.*
¿Tienes un empleo los fines de semana?	*Sí, trabajo en una tienda.* OR: *No, tengo que estudiar.*
¿Qué horas trabajas?	Trabajo de *nueve* a *cinco.*
¿Cuánto ganas?	Me pagan *cuatro libras la hora.*
¿Qué te parece el trabajo?	Es *bastante aburrido.*
¿Dónde recibiste tu experiencia laboral?	Trabajé en *una fábrica.*
¿Qué te pareció el trabajo?	*Fue muy interesante.*

Life in other countries

¿Has visitado España?	Sí, fui *el año pasado.* OR: No, *pero me gustaría ir.*
¿Cómo es el clima de España?	Depende de la región, pero generalmente hace más calor que aquí.
¿Qué diferencias hay en la comida?	En España se come mucha fruta y mucha verdura.
¿Qué platos españoles te gustan?	Me gustan *la paella y la tortilla.*
¿Cómo es el desayuno español?	Generalmente toman café con leche y un bollo.

As you can see, there is a good deal of overlap in the kinds of question to expect, but your teacher will use a mixture. There are many other possible questions which *could* be asked. Make sure you check what you cover during your lessons and listen carefully to what your teacher says about preparation for this section of the examination. In some cases there will be special information about a final selection of topics to be covered shortly before the examination itself.

Grades D–A*

If you are aiming at Grade D or above, you *must* be able to answer any of the questions listed above for Grades G, F and E, so make sure you check that you can. In addition you should remember the following points.

- **You are expected to say more.** The initiative lies with you much more than it does with the examiner. The questions asked will normally require more than a brief response. Your teacher, as the examiner, will ask questions of a more open nature, giving you a cue to talk on a particular topic. An example could be something like *Háblame un poco de tu familia* or *¿Cómo es tu casa?*. These questions are a clear invitation to you to say what you can, so at this level you must be prepared to string a number of sentences together on a variety of themes.
- **Quality of language is important.** In addition to marks for communication, you need to score some marks for 'quality of language' and this is your chance to 'show off' what you know. You should make your answers interesting in terms of content, vocabulary, idiom and structure. Remember, if you don't use it, you cannot be awarded credit for knowing it!
- **Use a variety of tenses.** For Grade D and above, you are required to show that you can use Past, Present and Future tenses. The examiner will be aiming to ensure that you have an opportunity to show that you can use different tenses, by asking questions about the past (e.g your last summer holiday) and the future (e.g. your plans for this year's holidays or your plans for next year). But it is not easy to ask such questions on every topic. So, as you prepare for the examination, you should think out ways of introducing other tenses yourself into every topic.
- **Express opinions and justify them.** You should be able to say what you like or dislike and why, what you think is right or wrong and why. Again, as you prepare for the examination topic by topic, think what you could have an opinion about and why. It could be as simple as why you don't like the colour of your dining room walls, why you do or don't like your school uniform, or it could be something that leads on to a much longer explanation, such as why you like your sister, complete with examples of

ways in which she has been kind to you or things she has done to help you. The important thing is to think out in advance what opinions you could express and how you will justify or explain them.

Using a variety of tenses

It is much easier for you to introduce different tenses than for your teacher to ask questions that make you use them. For example, if you have been asked to describe your sister, you can give a brief physical description, mention something about her character and then come on to her interests. In the process you can mention something she has done and something she will do:

> *Mi hermana tiene dieciocho años. Es bastante alta y delgada y tiene el pelo rubio y los ojos azules. Es muy simpática y me ayuda mucho. Por ejemplo, anoche me ayudó con mi deber de historia. Le gusta mucho el tenis y este sábado jugará en el equipo del club.*

Even quite unlikely subjects lend themselves to this approach. Talking about your bedroom, you can include information such as:

> *En la mesa hay una lámpara que mis padres me dieron el año pasado ... este verano pintaré las paredes. Si lo hago, mis padres me comprarán cortinas nuevas.*

Describing people

When you are asked to describe a person, you should aim to say three or four sentences on each of the following:

- Their physical appearance (height, colour of hair, eyes etc.).
- Their character (*simpático, divertido, inteligente, hablador*).
- Their likes and dislikes (including mention of something they have done and will do).

In the examination

Try to say a few sentences in answer to every question you are asked. Even the simple question, such as *¿Dónde vives?*, can be used as an opportunity to answer at some length, for example:

> *Vivo en las afueras de Birmingham, en un barrio bastante bonito donde hay varias tiendas y una biblioteca. La casa tiene tres dormitorios y un jardín y está a cuatro kilómetros del colegio. Por eso tengo que coger el autobús por la mañana. Llevo cinco años viviendo en esa casa. Antes vivíamos en el norte de Inglaterra.*

Your teacher may interrupt you with another question, because you are not allowed simply to recite a pre-learnt monologue, but if you have to be interrupted in order to stop you talking you are obviously doing well!

PRACTICE QUESTIONS

Below are some open-ended questions of the sort you should be prepared to answer. If your teacher gives you a list of possible questions, use that! Remember, you should be trying to give **full** answers even to the simpler questions. At the end of this set of examples, sample answers are given for two of the questions.

1. School or college

Háblame un poco de tu colegio.
¿Cuál es tu asignatura preferida? ¿Por qué?
¿Cómo es tu profesor de (*matemáticas*)?

2. Your home life

¿Cómo es tu casa?
¿Cómo es tu dormitorio?
¿Te gusta tu casa? ¿Por qué?

3. Your daily routines

¿Qué haces por la mañana?
Háblame un poco de las comidas en tu familia.
¿Cómo es un día típico en el colegio?

4. Food and drink

¿Cuál es tu plato preferido? ¿Por qué?
¿Prefieres comer en casa o en un restaurante? ¿Por qué?
¿Qué te parece la comida que dan en el colegio?

5. Yourself and your family

Háblame un poco de tu familia.
¿Cómo es tu hermano?
¿Cómo es tu padre/tu madre?

6. Your friends

Háblame de tu mejor amigo/a.
¿Tienes disputas a veces con tus amigos/as? ¿Por qué?

7. Free time, interests and hobbies

¿Qué haces en tu tiempo libre? ¿Por qué te gusta?
¿Qué hiciste el fin de semana pasado?
¿Qué vas a hacer el sábado por la tarde?
Háblame de tu programa preferido de televisión.
¿Cuál es la última película que viste? ¿Te gustó? ¿Por qué?
¿Cuál es el último libro que leíste? ¿Te gustó? ¿Por qué?

8. Your holidays

Háblame de tus vacaciones del verano pasado.
¿Cómo vas a pasar las vacaciones de verano este año.
¿Has visitado España? ¿Qué diferencias has notado entre Inglaterra y España?

9. Your home town, village or area

¿Cómo es . . . (*Nottingham*)?
¿Te gusta vivir allí? ¿Por qué?
¿Qué hay de interés en . . . (*Nottingham*)?

10. Shopping

¿Qué haces cuando vas de compras?
¿Por qué te gusta ir de compras?
Háblame de una cosa interesante que has comprado recientemente.

11. Travel and transport

¿Cómo es tu viaje al colegio?
Háblame de tu medio de transporte preferido.
¿Cuál fue el último viaje largo que hiciste? ¿Cómo fue?

12. Your future plans

¿Qué vas a hacer el año que viene? ¿Por qué?
¿Cuando termines por fin tus estudios ¿qué quieres hacer? ¿Por qué?

13. The world of work

¿Trabajas los fines de semana? Háblame de ese trabajo.
¿Cómo fue la experiencia laboral que recibiste?
Háblame del puesto de trabajo que te gustaría obtener.

14. Life in other countries

¿Qué países has visitado? ¿Qué diferencias has notado entre España e Inglaterra?
Háblame un poco de la región de *España* que visitaste.

SAMPLE ANSWERS

2. Your home life

¿Cómo es tu casa?
Mi casa es bastante moderna. Tiene tres dormitorios y un jardín. El salón no es muy grande pero es muy cómodo, con dos sillones y un sofá. La cocina es muy grande y a mi madre le gusta mucho. Es mucho mejor que la cocina de la casa donde vivíamos antes. Mi dormitorio es pequeño pero a mí me gusta porque es cómodo y bonito. El verano pasado pinté las paredes. Allí tengo mis libros y mis discos. Esta noche haré mis deberes en mi dormitorio.

Cuando miro por la ventana veo el parque, donde siempre hay gente . . . .

Notice that you do not have to use long, complicated sentences in order to display your fluency.

5. Yourself and your family

Háblame un poco de tu familia.
Somos cuatro en la familia: mis padres, mi hermana y yo. Mi hermana tiene catorce años y se llama Susan. Tiene el pelo largo y moreno y los ojos negros. Es simpática y bastante viva. Le gusta mucho la música pop y tiene muchos discos en su dormitorio. El sábado pasado fue a un concierto. También le gusta nadar. Irá a la piscina mañana. Mi padre es bastante tranquilo pero a veces se enfada si discutimos mi hermana y yo. Trabaja en un banco. Mi madre es enfermera . . . .

PRESENTATIONS – WHAT YOU NEED TO KNOW

For Edexcel, MEG and NEAB examinations you will have to make a short presentation of a topic from within the topic list in the syllabus. The main purpose of this is to build up your confidence by making sure that you have control of the beginning of the conversation and can decide in advance just what you want to say at that point.

- You will be allowed to take brief notes (about five short headings) into the examination room to remind you of the points you want to make.
- You will be allowed to speak for up to about a minute before you are asked a question about the topic.
- What you will say is probably very much the sort of thing that you would have said if you had been asked about the subject in the general conversation.
- Make sure you do not say everything you know about the subject. You are expected to carry on a conversation on the same subject for a minute or two after the end of your presentation.
- It is a good idea to give hints about points you could talk a little more about, so that you actually provoke the questions you have prepared yourself to answer.

As an example of this last point, you might be talking about your home village and have a few things you would like to say about the church. If in your presentation you say: *Uno de los edificios más interesantes es la iglesia* and then move on to a different point, the examiner will probably ask you why the church is interesting. This gives you the opportunity to say exactly what you have planned to say, but in answer to a question rather than in your prepared presentation. In this way you can be in control of the conversation as well as the initial presentation.

A STEP FURTHER

There are many ways of increasing your fluency. Most come down to actually speaking.

- Speak Spanish whenever you can, to anyone who will listen.
- Speak to your pets in Spanish!
- Imagine the conversation – the questions and your answers to them – while on your journey to school or college.
- Prepare the conversation questions carefully. Make sure you know the specialized vocabulary for your parents' jobs and your hobbies.
- Make good use of any mock Speaking test that is arranged for you. It is an excellent opportunity to gain valuable experience. Don't waste it by going in ill-prepared.

Take a topic from the list for conversation, think about it for a few minutes and then try talking about it in Spanish for a minute to a minute-and-a-half. Try to make it sound interesting. Would a Spaniard actually enjoy listening to you? When you are reasonably happy, try recording it on cassette. Then listen to the cassette and see if you can see ways of improving it. It will always sound more natural if you feel you are actually talking to someone, so it is much better if you don't write it all down and then read it aloud.

You could then make it into more of a conversation by recording on cassette the questions you think you could be asked on that topic and then playing the recorded questions and answering each one as fully as you can.

For role-play, imagine likely situations and think how you would work through them in Spanish. Try to include as many of the 'unexpected' or unprepared questions as you can, so that when you are in the examination there is less chance of being taken completely by surprise. You can imagine role-play situations at all sorts of times, particularly when you are travelling to or from your school or college.

Chapter 6

Reading

GETTING STARTED

Reading is probably the easiest of the four skills for most candidates, since the quality of your written Spanish is not assessed and you can work at your own pace, going back a number of times over the parts you are unsure about. It is also an easy skill to practise on an individual basis. It does not require special equipment, can be done almost anywhere and in long or short sessions. There is usually plenty of reading material available in schools, colleges, bookshops and libraries. On the other hand, it is a good idea to make sure you know what sort of reading matter you need to practise with.

The reading material you are expected to deal with is of the sort you would have to cope with in a Spanish-speaking country or when in contact in this country with Spanish-speaking people.

You are allowed to use a dictionary to cope with unfamiliar vocabulary and the G, F and E tasks will generally test only words that are listed in the board's Core Vocabulary list.

TOPIC	STUDY	REVISION 1	REVISION 2
The reading material			
The nature of the questions			
Answering the questions			
Understanding signs, notices, menus and programmes			
Coping with words you do not know			
G, F, E tasks			
D, C tasks			
Understanding longer texts			
The flexibility of Spanish word order			
The personal *'a'*			
B, A, A* tasks			
Examination questions			
Students' answers with examiner's comments			
Practice questions			
Answers to practice questions			

WHAT YOU NEED TO KNOW

The reading material

The types of reading material you will be expected to understand include:

- Public signs and notices.
- Simple instructions likely to be found in public places or on items bought in shops.
- Menus, price lists and labels on food and drink.
- Timetables (for school and public transport).
- Advertisements and publicity handouts.
- Brochures and guides.
- Town plans, simple maps and tickets.
- Magazine articles likely to be of interest to a sixteen-year-old.
- Post cards, notes and messages.
- Informal letters (from penfriends or from acquaintances of parents or friends).
- Formal letters (e.g. about accommodation or town twinning arrangements).
- Imaginative writing of the sort likely to be read by a sixteen-year-old.

The material is of the sort that British sixteen-year-olds might realistically have to deal with when they are:

- In a Spanish-speaking country.
- Reading a letter, post card or message from a Spanish-speaking person.
- Interpreting for someone who does not know Spanish well enough to understand the material for himself/herself.
- Reading material published in a Spanish-speaking country.

The texts will be printed in as realistic a form as can reasonably be expected within the limits of an examination paper. Signs will look like signs – not free-standing words. Brochures will look like brochures and may be direct copies of the originals, while some texts may be photocopied directly from Spanish newspapers and magazines. Letters will look reasonably authentic – and that means that informal letters are likely to be handwritten, so you need to be able to read Spanish handwriting. (Don't get too worried – the examining board will make sure they are legible!)

At Higher Tier the extracts will be longer (ranging up to about 350 words). There are more extended pieces from magazines and newspapers. Any letters and advertisements tend to be longer than at Foundation Tier. Where small ads and cinema guides are included, they tend to occur in groups, rather than individually, so that an individual question can be based on information taken from more than one or can require you to select the appropriate item or items from the group. There are likely to be few signposts or signboards in Higher Tier papers.

The nature of the questions

- You will be tested only on your understanding of the material. (You will not be expected to make any significant use of other skills, such as making calculations.)
- You write your answers on the question paper in the spaces provided.
- Answers (whether in Spanish or in English) are marked for the information given, not for the quality of the language.

A variety of different test-types are used. Up to 20 per cent of the questions will be in English. All other questions are in Spanish and must be answered either with Spanish words or with ticks, crosses, figures or letters. The sort of questions you can expect to find in the papers are:

- Questions in English.
- Questions in Spanish.
- True/false questions.
- Grids to be completed (with figures, words, ticks, crosses or letters).
- Multiple-choice questions.
- Multiple-choice sentence completions.
- Spanish sentences with gaps to be filled.

Questions about specific facts will normally be set out in the order in which the information is given in the texts but the questions testing your ability to identify the important themes, to identify relationships between ideas and to draw conclusions will come nearer the end, since they require you to look at the text as a whole.

In the Foundation Tier there is extensive use of pictures (mainly line drawings) which have to be matched with words in the texts.

In many cases the questions will be seeking an answer to the following:

¿Qué . . . ?	*What . . . ?*
¿Quién/Quiénes . . . ?	*Who . . . ?*
¿De quién . . . ?	*Whose . . . ?*
¿Dónde . . . ?	*Where . . . ?*
¿Adónde . . . ?	*Where . . . to?*
¿Cuándo . . . ?	*When . . . ?*
¿A qué hora . . . ?	*At what time . . . ?*
¿Cuánto/a . . . ?	*How much . . . ?*
¿Cuántos/as . . . ?	*How many . . . ?*
¿Cómo . . . ?	*How . . . ?*
¿Cómo es / son . . . ?	*What is / are . . . like?*
¿Por qué . . . ?	*Why . . . ?*
¿Para qué . . . ?	*For what purpose . . . ?*

These questions suggest some areas of vocabulary that you would be well advised to make sure you know.

- **What?** – almost anything! Check out particularly school subjects and extra-curricular activities, shopping, food and drink and free time activities.
- **Who?** – family and friends, jobs.
  – descriptions: physical appearance, size, age, etc.
- **Where?** – position, location of places and buildings (*delante de la iglesia, enfrente de Correos,* etc.) landmarks, countries, distances and directions (*la primera calle a la izquierda,* etc.).
- **When?** – time of day, days, weeks, months, dates, frequency, expressions of time (*hoy, ayer,* etc.), seasons, important holidays (e.g. *Navidad, Semana Santa*), beginning, middle, end.
- **How much?** – quantity, numbers.
- **How many?** – numbers.
- **How?** – expressions of speed, ways of doing things, means of transport, tools and implements, directions.
- **What . . . like?** – descriptions of people, buildings, towns and villages, school subjects, etc.
- **Why?** – reasons.

You are allowed to use a dictionary in the examination.

Answering the questions

- **Remember that you do not have to understand every word** – only the ones relevant to the question.
- **Make sure you read the question and that what you write does actually answer it.** If you are looking at a small advertisement and you are asked what you should do if you are interested in buying the article advertised, don't write down what the article is. What is almost certainly needed is a statement that you should ring a particular telephone number or go to a particular place (possibly at a particular time).
- **If you are told the setting, read it carefully.** It is there to give you some guidance and help and it will often point you towards the right answer. If you are told, for example, that you see a particular notice in your hotel bedroom, it is hardly likely to be telling you that this is a one-way street or that you may not park your car there!
- **Remember to answer English questions in English and Spanish questions in Spanish.** Answers in the wrong language will almost certainly score no marks.
- **Keep your answers as short as possible** (but do make sure you give all the necessary information). Whole sentences are not required. If you are looking at a sign that reads *Se prohibe fumar* and the question is 'What are you told not to do?', you certainly do not need to write: 'I am told not to smoke'. All that is required in this case is 'Smoke'.

- **Check how many marks there are for each question.** (This is usually shown in brackets at the end of the question.) The number of marks will give you a good indication of the number of items of information required. Look for the extra points but make sure you find them in the text! There could be three marks for saying 'He bought *(1 mark)* an interesting *(1 mark)* book *(1 mark)*', so make sure you include the details. (Sometimes there are more points to be made than marks allocated. In such cases it is quite common for, say, 2 marks to be given for any two of three possible points.)
- **Always give an answer.** Even if you have no idea, make an informed guess, based on what you have understood from the setting, the question and the Spanish words themselves. You never know, you might be right! Your chances of guessing the correct answer are particularly good in multiple-choice and true/false questions.
- **Don't list every possibility you can think of.** If, when looking at a shop sign, you are asked what sort of shop it is, there is no point in listing every sort of shop you can think of. The examiner is likely either to mark your answer wrong straightaway or to mark only the first answer. (The examining boards have their own rules for marking such answers.)
- **Remember to use your common sense.** If the answer you have given seems totally unlikely or ridiculous, it is almost guaranteed to be wrong. In the Students' Answers – Examiner's Comments section later in this chapter there is a good example of what can happen if you fail to apply common sense and bear in mind the setting and the question. The answer was actually written by a candidate under examination conditions.

Understanding signs, notices, menus and programmes

Signs and notices are often very brief, consisting of one, two or three words only. It is then important to understand those words. They normally do one of the following:

(a) Tell us what something is or where it is (by pointing towards it).
(b) Tell us what to do.
(c) Give us further information.

Signposts and signboards

It is a good idea to make sure you know the Spanish for the places that are often signposted in towns or inside public buildings and hotels and also the Spanish for places that have notices on them to inform us what they are.

The sort of signposts you will see in town include:

AYUNTAMIENTO	*Town Hall*
BIBLIOTECA	*Library*
CASTILLO	*Castle*
CATEDRAL	*Cathedral*
CORREOS	*Post Office*
ESTACIÓN	*Station*
MERCADO	*Market*
OFICINA DE TURISMO	*Tourist Office*
PARQUE	*Park*
PISCINA	*Swimming Pool*
PLAYA	*Beach*
PLAZA MAYOR	*Main Square*
PLAZA DE TOROS	*Bull Ring*
PUERTO	*Harbour*

The sort of signposts you will see in *hotels, offices, shops, stations* and *airports* include:

ADUANA	*Customs*
ASCENSOR	*Lift*
COMEDOR	*Dining Room*
CAJA	*Cash desk*
CAMBIO	*Exchange, Bureau de Change*
RECEPCIÓN	*Reception*
SALA DE ESPERA	*Waiting room*
SERVICIOS	*Toilets*

There are others that you will find in the vocabulary lists. It is well worth while making sure you will be able to recognize the names of different departments on a store guide.

The signs that tell you what something is include the different types of shops and also banks and any of the places that may be signposted in the town. It is useful to remember that the names of most shops have the ending *-ería*, e.g:

A shop selling *libros* is *una librería.*
A shop selling *pescado* is *una pescadería.*

Instructions

It is also useful to be able to recognize an instruction when you see one! Perhaps rather surprisingly, there is no agreed way in which the readers of public notices are to be addressed in Spanish. You will therefore find, often quite close together, signs that address you in the singular and others that address you in the plural; signs that address you in the familiar forms *(tú, vosotros)* and signs that address you more formally *(usted, ustedes)*. Finally there are signs that issue instructions quite simply by using the infinitive of the verb (e.g. *Bajar con cuidado* – Go down carefully).

You therefore need to be aware that any verb ending in

-a -an -ar
-e -en -er
-ir

could be an instruction. What is absolutely certain is that any verb ending in

-ad -ed -id

definitely **is** an instruction.

Thus the instruction 'Pull' on a door or handle could be given in any of the following ways:

TIRE	(*addressing the reader as* usted)
TIRA	(*addressing the reader as* tú)
TIREN	(*addressing the readers as* ustedes)
TIRAD	(*addressing the readers as* vosotros)
TIRAR	(*using the infinitive*)

Instructions **not** to do something often include the word *No* (e.g. *No fumar*) but they very frequently use the verb *prohibir* in some form or other. Thus the instruction not to smoke is likely to be expressed in one of the following ways:

Se prohibe fumar
Está prohibido fumar
Queda prohibido fumar
Prohibido fumar

More forcefully it may be linked with the word *terminantemente* (strictly):

Queda terminantemente prohibido fumar (*Smoking strictly prohibited)*

If all this sounds confusing, don't worry! You don't have to be able to reproduce all of these in Spanish. You simply have to recognize them as instructions and work out what they mean.

Further information

Signs giving further information can deal with a whole range of matters but among the most frequent are notices that:

- State that a place is open or closed.
- State hours, days or dates of opening.
- Give instructions on how to get there.
- State what is for sale.
- Publicize special offers.
- Publicize the specialities of restaurants and bars.

It is important, therefore to know the days of the week, the months, the seasons of the year and the words for the different parts of the day – and it is worth making a special point of checking very carefully all answers about these. It is surprising how many candidates make silly mistakes over days and seasons.

You also obviously need to know expressions such as:

abierto *open*	cerrado *closed*
se abre *opens*	se cierra *closes*
de. . . a. . . *from. . . to. . .*	desde. . . hasta. . . *from. . . until. . .*
se vende *for sale*	vendo *for sale* (= *I am selling*)
descuento *discount*	liquidación *clearance sale*
rebajas *price reductions* (= *sale*)	

The words for items of food and drink, clothing and other things you could be interested in buying are likely to be important.

You also need to be fully aware of expressions telling you where places are, e.g. *enfrente de Correos* (opposite – not in front of – the Post Office), *al lado del cine.*

Menus and programmes

Questions based on menus and programmes normally test understanding of individual words, by asking the price of an item or the time of a particular programme on radio or television, so you need to know the vocabulary of food and drink and of entertainment.

Coping with words you do not know

In coping with unknown words there are a number of strategies that can be adopted before you use up time by referring to your dictionary:

- Check if they are important for you to be able to answer the questions you have been asked. If they are not, don't worry about them!
- Are they similar to any words in English (or any other language you know)? If they are, does that lead you to a meaning that makes sense in the context?
- Do the other words and the meaning of the sentences around them give you a clue to their possible meaning?
- Does the question or the setting give you an indication of possible meanings?
- Does the word begin with a common prefix, e.g. *des-* or *in-* (which are the equivalent of the English 'dis-', 'un-', 'in-')? For example, *desagradable* means 'unpleasant'.
- Does the word end in a common suffix? It is helpful to be aware of the following:
  -mente is the equivalent of the English -ly (as in *desafortunadamente*: unfortunately).
  -ito (*-ita*) means 'little' (as in *casita*: little house).
  -ería usually means 'shop' (as in *pastelería*: cake shop).
  -ero (*-era*) means either 'person who deals with. . .' or 'container for. . .' (as in *camionero:* lorry driver; *florero*: vase).
  -ista usually means 'person who deals with or is involved in . . . ' (as in *maquinista*: machinist or engine-driver; *futbolista*: footballer; *taxista*: taxi-driver).
  -ura is often the equivalent of the English -ness (as in *blancura*: whiteness). (Note also: *hermosura*: beauty.)
  -izo is the equivalent of the English -ish, e.g. *rojizo*: reddish.
  -illo/-illa -ecillo/-ecilla, *-ecito/-ecita* all mean 'little', e.g. *mesilla*: small table, *panecillo*: bread roll (= little loaf).
- In the case of fruit, trees and orchards/groves, the following pattern is common:
  -a is the ending for the fruit (which is a feminine word)
  -o is the ending for the tree (which is a masculine word)
  -ar/-al is the ending for the orchard or grove
  – Thus:

manzana: apple	*naranja*: orange
manzano: apple tree	*naranjo*: orange tree
manzanar: apple orchard	*naranjal*: orange grove

- Will a change of one or two letters make the word look more like an English word that will make sense in the sentence? The following are worth trying:
  f – change to *ph* (as in *farmacia*: pharmacy; *foto*: photo).
  t – change to *th* (as in *tema*: theme).
  qu – change to *ch* (as in *máquina*: machine; *arquitecto*: architect).

-ción – change to *-tion* (as in *nación*: nation).
-cia – change to *-cy* or *-ce* (as in *agencia*: agency; *esencia*: essence).

- Additional letter substitutions that can be tried, in order to find a similarity with a word in English, French or other European language, include:
  ue – change to *o* as in *puerto*: port; or *fuerte*: strong (French: *fort*).
  ie – change to *e* as in *hierba*: grass (French: *herbe*).
  ll – at beginning of word change to *pl* as in *llover* (French: *pleuvoir*) or to *fl* as in *llamas*: flames.
  h – at beginning of word change to *f*.
  Sometimes two of these substitutions will work together. Thus, if you take the word *hierro* and apply the two suggested changes you find you now have *ferro*, which you may well recognize as having to do with iron (ferreous or ferrous). (*Hierro* means 'iron'.)
  It is also worth trying an exchange of *g* with *j* or *j* with *g* and an exchange of *b* with *v* or *v* with *b*.

If you know these strategies and can apply them effectively, you will save a considerable amount of time that would otherwise be spent looking words up in the dictionary.

G, F, E tasks

At this level:

- You are expected to demonstrate understanding of the main points of short items.
- You are expected to show understanding of some specific details of longer items.
- You will **not** be required to show any other skills, such as the ability to summarize or to draw conclusions.

D, C tasks

At this level, in addition to the skills required for Grades G, F and E, you are expected to show:

- Understanding specific details.
- Understanding of past, present and future tenses.
- An ability to identify points of view expressed in the texts.

Understanding longer texts

Longer texts (which are normally targeted at Grades D–A*) do not depend so much on understanding of individual words. You have more text to help you. On the other hand you do have to identify the key points and you are more likely to have to understand the verbs that are used.

- **Identify the tense from the verb ending.** It is quite important that you can tell whether the writer is telling you of something that regularly happens, is going to happen or has happened. For that reason you really do need to be able to **identify the main tenses** (Present, Future, Preterite). You may well receive help in this from the inclusion of other expressions such as *todos los sábados, el año que viene* or *la semana pasada* but you cannot be sure that there will always be help of this sort.
- **Identify who does, did or will do the action, also from the verb ending.** It is important to look at the endings of verbs in order to be sure who it is that does, did or will do the action. Do be careful here of verbs that end in -ó. *Llegó*, for example, means 'He (or she) arrived' – *not*, as all too many candidates decide under the pressure of the examination, 'I arrive(d)'.
- **Remember that the subject of the verb is regularly omitted in Spanish sentences.** You have to remember also that the **subject of the verb** (the person who does the action) is regularly omitted in Spanish.
- **Do not be misled by an object pronoun (*me, te, le, lo, la, nos, os, les, los, las*) coming before the verb.** *Me dio* . . . means 'He (or she) gave me . . . ' *not*, as many candidates decide, 'I gave . . . ' If you are in the habit of making mistakes of that kind, it is a good idea to make a special point of checking for them in every piece of reading work you do and to make a mental note to check for them in your examination answers.

It is also worth spending some time looking at two other key features of Spanish sentence structure:

- The flexibility of Spanish word order.
- The personal 'a'.

The flexibility of Spanish word order

Consider the following sentences and work out what you think they each mean:

(a) Mis padres compraron una mesa.
(b) Compraron mis padres una mesa.
(c) Compraron una mesa mis padres.
(d) Una mesa la compraron mis padres.

If you have applied the principle of using the verb ending to decide who did the action, you will have realized that all four sentences mean 'My parents bought a table'. In English the word order is critical: 'My parents' must come before 'bought' and 'bought' must come before 'a table'. Any variation in that will produce either a different meaning or complete nonsense. What would any of us make of a sentence such as 'Bought a table my parents'? Yet in Spanish the word order can be much more flexible and we have to make use of other 'markers', such as the verb ending, in order to understand the sentence.

Now consider these four sentences and decide what they mean:

(a) El hombre ve el perro.
(b) Ve el hombre el perro.
(c) Ve el perro el hombre.
(d) El perro lo ve el hombre.

In this case, as in the previous set of sentences, they all have the same meaning: 'The man sees the dog'. And yet, while we all know that a table cannot buy people, it is quite clear that a dog *is* capable of seeing a person. So why does none of the four sentences mean that the dog sees the man? The answer lies in the use of the personal '*a*'.

The personal '*a*'

Because of the flexibility of Spanish word order, an extra 'marker' is needed in order to make clear whether a person is the subject of the verb (the person who does the action) or the direct object of the verb (the person who is seen, helped, heard etc.). That 'marker' is the use of the word '*a*' before the direct object if the direct object is a person. So, if we wish to say that the dog sees the man, the possibilities are:

(a) El perro ve al hombre.
(b) Ve el perro al hombre.
(c) Ve al hombre el perro.
(d) Al hombre le ve el perro.

The same principle applies to *nadie, alguien* and *¿quién?*.

No vio a nadie = *He/she saw nobody*
No vio nadie = *Nobody saw*
¿A quién vio? = *Who(m) did he/she see?*
¿Quién vio? = *Who saw?*

It is perhaps worth mentioning that the personal '*a*' is also sometimes used when the direct object is an animal, in order to make the meaning clear:

- *Atacó el perro el gato* does not make clear which animal attacked the other.
- *Atacó el perro al gato* clearly means 'The dog attacked the cat'. The use of the personal '*a*' has ensured clarity.

A sound understanding of these two related points (flexible word order and the personal '*a*') will help you to avoid the sort of confusion that many candidates seem to have with some sentences in longer texts.

B, A, A* tasks

At this level, in addition to the skills shown for Grades G–C, you will be expected to show that you can:

- Identify the important points or themes within extended texts.
- Identify the relationship between ideas expressed.

- Draw conclusions from what you read.

The conclusions you are expected to draw are likely to refer to:

- The attitudes and emotions expressed in the texts (or likely to be felt by the people involved).
- The ideas implied (but not directly stated) in the texts.

These skills imply an ability to select what is relevant and disregard what is irrelevant.

It is obviously a good idea to make sure you know the vocabulary of emotions and attitudes (e.g. *triste, alegre, enfadado, preocupado*) but you must bear in mind that a genuine 'Attitudes and emotions' question does not normally have those words in the text. You may have to identify the attitude of someone who says *¡Qué asco! ¿Tú sabes cómo es eso?* In this case, the words for 'unhappy' or 'not enthusiastic' have not been used, but that is clearly the attitude of the Spanish writer.

EXAMINATION QUESTIONS

You are recommended to try the questions for yourself before you look at the Students' Answers with Examiner's Comments (pages 131–133).

G, F, E tasks

The first items in the examination are usually very short. There is often only one word to read. Typically the early sections will deal with signs and notices.

Question 1 You see this advertisement for a drink called Sinsa.

¡SED! ¡CALOR! ¡FATIGA!

beba **Sinsa**

CON SABOR NARANJA

* * *

Apropiado para todas las edades

De venta en farmacias

Necesario disolver el contenido del sobre en agua fría.

(a) What advice is given on line 2?

.... *(1)*

(b) What flavour is the drink?

.... *(1)*

(c) For what ages is the drink recommended?

.... *(1)*

(d) Where can you buy the drink?

.... *(1)*

(e) What advice is given about dissolving the contents of the envelope?

.... *(1)*

(MEG)

Question 2 Estos son los anuncios de 4 tiendas en el pueblo de Las Torres de Cotillas. Contesta a las preguntas escribiendo la letra apropiada para cada tienda.

FRUTERIA
LEO
Especialidad en todo tipo de frutas
C/. Narciso Yepes, s/n. - Telf.. 62 62 89
LAS TORRES DE COTILLAS
D

Por ejemplo: ¿Qué tienda buscarías para comprar salchichas? TIENDA B

(i) ¿Qué tienda buscarías para comprar naranjas? TIENDA ______ (*1*)
(ii) ¿Qué tienda buscarías para comprar panecillos? TIENDA ______ (*1*)
(iii) ¿Qué tienda buscarías para comprar jabón? TIENDA ______ (*1*)
(iv) ¿Qué tienda quiere que sus clientes lo pasen bien? TIENDA ______ (*1*)

(WJEC)

D, C tasks

Question 3 You are on holiday in Spain with your family and it is raining. You decide to go to the cinema and your family asks you to look at the film guide below and say which kind of film is showing at each cinema.

Guía de los cines

(a) COLISEUM. 'El tren.' Problemas en el oeste. El ferrocarril se acerca ... y los vaqueros no están contentos.
(b) LICEO. 'Recompensa.' Se declara un incendio forestal de tanta magnitud que no hay más remedio que utilizar explosivos para cortarlo. Ofrecen una recompensa a quien se arriesgue a transportarlos.
(c) ARCADIA. 'Voces de muerte.' La verdadera historia de Edward Chapsan, un agente doble que trabaja sin descanso contra los rusos.
(d) ASTORIA. '¿Quo vadis?' Adaptación de la novela de Henry Sinkiewicz sobre el encuentro entre un radiante soldado romano y una frágil cristiana.
(e) FILMOTECA. 'Mi hermana Elena.' Está muerta ... pero vuelve a medianoche.
(f) MODERNO. 'Providencia.' Historia relacionada con los vuelos espaciales del futuro.

Your family tells you that they are particularly interested in:

comedy films
adventure films
horror films
spy films
science-fiction films
westerns
romantic films

Write in the spaces provided the type of film being shown in each cinema. The first has been done for you.

(a) At the Coliseum, there is a . . western . . . . film. (*1*)
(b) At the Liceo there is a . . . . film. (*1*)
(c) At the Arcadia, there is a . . . . film. (*1*)
(d) At the Astoria, there is a . . . . film. (*1*)
(e) At the Filmoteca, there is a . . . . film. (*1*)
(f) At the Moderno, there is a . . . . film. (*1*)

(MEG)

Question 4 Lee el anuncio y contesta las preguntas en español.

Gran Festival de Circo 1988

Junto a la plaza de toros de Las Ventas.
Teléfono 246 88 80. Un moderno circo con calefacción. ¡Sensacional! ¡Fabuloso! Hasta 30 atracciones.

Sábados y festivos 12 mediodía, 4.30 y tarde.
Viernes 6.30 y 8.45 tarde.
Los demás días, 6.30 tarde.
Taquillas, desde las 10 horas.

(a) ¿Dónde está situado el circo?
....
.... (2)

(b) ¿Cómo es el circo?
....
.... (2)

(c) ¿A qué hora comienza el espectáculo los miércoles?
....
.... (2)

(d) ¿Cuándo se puede sacar entradas?
....
.... (2)

(*Total: 8 marks*)

(NICCEA)

B, A, A* tasks

Question 5 Lee este boletín meteorológico.

Gijón

Despejado

La predicción apunta a cambios.
Máxima: 28°. Mínima: 19°

Mañana: Chubascos frecuentes.
Máxima: 25°. Mínima: 18°

Madrid

Seguirá como ayer

Sin cambios. Máxima: 38°
Mínima: 20°

Mañana: Igual. Máxima: 38°
Mínima: 21°

Sevilla

Ambiente caluroso

Predominio del sol y del calor.
Máxima: 41°. Mínima: 23°

Mañana: Sin cambios. Máxima: 41°
Mínima: 22°

Bilbao

Alguna niebla

Otra vez alguna niebla matinal es lo único reseñable. Máxima: 31°
Mínima: 19°

Mañana: Algo más de calor.
Máxima: 33°. Mínima: 20°

Barcelona
Pocas nubes Todo igual, cielos casi despejados. Máxima: 31°. Minima: 22° Mañana: Lo mismo. Máxima: 30° Mínima: 22°

Lee estas frases que describen el tiempo en cada ciudad.

(a) El tiempo de mañana cambiará, dando lugar a un tiempo más caluroso.
(b) Seguirá el tiempo soleado con temperaturas altísimas.
(c) El tiempo seguirá con muy poca nubosidad.
(d) El tiempo será parecido al del día anterior.
(e) Mañana, habrá mucha lluvia.

Pon la letra (a, b, c, d, o e) en la casilla que le corresponde.

MADRID ☐ SEVILLA ☐ GIJON ☐
BARCELONA ☐ BILBAO ☐

(5)
(NICCEA)

STUDENTS' ANSWERS WITH EXAMINER'S COMMENTS

G, F, E tasks

Question 1

Student's answer

(a) *Drink Sinsa*
(b) *Orange*
(c) *Adults*
(d) *Pharmacy*
(e) *Dissolve in cold soapy water*

Examiner's comments

(a) Good.
(b) Good.
(c) No. '*Todas las edades*' means 'all ages'.
(d) Yes. Most people would say 'chemist's'.
(e) Really! This is a drink – have you forgotten that? Everything is right except for 'soapy' but you really can't expect a mark if your interpretation of the instructions would lead you to do something quite so ridiculous! Incidentally, 'sobre' means 'envelope'.

Question 2

Student's answers

(i) *D*
(ii) *C*
(iii) *B*
(iv) *B*

Examiner's comments

(i) Good. You recognized naranjas as fruta.

(ii) No. *Panecillos* are bread rolls. You could have checked in your dictionary instead of guessing.
(iii) No. The answer is C. *Jabón* is soap; I suspect you confused it with *jamón*.
(iv) Good.

D, C tasks

Question 3

Student's answers

(b) *comedy*
(c) *spy*
(d) *romantic*
(e) *horror*
(f) *adventure*

Examiner's comments

(b) Wrong. It is not clear why you chose this answer. It looks like a process of elimination. The correct answer is 'adventure'.
(c) Correct.
(d) Correct.
(e) Good. You have clearly identified this as a ghostly return!
(f) No. It does involve adventure but space travel is normally seen as science-fiction. If you had given the right answer to Question 1 you would probably have chosen correctly here.

General comment: These questions may seem comparatively easy but they do all involve drawing conclusions from the text (a specific Higher Level skill). Notice that the words for 'adventure', 'spy', 'romance', 'horror' and 'science-fiction' do not occur in the film guide.

Question 4

Student's answers

(a) *Está situado en Las Ventas.*
(b) *Es sensacional, fabuloso.*
(c) *Comienza a las 6.30.*
(d) *Se puede sacar entradas los demás días.*

Examiner's comments

(a) This is insufficient for two marks. You needed to add *junto a la plaza de toros* in order to earn the second mark.
(b) This is not really what was wanted but you ought to get one mark. The main idea was that this is *un circo moderno con calefacción*.
(c) When two marks are available you should always look carefully to see what might be expected for the second mark. In this case, one mark was for *de la tarde*. It may seem unfair that you don't get full marks for this, when it is obviously not going to be 6.30 in the morning, but on the other hand you have only given a single detail, which can hardly justify two marks.
(d) No. You have missed the point. *Taquillas* means 'box office' and you are told it is open *desde las diez*.

You do not have to write full sentence answers. You could omit all the verbs here, but you do need two details for two marks.

B, A, A* tasks

Question 5

Student's answers

Madrid: *b*
Barcelona: *c*
Sevilla: *d*
Bilbao: *a*
Gijón:

Examiner's comments

You are right about Barcelona and Bilbao. There is some similarity between the forecasts for Madrid and Sevilla, since both include the phrase *sin cambios*. The key to distinguishing between them is in the very high temperatures in Sevilla. You should never leave a question unanswered, as you did for Gijón. You presumably failed to see the link between *chubascos* and *lluvia*, but you should always offer an answer – your guess might be right!

PRACTICE QUESTIONS

Suggested answers to these questions are on pages 146–148.

G, F, E tasks

Question 6 You have just arrived in Spain by plane and you want to take a bus into the town centre. Which sign should you follow?

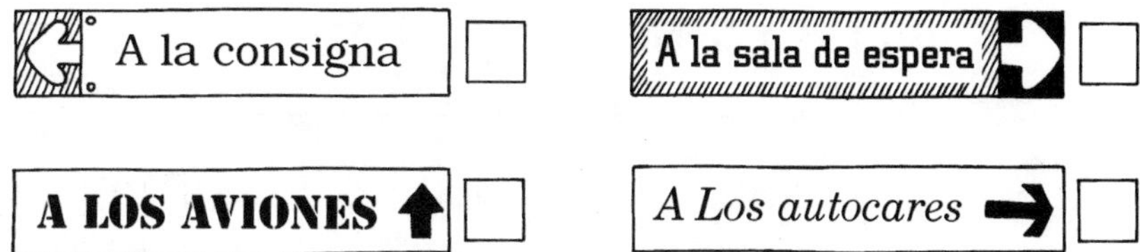

(MEG)

Question 7 You reach your hotel and you are trying to find your room on the seventh floor. Which sign should you look for?

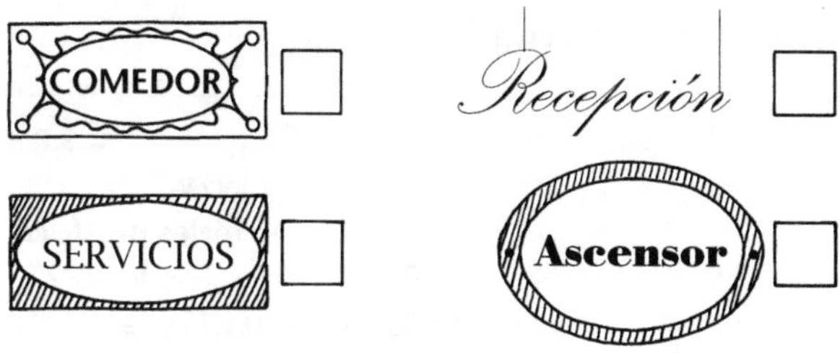

(MEG)

Question 8 You are about to enter a shop and you see this sign on the door.

What does the sign tell you? .... *(1)*
(MEG)

Question 9 You want to buy some meat. Which sign would you follow?

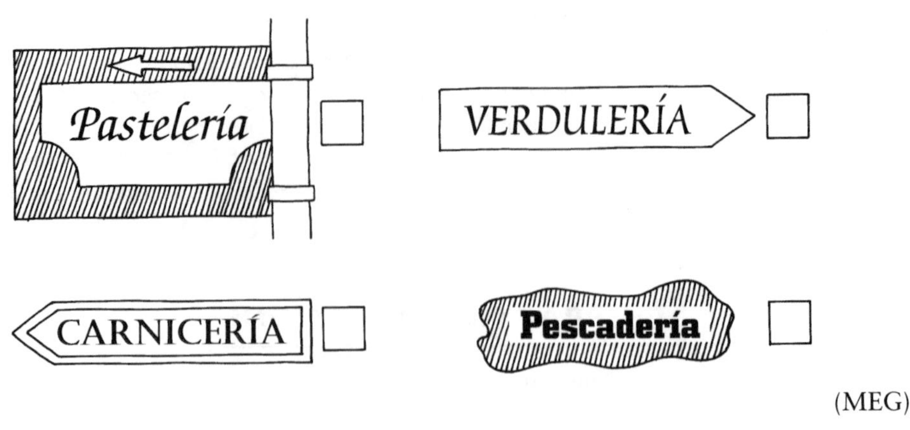

(MEG)

Question 10 Haces las compras. Pon una marca (✓) en la casilla correcta.

A SUPERMERCADO

B CORREOS

C LIBRERIA

D JOYERIA

(a) Quieres comprar sellos	A ☐	B ☐	C ☐	D ☐
(b) Quieres comprar revistas	A ☐	B ☐	C ☐	D ☐
(c) Quieres comprar comestibles	A ☐	B ☐	C ☐	D ☐
(d) Quieres comprar un reloj	A ☐	B ☐	C ☐	D ☐

(4)
(NICCEA)

Question 11 TELEDIARIO

Canal Plus

18.00	Tom y Jerry
18.30	Los Animales de Africa
19.00	Noticias: Telediario 2
19.30	Deporte: Liga española, Real Madrid – Athletic Bilbao
21.30	Concierto: Pavarotti en Madrid
23.30	Deporte: Boxeo
24.00	Noticias: Telediario 3
00.30	Cine Club: Entrevista con el vampiro
03.30	Despedida y cierre

Escribe la hora adecuada del programa.

Ejemplo: los dibujos animados	18.00
(a) fútbol	
(b) música	
(c) naturaleza	
(d) películas de horror	

(4)
(Edexcel)

Question 12

CAMPING OLIDEN

RESTAURANTE

SUPERMERCADO

PISCINA Y TENIS

Carretera General Madrid–Irún, Km 476

Teléfono 49 07 28 OYARZUN

¿Qué puedes hacer en este camping? Pon una ✗ en las 3 casillas adecuadas.

Ejemplo

✗

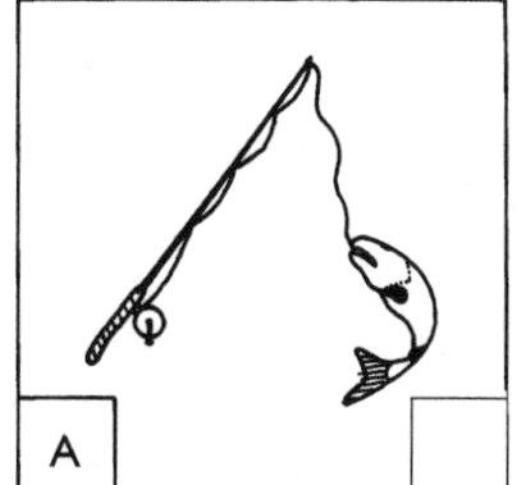

A

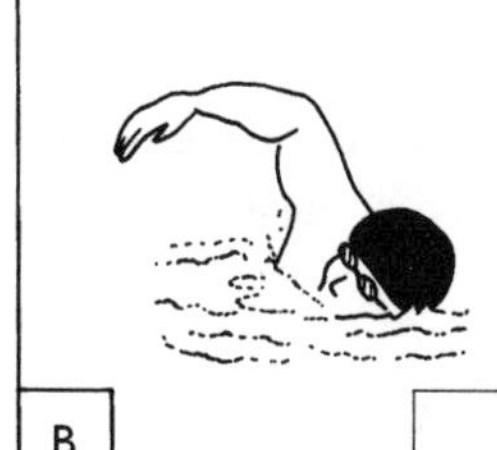

B

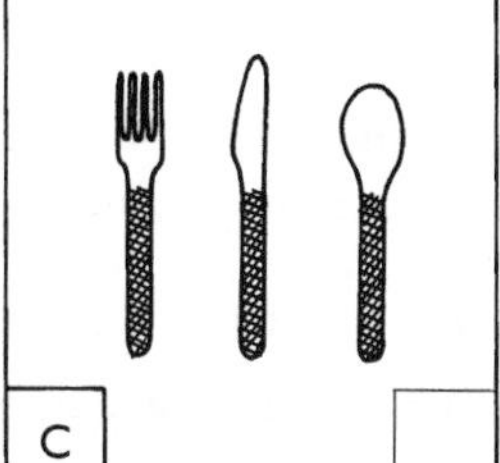

C

D

E

(3)

(Edexcel)

Question 13

Lee este folleto que da detalles sobre un hotel.

HOTEL VELAZQUEZ

AVDA DE MONTEMAR 70
TORREMOLINOS
TELF: 38 62 11

Situación En la zona de Montemar en las afueras de Torremolinos.
A 300 metros de la playa.

MAYO–
SEPTIEMBRE

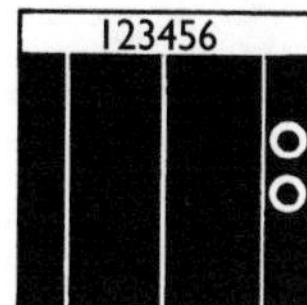

Indica si la frase es verdad o mentira.
Pon una marca (✓) en la casilla correcta.

(a) El hotel está en el centro de la ciudad.

Verdad ☐ Mentira ☐

(b) Se puede cenar en el hotel.

Verdad ☐ Mentira ☐

(c) Se puede subir a la habitación en ascensor. Verdad ☐ Mentira ☐

(d) Se admiten perros. Verdad ☐ Mentira ☐

(e) Se puede reservar una habitación en enero. Verdad ☐ Mentira ☐

(f) Cada habitación tiene un baño. Verdad ☐ Mentira ☐

(g) El hotel tiene su propio aparcamiento. Verdad ☐ Mentira ☐

(h) No se permite beber alcohol en el hotel. Verdad ☐ Mentira ☐

(8)
(NICCEA)

Question 14

Tu amigo español sigue una dieta porque quiere perder unos kilos. Tú le muestras este artículo que tiene una lista de cosas que no se deben hacer si se quiere adelgazar.

COMO SEGUIR LA DIETA CON EXITO

6 TRUCOS PARA LOS QUE QUIEREN ADELGAZAR

1. Para no comer comida frita, quita la sartén de la cocina.
2. Es mejor servir las porciones pequeñas en platos pequeños. ¡Así parecen mayores!
3. Está prohibido tener sal sobre la mesa.
4. Si no tienes que preparar la comida, ¡quédate fuera de la cocina!
5. Sírvete en la cocina y come lejos de la cocina.
6. ¡No hagas las compras! Si un amigo te compra la comida, ¡no puedes comprar dulces!

Identifica los **6** consejos mencionados en el artículo, poniendo los números 1–6 en las casillas correctas.

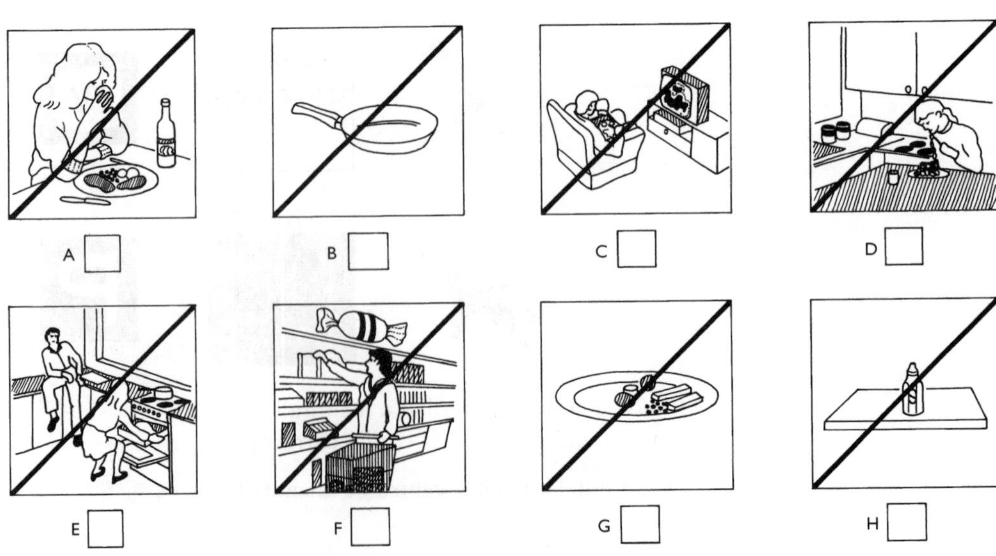

(6)
(MEG)

Question 15

A Me llamo Dolores Hernández, tengo 15 años. Deseo cartearme con chico/chica extranjero/a entre 13 y 16 años. Toco la flauta, me gustan los animales y la naturaleza.

B Me llamo Felipe Murillo. Tengo 15 años y deseo cartearme con chicos/chicas del mundo entero de 12 a 15 años y que hablen español e inglés. Pasatiempos: el ciclismo, los sellos y los dibujos animados.

C Me llamo Ana González, tengo 16 años. Quisiera cartearme con chico/chica a quien le gusten la lectura, la natación, el tenis, el baloncesto y el cine. Escribe en inglés o en español.

D Me llamo Pedro Puente y tengo 14 años. Quiero cartearme con chico/chica de Estados Unidos o de Canadá, de 12 a 15 años. Me gustan la lectura, la música y la historia.

Empareja los símbolos con las personas.

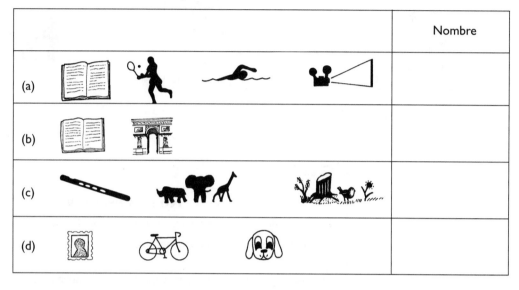

	Nombre
(a)	
(b)	
(c)	
(d)	

(*4*)
(SEG)

Question 16

Tu amigo español te escribe una carta.

> Hola amigo:
>
> ¡La semana pasada fue interesante!
>
> El lunes llegué muy tarde a mi trabajo. ¡Mi jefe no estaba contento!
> El martes jugué al tenis. ¡Perdí!
> El miércoles fui a Madrid en tren y el viaje fue excelente.
> El jueves mis padres estaban enfadados conmigo y no salí.
> El viernes ¡mi tío me dio mucho dinero!
> El sábado mi amiga dijo que no quiere salir conmigo.
>
> ¡Qué semana!
>
> Adiós
>
> Hasta pronto
>
> Pepe.

¿Qué aspectos de la semana de Pepe han salido bien y qué aspectos han salido mal? Pon una ✓ en la casilla correcta.

Example

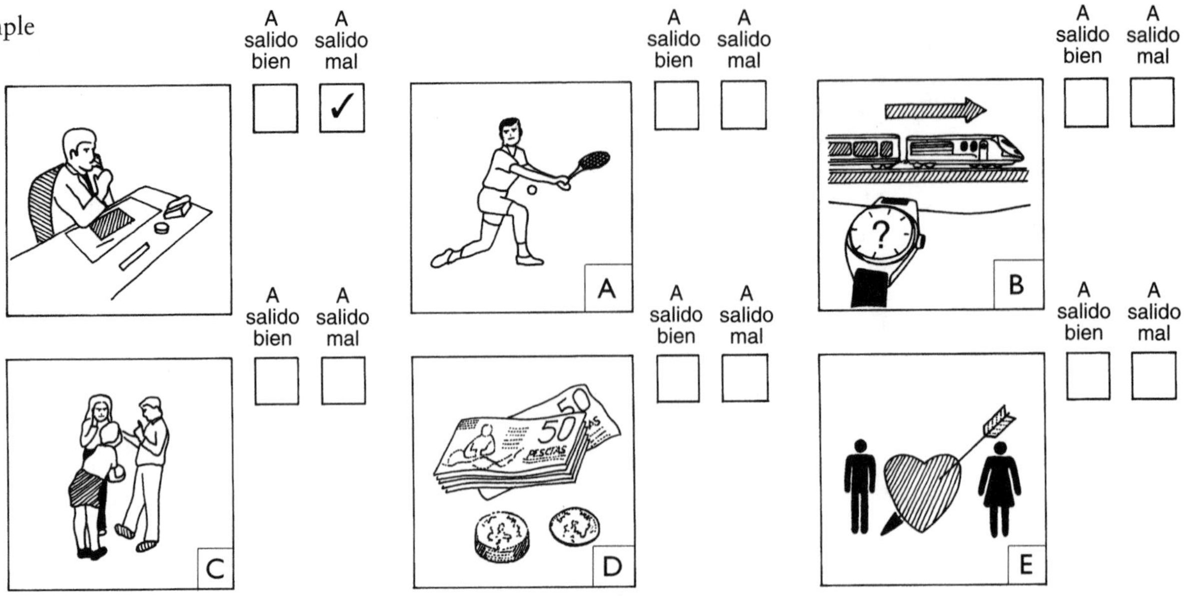

	A salido bien	A salido mal
Example		✓
A		
B		
C		
D		
E		

(5)
(MEG)

D, C tasks

Question 17

No leas esta revista

Nace «Lourdes a las cinco». Una nueva revista diaria que no debes leer.

Escúchala de 5 a 7, de lunes a viernes, en cualquiera de las 70 emisoras de la Cadena Rato.

Lourdes Zuriaga dedica su gran experiencia periodística en televisión y otros medios, para presentar dos horas diarias de radio-revista.

El mundo de la cultura y de los pasatiempos. Las últimas noticias en cine, teatro y música. Entrevistas a los personajes de mayor actualidad. Conexiones en directo a través de unidades móviles ...

¿VERDADERO o FALSO? Pon una X en la casilla adecuada.

	VERDADERO	FALSO
(a) Tienes que leer esta revista.		
(b) Se puede escuchar 'Lourdes a las 5' todos los días.		
(c) El programa consiste en 2 horas de información.		
(d) Lourdes Zuriaga tiene mucha experiencia en el mundo de la televisión.		
(e) Hay todo tipo de información.		
(f) Todo el programa se realiza en un estudio.		

(6)
(Edexcel)

Question 18

Escribe las palabras siguientes en el orden correcto.

(a) calle una Vivo estrecha de Correos cerca en.

....

.... (2)

(b) casa con es Mi grande bastante terraza una.

....

.... (2)

(c) edificio pisos de Es dos un moderno.

....

.... (2)

(*Total: 6 marks*)

(NICCEA)

Question 19

Tu familia va a pasar el verano en Cantabria con unos amigos españoles. Te mandan información sobre la casa y la región.

Lee la carta y contesta a las preguntas poniendo una ✓ en la casilla correcta.

León
10 de mayo 1995

Queridos amigos:

Ya hemos confirmado el apartamento para el verano y os escribo para daros todos los detalles.

Está precisamente a orillas del mar al lado de un bosque. Tiene salón, comedor, cocina y cuatro dormitorios, dos con baño y ducha. También hay un cuarto de baño.

El apartamento está completamente amueblado con buen gusto pero tendremos que llevar nuestras sábanas y toallas.

La limpieza está a cargo de una muchacha que viene diariamente. La he conocido ya y es muy simpática.

Un autobús sale cada quince minutos para el centro de la ciudad y el trayecto dura unos cuarenta minutos. También se puede tomar el tren pero esto sale caro y, además, la estación está bastante lejos.

En las inmediaciones hay facilidades para pescar e ir a caballo.

El alquiler mínimo es de dos meses y por eso mi madre, mi hermana y yo vamos a trasladarnos allí a principios de julio. Papá vendrá más tarde.

Sin más por ahora

Un abrazo de vuestro amigo

Juan Carlos

Ejemplo

Queridos amigos:

Ya hemos confirmado el apartamento para el verano y os escribo para daros todos los detalles.

	No se recomienda	Es posible	No es posible	Es necesario	No es necesario
Confirmar que queremos alquilar el apartamento					✓

	No se recomienda	Es posible	No es posible	Es necesario	No es necesario
1. Ir a la costa en coche.					
2. Llevar sábanas y toallas.					
3. Limpiar la casa todos los días.					
4. Ir al centro ciudad en tren.					
5. Preparar la comida.					

	No se recomienda	Es posible	No es posible	Es necesario	No es necesario
6. Ir de pesca.					
7. Quedarse dos semanas.					
8. Dormir en una habitación con ducha.					

(MEG)

Question 20 En un periódico español, estás leyendo la sección de sucesos nacionales e internacionales. Lee los artículos, y contesta a las preguntas **en español**.

SUCESOS DIVERSOS

1. DOS DIAS CON UN TENEDOR EN EL ESTOMAGO
María José Fernández Ledo, de veintitrés años, vecina de Bornalle-Abilleira, estaba preparando una tortilla en su casa, y de manera fortuita introdujo un tenedor en la boca. Cuando quiso aspirar tragó el utensilio completo, que tenía veinte centímetros de largo. Permaneció todo un día sin decir nada, hasta que finalmente contó los hechos a su familia, que determinó llevarla al hospital de Santiago de Compostela, en donde fue intervenida con éxito.
María José dijo que durante los días que tuvo el tenedor en su estómago sólo notó dolor en el hombro derecho cuando se sentaba.
2. SANTIAGO DE COMPOSTELA
Contra el parecer de todos los médicos. Mónica Vivas Hernández ha cumplido hoy cien años. Mónica que vive en Vigo, nació en Salamanca. A los 22 meses, perdió a sus padres en un accidente. Mónica no se casó nunca.
3. RECORD BELGA
DISC-JOCKEY TRABAJA DIEZ DIAS SEGUIDOS
Bruselas – Un joven escocés, Tim Woods, de 29 años de edad, presentó discos, en una discoteca bruselense durante 10 días seguidos, batiendo el récord mundial de 'disc-jockey', según informa Efe.
4. LADRON DETENIDO EN CUENCA
Drama ayer en la Calle Mayor de Cuenca. Armado con un fusil, Daniel Ortega atacó la oficina de Correos exigiendo un millón de pesetas. Al salir del edificio con el dinero, no logró arrancar su coche y tuvo que escapar a pie. Fue detenido poco después.
5. VEINTE MUERTOS EN UN CINE EN COLOMBIA
Serían sobre las siete de la tarde del lunes pasado cuando corrió la voz de horror, muertos y fuego. Una serie de voces que alarmaron a toda la ciudad. Como reportero-redactor del Diario de Bogotá tuve la suerte de ser de los primeros en llegar al lugar del suceso. En la puerta de entrada y de salida del Cine de la Paz, se veía un montón de seres humanos gritando como locos, forzando por salir de aquel sitio terrible. La voz de un loco había gritado ¡fuego! durante la película. Por supuesto no había ningún incendio pero veinte personas, en su mayoría jóvenes y niños, perdieron la vida en el pánico al tratar de salir.

Artículo 1

(a) ¿Qué hacía María cuando ocurrió el accidente?
.... *(1)*

(b) ¿Dónde le dolía durante el día siguiente?
.... *(1)*

Artículo 2

(c) ¿Por qué se ha publicado hoy el informe sobre Mónica?
.... *(1)*

Artículo 3

(d) ¿Qué ha hecho Tim Woods exactamente?

.... (*1*)

(e) ¿De qué nacionalidad es?

.... (*1*)

Artículo 4

(f) ¿Por qué fue arrestado tan fácilmente Daniel Ortega?

.... (*1*)

Artículo 5

(g) ¿Cuál fue la causa de los veinte muertos en el cine?

.... (*1*)

(*Total: 7 marks*)

(MEG)

Question 21

Lee la información para los pasajeros en avión y contesta las preguntas **en español.**

VIAJE COMODO

Equipaje de Mano

A causa de la seguridad y comodidad en el avión tenemos que limitar el equipaje de mano de nuestros pasajeros. No obstante, bajo su custodia, y sin pagar más, Vd. puede llevar en cabina: una maleta cuyas medidas no superen los 100 cm (45 × 35 × 20 cm) y la mayor de sus dimensiones sea 55 cm, un bolso o cartera; un abrigo o manta de viaje; un paraguas, una máquina fotográfica y libros para el viaje. Los abrigos y los objetos más ligeros póngalos en los portaequipajes situados en la parte superior de la cabina, y el resto del equipaje debe ir bajo la butaca anterior a la suya.

Por último, les recomendamos que no metan en su equipaje de mano objetos como cuchillos, tijeras y armas, ya que les serían cogidos por los controles de seguridad antes de subir al avión.

(a) ¿Por qué se puede llevar en cabina sólo poco número de objetos?

....

.... (*2*)

(b) ¿Qué ropa se puede tener en el equipaje de mano?

....

.... (*1*)

(c) ¿Qué equipaje hay que poner debajo de una butaca? (Escribe **un** objeto).

....

.... (*1*)

(*Total: 4 marks*)

(NICCEA)

Question 22

In the United States, an experiment in the use of multi-media technology has been taking place, with great success.

LA TELEVISION INTELIGENTE

Los Willard escogieron en su televisor una película entre más de cincuenta que les ofrecía el cable de Time Warner. Luego, Karl decidió hacerse un sandwich y congeló la imagen en pantalla.

Aprovechando esto, Brad, 12 años, escogió un juego de vídeo de realidad virtual . . . pero su hermana Jacklyn le quitó el mando a distancia: quería conectar con Shopper Vision. En el supermercado tridimensional de la tele, Jacklyn encontró el champú que buscaba, y lo encargó para que se lo enviasen a domicilio al día siguiente.

Entonces Karl regresó, pero un amigo llamó al televisor para proponer una partida de naipes, que todos luego jugaron interactivamente.

Así nació la televisión del siglo XXI: una red inteligente e interactiva por la que los telespectadores se convertirán de auditorio pasivo en protagonistas de un mundo virtual en el que casi todo es posible.

You read this article in a Spanish newspaper and decide to use it as part of your class presentation. Write notes in **English** under the following headings.

(a) How the new TV system helped the Willards to plan their viewing for the evening.
.... *(1)*

(b) Why Karl delayed the start.
.... *(1)*

(c) How Brad took advantage of the delay.
.... *(1)*

(d) What use Jacklyn made of the technology.
.... *(1)*

(e) What further interruption occurred, and how it altered their plans for the evening.
....
.... (2)

(f) The major change for television viewers made possible by the new system.
....
.... (2)

(*Total: 8 marks*)
(Edexcel)

B, A, A* tasks

Question 23 En cada casilla pon la letra del párrafo que corresponde a la frase.

1. ***Noticia recibida de la policía de Sevilla.***
2. ***La chica en peligro mortal.***
3. ***La tragedia sucedió en una de las atracciones más populares.***
4. ***La culpa fue de la chica herida.***
5. ***Golpe en la cabeza.***
6. ***La tristeza de los sevillanos.***

Ejemplo: **1**	**2**	**3**	**4**	**5**	**6**
D					

A
El accidente entristeció a todos los ciudadanos que se divertían en la Feria.

B
El accidente ocurrió en la montaña rusa, una de las atracciones favoritas de la Feria.

C
Según los propietarios, el accidente fue ocasionado por una imprudencia de la joven.

D
SEVILLA – Una joven de 16 años resultó gravemente herida en un accidente ocurrido en la Feria de Sevilla, según nos informó ayer la Policía Local.

E
Al parecer, la joven se levantó, de modo que a gran velocidad se dió con la cabeza contra la estructura metálica de la montaña rusa.

F
La joven fue trasladada al hospital, donde los médicos dicen que se encuentra gravemente enferma.

(*5*)
(Edexcel)

Question 24

Tu amiga Beartriz ha hecho este test.
¿Cómo es Beatriz según cada contestación? Pon una 'X' en la casilla correcta.

1 ¿Serías capaz de aparecer en un vídeo musical?

- a Sí, pero sólo si es de mi grupo preferido.
- (b) No, me daría muchísimo corte.
- c Sí, sería vivir una experiencia que quizá nunca volvería a repetir.

ejemplo
Beatriz es

Tímida	X
Deportista	
Músico	
Valiente	
Religiosa	
Generosa	

2 Imagínate que has ganado un millón de pesetas. ¿Qué harías con el dinero?

- a Me pondría a contar el dinero muchas veces y me pensaría mil y una posibilidades para gastármelo en caprichos.
- b Lo ingresaría, en mi cuenta de ahorros, para que me rente, ya que en estos momentos no deseo comprarme nada.
- c Me gastaría la mitad en ropa y en mejorar mi físico. El resto lo dejaría para disfrutar de unas maravillosas vacaciones.
- (d) En primer lugar invitaría, por fin, a todos mis amigos a una fiesta.

2 Beatriz es

Tímida	
Deportista	
Músico	
Valiente	
Religiosa	
Generosa	

3 ¿En qué te gustaría ser una auténtica especialista?

- a En informática.
- b Domando felinos salvajes.
- c Hipnotizando personas.
- d Hablando muchos idiomas.
- e Leyendo la mano.
- (f) Tocando algún instrumento.

3 Beatriz es

Tímida	
Deportista	
Músico	
Valiente	
Religiosa	
Generosa	

4 ¿Sientes miedo de la oscuridad si estás sola?

- (a) No.
- b Sí, muchísimo.
- c A veces.

4 Beatriz es

Tímida	
Deportista	
Músico	
Valiente	
Religiosa	
Generosa	

(3)
(NEAB)

Question 25

Lees este artículo.

Cada país europeo castiga con penas distintas a los 'narcos'

Un narcotraficante detenido en Bélgica es castigado con cinco años de prisión. Si es arrestado en Alemania, la pena será de 15 años. Pero si ha cometido el delito en el Reino Unido, la condena será de cadena perpetua. Un drogodependiente no podrá curarse en centros de El Patriarca en Bélgica, porque allí fueron cerrados por 'falta de higiene' y 'malos tratos'. Pero sí podrá hacerlo en España, donde esta asociación funciona regularmente, con excepción de Cataluña. A partir de ejemplos de este tipo se ha planteado en Bruselas un debate sobre la necesidad de contar con un convenio común europeo sobre la droga.

(a) Rellena la tabla con la información correcta según el artículo.

	PAIS	SENTENCIA
(i)	Bélgica	....
(ii)	Alemania	....
(iii)	Reino Unido	....

(3)

(b) ¿Por qué cerraron los centros de El Patriarca en Bélgica?

....

.... *(2)*

(c) ¿En qué parte de España no se puede curarse en los centros?

.... *(1)*

(NEAB)

Question 26

Las frases de abajo son definiciones de palabras que se encuentran en el artículo. Busca en el texto las palabras definidas.

Veinte mil duros para un día en la Sevilla de la Expo

Sevilla **M.J.F.**

El coste de la estancia durante un día en la Sevilla de la Exposición Universal para una familia media forastera formada por un matrimonio con dos hijos y que decida alojarse en un hotel de tres estrellas se aproximará a las cien mil pesetas, según los cálculos que ya se realizan en el sector turístico sevillano. El presupuesto de esta familia prototípica para ese día de visita en la Sevilla del 92 sería el siguiente:

-Alojamiento en un hotel de tres estrellas a razón de dos habitaciones dobles por un precio unitario de 20.000 pesetas. Total, 40.000 pesetas una noche.

-Desayuno en el hotel para toda la familia: 3.800.

-Cuatro entradas de un día para visitar la Expo, a razón de cuatro mil pesetas por cabeza. Total, 16.000 pesetas.

-Desplazamiento a la Expo en taxi o tarifa del aparcamiento en caso de ir con vehículo propio: 1.000 pesetas.

-Almuerzo en el recinto de la Exposición Universal a razón de 3.500 pesetas el cubierto: 14.000 pesetas.

-Cena en la misma isla de la Cartuja al mismo precio por cubierto: 14.000 pesetas.

-Telecabina, torre panorámica y «souvenir» baratito: Mínimo, 10.000 pesetas.

No se contabilizan gastos diversos y más que probables, como consumiciones en los bares, kioscos y otros.

(a) monedas de cinco pesetas

.... *(1)*

(b) tiempo que permanece una persona en un sitio

.... *(1)*

(c) marido y mujer

.... *(1)*

(d) al precio de

.... *(1)*

(e) comida de los restaurantes a precio fijo

.... *(1)*

(WJEC)

Question 27 You read the following letter in the agony column of a Spanish magazine. It reminds you of the elder brother of a friend of yours, so you tell your friend the main points.

> Querida Dolores:
>
> ¡Acabo de darme cuenta de que mi hijo se ha convertido en un Yuppy! Tiene todas las características. Se dedica al dinero y a tener éxito. No almuerza por falta de tiempo y trabaja después de la jornada laboral.
>
> Viene raras veces a casa. Tiene su propio 'pisito' que ha sido fotografiado por una importante revista de decoración. Todo esto es aceptable pero lo que no puedo tolerar es que se dedica a analizar cuatro o cinco veces a la semana el valor de la vida que lleva.
>
> Por otra parte, el 'Yuppy' debe cobrar un sueldo fenomenal; pero mi hijo no se encuentra en esa categoría.
>
> Y ¡no me hables de la igualdad entre el hombre y la mujer! Según mi hijo, por ejemplo, si un hombre en su oficina tiene colocadas encima de su mesa las fotos de su esposa e hijos, es un hombre responsable que se preocupa por su familia. Pero si una mujer tiene tales fotos, entonces según mi hijo, su familia tiene prioridad sobre su trabajo. Si un hombre falta al trabajo por enfermedad, debe encontrarse muy mal. Si una mujer hace igual, 'tendrá un resfriadito'.
>
> ¿Qué se puede hacer con tal hijo?
>
> M J Avila

(a) When did the writer realize that her son was a yuppy? Tick **one** box only

A ☐ A long time ago.
B ☐ Last summer.
C ☐ Very recently.
D ☐ A few months ago. *(1)*

(b) Apart from money, what does her son dedicate his life to?

.... *(1)*

(c) Which statement best describes her son's attitude to his accommodation? Tick **one** box only.

A ☐ He only goes to his flat rarely because he is ashamed of it.
B ☐ He lives in a fashionable flat which has attracted publicity.
C ☐ He lives in a fashionable flat and does not draw attention to it.
D ☐ His flat is in need of decoration.

(1)

(d) How does the writer's son show himself to be sexist? Give two examples.

(i) ....
.... *(1)*

(ii) ....
.... *(1)*

(Total: 5 marks)

(MEG)

Question 28 Lee el artículo sobre las Playas de Bandera Azul.

PLAYAS BANDERA AZUL

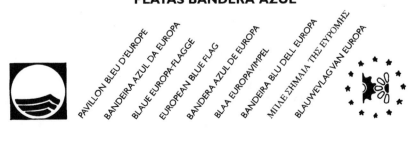

¿Qué espera de usted una Playa Bandera Azul?

> «Muchos millones de ciudadanos europeos viajan cada año para pasar sus vacaciones en las playas de otros países. No han esperado a 1992 para percibir toda Europa como su país. La Campaña Bandera Azul, con su objetivo de conseguir playas limpias y seguras en todas partes y para todo el mundo, es un signo real de solidaridad y una contribución práctica a la Europa de los ciudadanos.»
>
> (*Carlo Ripa di Meana, Italia, Miembro de la Comisión de las Comunidades Europeas, responsable del Medio Ambiente.*)

(a) Completa la siguiente frase rellenando el espacio en blanco con las palabras correctas: Según Carlo Ripa di Meana millones de ciudadanos europeos pasan sus vacaciones . . . (*1*)

(i) en el interior de otros países
(ii) cerca de una gran ciudad
(iii) lejos del ruido
(iv) en la costa

(b) Algunas de las características esperadas de una Playa Bandera Azul se encuentran en la lista que sigue. Pon una cruz en la casilla al lado de las características en que piensa Carlo Ripa de Meana. Tienes que poner 4 cruces. (*4*)

(i)	Limpieza de arena	☐	(vi)	Servicios sanitarios	☐
(ii)	Tiendas de recuerdos	☐	(vii)	Sitios para hacer camping	☐
(iii)	Restaurantes cerca de la playa	☐	(viii)	Pédalos	☐
(iv)	Sitios para jugar a los deportes	☐	(ix)	Recogida de basura	☐
(v)	Aguas limpias para bañarse	☐			

(WJEC)

ANSWERS TO PRACTICE QUESTIONS

G, F, E tasks

(Answers)

Q6 A los autocares.
Q7 Ascensor.
Q8 (The shop is) closed.
Q9 Carnicería.
Q10 (a) B
(b) C
(c) A
(d) D
Q11 (a) 19.30
(b) 21.30
(c) 18.30
(d) 00.30
Q12 X against B, C and E (*1 mark each*)
Q13 (a) Mentira
(b) Verdad
(c) Verdad
(d) Mentira
(e) Mentira
(f) Mentira
(g) Verdad
(h) Mentira
Q14 A
B 1
C
D 5

E 4
F 6
G 2
H 3

Q15 (a) Ana (C)
(b) Pedro (D)
(c) Dolores (A)
(d) Felipe (B)

Q16 A. Ha salido mal
B. Ha salido bien
C. Ha salido mal
D. Ha salido bien
E. Ha salido mal

D, C tasks

(Answers)

Q17 (a) Falso
(b) Falso
(c) Verdadero
(d) Verdadero
(d) Verdadero
(f) Falso

Q18 (a) Vivo en una calle estrecha cerca de Correos
(b) Mi casa es bastante grande con terraza
(c) Es un edificio moderno de dos pisos

Q19 1. No es necesario
2. Es necesario
3. No es necesario
4. Es posible
5. Es posible
6. Es posible
7. No es posible
8. Es posible

Q20 (a) Cocinando *OR* preparando una tortilla
(b) Hombro derecho
(c) Tiene 100 años
(d) Tocó discos durante 10 días seguidos
(e) Escocés
(f) No logró arrancar su coche
(g) El pánico *OR* Un loco gritó '¡Fuego!'

Q21 (a) (Para tener) seguridad
(Para tener) comodidad
(b) Un abrigo *OR* una manta
(c) Una maleta *OR* una bolsa *OR* un bolso *OR* una cartera

Q22 (a) It allowed them to select from about 50 films
(b) He wanted to make a sandwich
(c) He chose a virtual reality video game
(d) She found the shampoo she wanted *OR* Had shampoo delivered
(e) A friend called through the TV and they played cards together
(f) They are no longer passive viewers but can take an active part

B, A, A* tasks

(Answers)

Q23 2–F
3–B
4–C
5–E
6–A

Q24 2. Generosa
3. Músico
4. Valiente

Q25 (a) (i) 5 años de prisión
(ii) 15 años de prisión
(iii) Cadena perpetua
(b) Falta de higiene
Malos tratos
(c) Cataluña

Q26 (a) duros
(b) estancia
(c) matrimonio
(d) a razón de
(e) cubierto

Q27 (a) C
(b) *EITHER* power *OR* success
(c) B
(d) His attitude to family photos (on men's and women's desks)
His assumption that women are not really ill when off work

Q28 (a) (iv)
(b) X against (i), (v), (vi), (ix)

A STEP FURTHER

Make a list of any more buildings in a town that might be signposted or have signboards on them. Check that you would understand the Spanish if you saw those signs. Look through your text book for any more signs that you might see displayed in Spain. Then find half-a-dozen signs giving instructions and see if you can write down the other ways those instructions could have been expressed (addressing the people in the singular or plural, in familiar or formal ways, or using the infinitive).

Using the advice given in this chapter, make sure you can recognize the different verb tenses.

Look in a Spanish newspaper for some advertisements, particularly restaurant advertisements and small ads of items for sale. Can you understand the key points? Note down any phrases you find that you think might be helpful in understanding other similar advertisements in the future.

It is a good idea, from time to time, to take a Spanish newspaper or magazine, look at a few pages, particularly advertisements and news items (and possibly letters to the editor), and see how much you can understand without using a dictionary. Make a list of, say, 20 words that you had never seen before but that you were able to understand, simply from the context, the pictures, similarity with other words you know or by applying other techniques suggested in this chapter. Then look for about half-a-dozen sentences in which the subject comes after the verb (*see* Flexibility of Spanish Word Order, p. 127) and half-a-dozen sentences in which you can see the personal *'a'* being used.

Chapter 7

Writing

GETTING STARTED

Writing plays a very important part in learning a language. You do not have to produce perfect Spanish in order to score full marks. For the Foundation Tier, the emphasis is on 'getting the message across', which carries more marks than the quality of the Spanish used. The key questions are: **'Have you done all the tasks set?'** and **'Would a Spanish-speaker with no knowledge of English actually be able to understand what you have written?'**

For the Higher Tier, the examining boards are interested in:

- whether you 'get the message across';
- the accuracy of your Spanish;
- the overall quality and variety of expression.

Higher Writing is not intended to be easy but, if you know what is required, there is much you can do to prepare for the examination and to ensure that you gain positive marks.

If you are taking the Writing Coursework option (*see* Chapter 8), this chapter is still very relevant to you, as the tasks you will perform and the way your work will be assessed will be very similar to what happens in the Writing examination.

TOPIC	STUDY	REVISION 1	REVISION 2
The nature of the tasks			
Preparing for the examination			
In the examination			
Answering the questions			
Coping with problems			
G, F, E tasks			
D, C tasks			
Marking schemes/criteria for assessment			
The 'instant writing kit'			
B, A, A* tasks			
Examination questions			
Students' answers with examiner's comments			
Practice questions			
Specimen answers to practice questions			

WHAT YOU NEED TO KNOW

The nature of the tasks

In many cases, the tasks you have to do are the kind of things you have done to help you with learning the other skills. In the Foundation Tier they are designed to be fairly straightforward and predictable. Foundation Writing is not intended to be any more difficult than any of the other Foundation Tier tests.

All the examining boards require candidates to write a letter, normally within the Grade D and C tasks. The G, F and E tasks include writing lists, form-filling, writing diary entries, messages and post cards. In some cases this will involve filling gaps in a pre-printed text, or writing captions for pictures. Not all these types of task will be set each year.

B, A and A* tasks normally involve writing a short article, account or material for a brochure, though sometimes a second letter may be set. In all exercises there will be instructions as to what you should include, and how much you are required to write. Often the answer you have to provide will be outlined in Spanish and by means of pictures. You may be required to write a reply to a message, post card, or letter written in Spanish, so it is a good idea for you to get practice in reading and understanding Spanish handwriting.

Preparing for the examination

- Check the topic areas.
- Learn the vocabulary and structures required.
- Study as many specimen papers and past examination papers as possible.
- Devise a checklist which suits you, in order to check your work for accuracy and mistakes before and during the examination.
- Write as many practice letters and accounts as you can before the examination. Work to the times allowed in the examination and use your checklist.

Vocabulary

You cannot suddenly expect to sit down and learn 1500–2000 words. Be systematic and learn vocabulary regularly and in short bursts. 'A little but often' is a sensible approach. In addition, make sure you know how to use your dictionary correctly. More detailed advice on learning vocabulary and using a dictionary is given in Chapter 3.

Devising a checklist

It is important that the checklist you adopt is simple but thorough and that it also suits you. It should take particular account of the mistakes you make most frequently.

Outlined below is an example checklist for you to consider.

1. Have you answered the question including all the relevant information?
2. Have you kept within the word limits?
3. Have you checked your work for accuracy?

Verbs

- Do your verbs agree with their subjects?
  Mi hermana fue . . . *Mis padres fueron . . .*
- Have you chosen the right tense? In particular:
  Preterite for events; imperfect for states of affairs/habitual action.
- Have you chosen the right form of the verb?
  Entré (I went in). *Entró* (He/she went in).

Gender

- Do the articles agree with the nouns in number and gender?
  Las casas. *Un café.*
- Do pronouns agree with the nouns they replace?
  El hombre tenía una bolsa. La *dejó en el banco.*

Adjectives

- Do your adjectives agree with the nouns they describe?
  Una catedral antigua. *Unos folletos interesantes.*

Spellings

- Have you obeyed the key spelling rules?
  Particularly for *-c- -z- -qu- -j- -g-*
  Hice but *Hizo*
  Toqué but *Tocó*
  Jugué but *Jugó*
  Cogí but *Coja usted*
- Have you obeyed the accent rules?
  Particularly for verbs of the *pretérito grave* group
  Dije Dijo; *Puse Puso; Vine Vino*; *Estuve Estuvo* etc.

In the examination

It is helpful to have a plan of action – the things to do once you have been told that you may start the examination. Your teacher will no doubt have discussed the importance of this but here again are some useful reminders and suggestions that are worth considering.

1. Make a quick **note of any memory aids** or checklists you may wish to refer to, including **key expressions** you particularly hope to be able to use or expressions in which you have often made mistakes.
2. **Read the instructions** on the question paper carefully, and make a sensible choice (where appropriate) from the questions available.
3. **Allow enough time** for each question.
4. Allow enough time to **re-read and check** your work.
5. Check that you have answered **all aspects of the question.**
6. Check that you have kept **within the word limits.**
7. Finally, **check your work carefully for ACCURACY** – use your checklist.

Answering the questions

- **Plan** what you are going to write before you launch into the writing itself. This is especially important if you have to write your answer in a limited space, e.g. on a blank post card or notepad. There should be 'rough paper' for you to draft your answer. Make a note of key vocabulary and expressions to be included.
- You will need to **communicate the information** required in such a way that the person for whom the list, message, post card, letter, report or account is intended can understand clearly what you mean.
- Make sure that you **include all necessary information.** If there are five points listed for you to mention in your note, message, post card or letter, deal with all five. If you attend to only three, you can qualify for only three-fifths of the marks available.
- Make sure that what you write is **relevant to the question**. Reproducing material learnt by heart, however correct, will gain you no marks if it is not relevant to the question. If you have to write an account of an incident you saw in the street, the examiner does not wish to have to read a detailed account of the meal you had in a restaurant just before the incident. He or she is likely to put a red line straight through the irrelevant material and all you will then have achieved is to reduce the number of words in which you can show how good you are at writing Spanish.
- **Write clearly and legibly**. A well-presented script creates a favourable impression on examiners and is easier for them to mark. Anything they cannot read will obviously gain no marks! If you notice a mistake and wish to correct it, do so clearly and neatly. You will not get credit for anything an examiner cannot decipher!
- **Do not write anything in English.** You will be given credit only for what is written in Spanish, so don't just write an English word when in difficulty.
- **Use Spanish that you know**. Although it is sometimes tempting, don't think of what you want to say in English sentences and then try to translate them into Spanish. That is a recipe for disaster! It is a good idea to learn and remember vocabulary and grammar in set phrases and then to use the phrases as 'building blocks'. You almost certainly already do this to some extent. You know *quiero* means 'I should like' and you

know the Spanish for many items and for several expressions of quantity, so you can use *quiero* to ask for a whole range of things, including, for example, *Quiero un kilo de tomates*.

- It is important to **'show off' what you know**. The examiner can only award marks for what you have written, so make sure you reveal your knowledge as fully as you possibly can, in terms of range of vocabulary, idiom, construction, etc.
- Use your dictionary as little as possible to look up Spanish equivalents of English words. **Check very carefully the real meaning of any unfamiliar words you look up in the dictionary**. (*See* 'Using the dictionary' in Chapter 3.)
  IF YOU AREN'T SURE ABOUT IT, DON'T USE IT.
- Do use the dictionary, when necessary, to **check spellings and genders**.
- **Keep within the word limits** set for the question.
- **Try to use interesting material** wherever you can, but make sure it is relevant.
- Make sure you **check your work thoroughly**.

Coping with problems

With a dictionary you are not supposed to have major problems of vocabulary, but there could well be occasions when you are unsure which word to choose. It is usually disastrous to pick one at random, so, when in doubt, think how you can get round the difficulty:

- Do you know the opposite expression? If you were worried which word to use for 'stupid', you could say *no muy inteligente*.
- Can you explain what you mean without the key word? If you cannot remember whether you should say *se está bañando* or *está bañándose* (both are actually correct!), **you can still give the message that someone is bathing by writing:** *Está en la piscina* **or** *Está en el mar*.
  If you have to say that someone is going to telephone the day after tomorrow and you cannot remember or find *pasado mañana*, why not head your note *Lunes* and write: *Va a telefonear el miércoles?* (It's cheating, really! But it conveys the message very effectively.) If you are unsure how to use the word *hace* in order to say 'two hours ago', head your note with a time, *las 4 y media*, and refer to the event happening *a las dos y media*.
- Can you explain by using the word for a similar item? If you are unsure of the word for an overcoat (*abrigo*), you could write: *una chaqueta muy larga*. That might work but you would guarantee successful communication if you added . . . *que se usa para salir en invierno*.

An additional area that is worth considering is what to do if you are **uncertain of the correct form of a verb**. Let us suppose you wish to use the verb *poner*. You remember there is something unusual about it in the preterite tense but cannot remember exactly what form it takes. You may be able to check it in the verb section of your dictionary, but you could always use the verb *decidir* before it. Instead of writing: *Puse la bolsa en el suelo* you write *Decidí poner la bolsa en el suelo*.

Other verbs that you could use in this way include:

empezar a	e.g. *Empecé a andar*	I began to walk
tratar de	e.g. *Traté de explicar*	I tried to explain
no querer	e.g. *No quise decir . . .*	I refused to say . . .

It is a good idea to practise these strategies.

G, F, E tasks

Writing lists

Writing a list is really not much more than showing that you know certain items of vocabulary. Check the topic areas to be tested and learn the words! You can help yourself to learn the vocabulary by actually testing yourself regularly. You can also devise your own test lists to fit in with the kind of exercise you may have to complete in this section of the examination. Advice on learning vocabulary is given in Chapter 3. If you know the words, you will save a great deal of time that would otherwise be spent looking them up in the dictionary. You will also avoid all those mistakes that come from choosing the wrong one from a whole list in the dictionary.

The sort of list you will be required to write is likely to centre on the topic areas of shopping, clothing and personal belongings and free-time activities, though these may not be the only topics tested. Possible lists could be:

- Shopping for food and drink, e.g. for a party or picnic.
- Shopping for presents, e.g. to take home from Spain.
- Describing the contents of a lost bag or case.
- Activities undertaken, or to be undertaken, with a Spanish-speaking friend.

Apart from knowing the individual words, you may be required to give further information, e.g. stating an appropriate quantity or amount (for food and drink), using adjectives of size and colour or stating ages, e.g. to describe clothing. You could also be asked to name the shop where you would buy each item.

Remember to make sure that what you include in your list makes sense for the task. For instance, if you are writing a shopping list for a picnic, it is unlikely that you would expect to buy a ready-made paella! Nor is it likely that you would wish to take ten different things to drink and nothing to eat!

Make sure you do not repeat yourself. Each item you list will gain a mark only once. If you have to list five items of food and drink and the quantities of each, you could ask for

un paquete de . . . *una botella de . . .*
un kilo de . . . *un litro de . . .*
una lata de . . .

Form-filling

Form-filling often involves you in understanding the Spanish instructions or questions, so make sure you are clear about the difference between *nombre* (first name) and *apellido* (surname). You also need to understand *edad* (age), *fecha* (date), *domicilio* (home address), *firma* (signature). Dates you may be asked for include: *fecha de nacimiento* (date of birth), *fecha de llegada* (date of arrival), *fecha de salida* (date of departure). You could also be asked to list members of your family, any pets, your interests, subjects studied, likes and dislikes in food and drink, etc.

This is an area where the dictionary can be very useful if there is a word on the form that you do not understand or are not sure about.

Diary entries

Diary entries tend to be like lists, with the emphasis on activities and on the places where those activities take place. If the activities listed are plans for the future (e.g. what you will do on the different days when your penfriend will be staying with you), an infinitive will normally communicate very well, e.g.:

Jueves: Ir al centro. Comer en un restaurante.

If the diary entries are a record of what you have done, you will need to use the preterite tense, e.g:

Viernes: Fuimos a Londres. Visitamos la Torre.

You might get away with a noun, e.g.

Viernes: Excursión a Londres. Visita a la Torre.

The one danger with that is that there could be situations in which it was not clear whether the entry referred to something already done or something planned for the future.

Writing messages

The messages you have to write may not involve writing complete sentences – simple notes may be sufficient. Be careful, as always, to **check all the instructions** very carefully and cover all the tasks.

Again, refer to the topic areas tested by your Examining Board.

Some obvious possible messages could include:

- Leaving instructions for a Spanish-speaking visitor explaining to him/her how to get to a particular place.

- Noting down a telephone message, e.g. Pablo rang up, he wants to go to the cinema tonight; the film is very good; please can you ring him; he is at home until 6 o'clock.
- Explaining why you have gone out and where, when you will be back, etc.
- Making arrangements for some kind of activity, e.g. planning a trip to town, to a concert, football match.

In order to be able to leave the right kind of message, you will need to be able to give details such as:

- Directions and places, e.g. *la primera calle a la derecha, todo recto, en el café.*
- Methods of transport, e.g. *a pie, en autobús/en tren/en taxi.*
- Times and dates, e.g. *a las cuatro y media, por la tarde, el viernes.*
- Duration, e.g. *durante cinco minutos, durante media hora.*
- Activities of interest, e.g. *ir al cine, ir a un concierto, jugar al tenis.*
- Simple instructions/suggestions/invitations, e.g. *¿Quieres ir a la discoteca?*

The above is not intended to be a complete list, but rather to show some examples of the kind of message to expect.

One area that can be a problem is verb tenses. You **must** make clear whether María has gone to the disco (*Ha ido a la dicoteca* OR *Está en la discoteca*) or is going to go (*Va a ir a la discoteca* or simply *Va a la discoteca*).

Writing post cards

As before, check all the instructions fully. You may have to write your answer on a blank post card printed in the question paper. This means you have to plan what you are going to write very carefully, and stick closely to the word limits.

It is normal to name the place (not the full address) you are writing from and put the date (in Spanish!) at the top. A good opening is *¡Hola!* or possibly *¿Qué tal?* Obviously, you also sign the card at the end. You may choose to write *Un abrazo de* before your signature. What comes in between the opening and the end will depend on what you are told to do in the question paper but there are some fairly obvious things that you could be required to say:

- Where you are.
- What sort of accommodation you are in (hotel, campsite, youth hostel etc.).
- When you arrived.
- Who you are with.
- How long you are staying there.
- What the weather is like.
- What you do (e.g. every day).
- What you have done since your arrival.
- What you plan/want to do (tomorrow, next week).
- What the food is like.
- What the hotel, campsite etc. is like.
- People you have met there.
- Whether/why you are enjoying yourself.

D, C tasks

The nature of the tasks

For Grades D and C you are required to write a passage in continuous sentences, normally of about 80 to 100 words. It is very likely to be a letter, so make sure you know how to begin and end a letter correctly (see below). There may even be some marks allocated for the beginning and ending of your letter, so make sure you do get those marks; they are among the easiest marks to acquire, provided you have prepared yourself properly.

At this level you are expected to use **different tenses** appropriately to write about **past, present and future** events.

You are also expected to express **opinions**.

Writing letters

It is important to be sure from the outset whether your letter is:

(a) **Informal** – to a friend of about your own age.
(b) **Semi-formal** – to an adult acquaintance.
(c) **Formal** – to someone in an official position whom you do not know well.

This will determine how you begin and end the letter. In all cases, though, you will begin by putting the name of the place you are writing from (not the full address) at the top right-hand corner, followed by the date. All letters end, of course, with a signature.

Informal letters

These **begin**:

Querido . . . : (*with a boy's name in place of the dots*) OR
Querida . . . : (*with a girl's name in place of the dots*)

You need to have two or three Spanish boys' names and two or three girls' names you can be sure of spelling correctly.

A typical **ending** is:

Un abrazo de . . . (*followed by the signature, on the next line*).

The content of the letter will be very similar to the subjects listed for post cards, but you will have to write rather more. You could well be asked to give information about yourself, your family or your house, about a recent incident (such as a party, a meal out, an accident), about your school or college. You might have to issue, accept or decline an invitation or make arrangements to meet the other person. You might have to thank your friend for a present or you might have to thank him/her and his/her parents for a good holiday at their house and say something about your return journey.

Remember, in an informal letter you address the person you are writing to as *tú*.

Semi-formal letters

A good **beginning** for these is:

Estimado . . . : (*with a man's name in place of the dots*)
Estimada . . . : (*with a woman's name in place of the dots*)

The names need to have a title (*señor/señora* + surname OR *don/doña* + first name), e.g.:

Estimado don José:

It is also a good idea to have two or three typical Spanish surnames you can guarantee to spell correctly (e.g. *Díaz, Rodríguez* or *Gómez*).

A typical **ending** for this sort of letter is:

Un afectuoso saludo de . . . (*followed by the signature, on the next line*).

The content is likely to be very much like that listed for informal letters but remember that you address the person you are writing to as *usted* (or *Vd.*).

Formal letters

These normally **begin**:

Muy señor mío: (= *Dear Sir*)
Muy señores míos: (= *Dear Sirs*)
Distinguida señora: (= *Dear Madam*)

Typical **endings** would be:

Le saluda atentamente (*followed, on the next line, by the signature*) to a man.
Les saluda atentamente (*followed, on the next line, by the signature*) to more than one person.
Reciba un respetuoso saludo de (*followed, on the next line, by the signature*) to a woman.

The content of such a letter is likely to be a request for information about holiday facilities, booking accommodation, making arrangements for a visit as part of town twinning, reporting or enquiring about lost property or possibly complaining about things that were unsatisfactory at the hotel you stayed in. It could also be a letter of application for a job (usually in response to an advertisement).

Remember that you address the person you are writing to as *usted* (or *Vd.*).

Marking schemes/criteria for assessment

The examining boards seek to reward answers by marking positively across three main areas. In some cases the emphasis is slightly different, and the three areas listed below are sometimes merged to form just two areas. Find out exactly what your board is doing. You may also be able to obtain a copy of their marking scheme. The three main areas are:

1. Communication.
2. Accuracy.
3. Quality of expression.

It is worth considering these aspects in more detail.

1. Communication

This refers to the extent to which the relevant information is conveyed to the reader. Do you cover all the tasks and make yourself understood? Remember, if there are five tasks specified and you include only three of them in your letter, you can be awarded only three-fifths of the marks for communication (and, because communication is the main purpose of writing, there could also be a rule that says you cannot be awarded more than that proportion of the marks for accuracy and quality of expression).

2. Accuracy

This refers to the extent to which grammatical accuracy helps to convey the relevant information. Do you just manage to get the message across, or are you able to communicate the message clearly in largely correct Spanish? Do your verbs agree with their subjects? Have you used the correct forms and tenses? Do your adjectives agree with their nouns? Is your spelling correct?

Remember that you must show that you can use different tenses.

3. Quality of expression

This is the extent to which the language you use helps to make your writing interesting and appropriate to the task. Do you use a variety of vocabulary, idioms, grammatical structures? Does your writing show coherence as a whole?

The 'instant writing kit'

Writing with variety and accuracy can be made much easier if you have your own set of useful phrases that you know are correct and that you can use in a wide range of different situations. You do not have to find or invent a whole lot of new structures for each writing task you do. You can develop your own **'Instant Writing Kit'**.

It is a good idea to see how many of the useful phrases you used in your last piece of written work can be re-used in the next – but do make sure that what you write is relevant to the task in hand.

Some people find it helpful to write the essential facts in as few words as possible and then to add useful phrases to improve the style of their writing, while bringing the total number of words up to the limit set.

As an example, let us consider part of a letter in which you have to mention a recent event. You decide to mention the meal you had in a restaurant to celebrate your friend's birthday, so you write:

Fui a un restaurante. Era el cumpleaños de mi amigo.

You now try to slot as many additional pieces of good (and relevant) Spanish as you can into those two sentences:

La semana pasada, precisamente el jueves por la tarde, fui con mi amigo David a un restaurante muy bueno y bastante famoso. Era el cumpleaños de mi amigo, que tiene dieciséis años, es muy simpático y vive a unos tres kilómetros de mi casa.

A quick check now reveals that your original 10 words have become 42. More importantly, the extra 32 words are all expressions you know to be correct Spanish, the sentences have become more interesting and the quality of the writing has been improved. (And, although all the additional expressions can be pre-learnt, it is not possible for an examiner to decide you have introduced irrelevant material.) The sentences look more complex but, in fact, you have used a sort of 'building block' technique. In the first sentence the following expressions:

la semana pasada,
por la tarde,
con mi amigo David,
muy bueno,
bastante famoso,

can each be included or omitted without in any way affecting the structure of the sentence itself. The one exception is *precisamente el jueves*, which clearly depends on *la semana pasada* for its meaning and which is essential if *por la tarde* is to have any real meaning. Each of the phrases includes more than one item that will improve your mark for quality of language. For example, *por la tarde* includes the correct agreement of *la* with *tarde* and good use of the preposition *por*. The phrase *bastante famoso* includes the correct (masculine singular) agreement of *famoso* with *restaurante* and good use of the adverb *bastante*.

You can build up your own set of useful phrases, beginning with the ones above and including the phrases added to the second sentence. Remember, you are dealing in phrases, not whole sentences.

Just to get you started, here are a few more suitable phrases:

(des)afortunadamente *(un)fortunately*
Hace dos semanas *two weeks ago*
tres horas más tarde *three hours later*
como llovía *as it was raining*
como hacía buen tiempo *as the weather was fine*
con mucho cuidado *very carefully*
sin dificultad *without difficulty*
bastante despacio *quite slowly*
no obstante *nevertheless*
a pesar de la dificultad *in spite of the difficulty*
cuando me di cuenta *when I realized*

B, A, A* tasks

For these grades a further writing task of 120 to 150 words is set. As for Grades D and C, candidates are required to narrate events and express opinions. You are also expected to justify ideas and points of view. The task is likely to require descriptive or imaginative work, including the use of a range of tenses. It could be a report of an event, an article for a magazine or some sort of publicity material. It might be a letter or part of a letter. If it is a whole letter, you must begin and end it correctly. If it is not a whole letter, don't waste time and words making it look like one.

The skills involved are really the same as those required for D and C tasks (with the addition of **justifying ideas and points of view**), so we shall not be considering them separately, but the **number of words** to be written is **greater** and there is an expectation that candidates will demonstrate a higher level of **accuracy** and a **wider range of expression** than would be expected of a Grade C candidate.

EXAMINATION QUESTIONS

You are recommended to try the questions yourself before looking at the Students' Answers with Examiner's Comments, which are on pages 160–163.

G, F, E tasks

Question 1 ***List question***

Estás en un camping. Haz una lista de la comida y las bebidas que vas a comprar.
Ejemplo: *Queso*

1. ....
2. ....
3. ....
4. ....
5. ....
6. ....

Question 2 ***Diary question***

Tu amigo/a español/a te va a visitar. Le mandas una lista de tus planes para la semana.

Día	*Actividad*
Lunes	**Ejemplo:** *Salir al restaurante*
Martes	
Miércoles	
Jueves	
Viernes	
Sábado	
Domingo	

Question 3 ***Message***

Estás en casa de tu amigo/a español/a. Vas a salir esta mañana sin él/ella. Escríbele una nota (aproximadamente 30 palabras). Dile:

- Adónde piensas ir.
- Cómo vas a viajar.
- Por qué tienes que ir allí.
- A qué hora vas a salir.
- A qué hora vas a volver. (Edexcel)

Question 4 ***Post card***

Estás de vacaciones. Escribe una postal (30–40 palabras) a tu amigo/a en España. Incluye la información siguiente:

- Dónde estás.
- El tiempo que hace.
- Descripción del hotel.
- Lo que has hecho.
- Lo que vas a hacer mañana.

D, C tasks

Question 5 ***Informal letter***

Tu amigo/a español/a te ha escrito felicitándote en tu cumpleaños. Escríbele una carta incluyendo la información siguiente:

- adónde fuiste en tu cumpleaños
- lo que hiciste
- el regalo de tus padres

- la música que te gusta
- dónde la oyes
- detalles de otros dos regalos que recibiste
- por qué te gustó cada uno
- lo que harás la semana que viene

Question 6 *Replying to an informal letter*

Lee la carta de tu amiga española.

Escribe una carta a Juana, según los puntos indicados abajo. Hay que escribir 80 palabras, más o menos.

(a) Contesta todas las preguntas en la carta de Juana.
(b) Escribe lo que tomaste en el almuerzo del domingo pasado (comida y bebida).
(c) Haz dos preguntas a Juana sobre la comida española

Albacete, 3 de mayo

¡Hola!

Muchas gracias por tu carta que recibí hace unos días. Va a alegrarnos mucho darte la bienvenida en el mes de julio. Mi madre quiere saber algo de tus costumbres en casa.

Por ejemplo, ¿a qué hora te levantas cuando no hay clase? Nosotros comemos poco en el desayuno. ¿Y tú? ¿Qué te gusta más comer al mediodía? En España cenamos muy tarde – a las diez por regla general. ¿Comes mucho por la noche? Aquí la tortilla es estupenda – ¿La has comido alguna vez? Se dice que los ingleses no beben mucho vino en casa. ¿Qué te gusta beber?

Bueno, espero con impaciencia tu visita.

Recuerdos a tus padres,

Juana

(30)
(NICCEA)

Question 7 *Formal letter*

Dejaste un artículo en un tren español. Escribe una carta a la RENFE, incluyendo la información siguiente:

- descripción del artículo
- por qué no lo quieres perder
- el tren en el que lo dejaste
- por qué no has podido ir a la oficina de objetos perdidos
- lo que deben hacer si lo tienen

B, A, A* tasks

Question 8

Tu hermana está en el hospital después de un accidente de bicicleta causado por un animal. Escribe un párrafo contando lo que ocurrió y tu visita al hospital. Explica y justifica tu opinión sobre el incidente.

STUDENTS' ANSWERS WITH EXAMINER'S COMMENTS

G, F, E tasks

Question 1

Student's answer

1. *el pan*
2. *la hamburgesa*
3. *el ramon*
4. *la agua de minerale*
5. *la cerveza*
6. *el vino*

Examiner's comments

1. Fine.
2. There should be a *u* after the *g*, but the meaning is absolutely clear.
3. No. I think you meant *jamón*, but what you have written is meaningless.
4. The Spanish is not very accurate – the word *de* should not be there, nor should the final *e* – but the answer would be very clear to a Spaniard. (You should use *el* before a stressed *a*, even for feminine words, but in fact there was no need to put *el* or *la* with any of these answers.)
5. *Good.*
6. *Good.*

Question 2

Student's answer

Martes: *Ir al parque*
Miércoles: *Juego al tenis*
Jueves: *Comprar régalos*
Viernes: *Visitar cathedral*
Sábado: *Ir al cine*
Domingo: *Voy al parque*

Examiner's comments

Martes:	Fine.
Miércoles:	Would be better as *jugar al tenis*, but acceptable.
Jueves:	Fine (though the accent should not be there).
Viernes:	Fine (though *catedral* does not have an *h* in Spanish).
Sábado:	*Good.*
Domingo:	This is really the same as your first answer. You can't count it twice. (*Total mark: 5 out of 6.*)

Question 3

Student's answer:

Voy a las tiendas. Viajar en autobús. Comprar regalos para mi famillia.
Salir: a las diez horas y quarto.
Volver: a las mediodía.

Examiner's comments

This answer communicates well and you will score good marks for that. The use of *Voy* in the first sentence makes quite clear it is you who are going. (If you had written *Ir a las tiendas*, the whole message would have been less clear.) Ideally you would have put *Voy a* at the beginning of each sentence. *Autobús* should have an accent. *Familia* has only one *l*. The word *horas* should be omitted from the time and *cuarto* is spelt with a *c* not a *q*. The last part should be *al mediodía*. (I hope you meant this to be the middle part of the day – between, say, 12.00 and 2.00 – and not 'midday'. Since your answer makes sense, we must assume that what you intended is what it says.)

Question 4

Student's answer

Estás (1) en Alicante. El tiempo (2) hace muy bueno y mucho calor. El hotel es grande y moderno. Has ido (3) mucho a la playa. Mañana ir (4) de compras y comer en un restuarante (5).

Examiner's comments

Even though most Spaniards would probably understand you, that is not certain, since you have told your friend the s/he (instead of you) is in Alicante and has gone to the beach. For this reason you cannot be given good marks for communication. Specific language points:

1. You should have *Estoy* instead of *Estás*.
2. You should omit *El tiempo*.
3. It should be *He ido*.
4. This is not actually a sentence and does not make absolutely clear who will go and eat. If you insert *voy a* before *ir* it will solve the whole problem.
5. Correct spelling: *restaurante*.

D, C tasks

Question 5

Student's answer

Southampton,
el 3 de julio

Querido José:
Gracias por tu amable carta. En mi cumpleaños fui con mis padres y mi hermano a un restaurante. El restaurante es bastante grande y muy bueno. Había mucha gente allí. Comimos estupendamente. Quiero volver allí el año que viene porque me gustó tanto.

Mis padres me daron (1) un estéreo magnífico. Me gusta mucho la musica (2) rock. Tengo muchos de (3) discos y los eschucho (4) en mi dormitorio. Mi dormitorio es grande y bonito. Tiene las paredes azules y las cortinas grises. Hay una cama, un armario, una mesa y una silla. También tengo allí muchos libros.

Un abrazo de
Jeffrey

Examiner's comments

This is a piece of very accurate Spanish, with only three real errors and a missed accent: (1) *daron* should be *dieron*; (2) accent missed on *música*; (3) *de* should not be there; (4) misspelling of *escucho*. The style is simple but there are several adjectives, all agreeing correctly with the nouns they describe, and there is good use of *bastante* and *estupendamente*. Overall it looks a good performance. But just a minute! The description of the bedroom is totally irrelevant to the question – so there can be no marks at all for those 29 words. The description of the restaurant and the wish to go there again can probably be accepted as just relevant, but there is no mention of two other presents received, why you liked them or of what you will do next week. So, of the ten things required in the instructions, five are missing and you cannot really expect to score more than half marks. By omitting all reference to next week, you have also failed to show your ability to refer to future events (which is one of the expectations for Grade C).

Question 6 *Student's answer*

Belfast,
el 15 de mayo

Querida Juana:
Muchas gracias por tu carta que recibí la semana passada (1).
Normalemente (2) me levanto a las ocho y media cuando no hay clase. En el desayuno como tostadas y bebo té. Al mediodía como carne y patatas. Por la noche no como mucho.
El domingo passado (3) comí un filete con patatas fritas y guisantes y bebí Coca-Cola. Me gusta mucho la Coca-Cola.
Se bebe mucho vino con la comida en España? (4) A que (5) hora comes en casa?

Recuerdos a tus padres,
Chris

Examiner's comments

Quite a competent performance, which will score good marks, even though you have failed to answer the question about Spanish omelette. (You also appeared to have overlooked the question about what you like to drink, but then covered it later.) Specific language points: (1) only one *s* in *pasada*; (2) the correct spelling is *normalmente*; (3) at least you are consistent, so the second misspelling of the same word should not count against you; (4) you have omitted the opening question mark (¿) for both your questions. (5) the accent is missing from *qué*.

Question 7 *Student's answer*

Birmingham,
el 3 de septiembre

Querido señor:
La semana pasada fui en el tren de Sevilla a Madrid. Viajó (1) el lunes en el tren de la tarde que sale de Sevilla a las dos y media y dejó (2) una bolsa de cuero color marrón cuando bajé. Me gusta mucho la bolsa porque me la regaló mi hermana mayor por Navidad. Contiene tres libros, ropa y varias postales de Madrid. No fue posible ir a la oficina de objetos perdidos porque tenía que volver a Inglaterra al día siguiente.
Si usted encuentra la bolsa, por favor mandarla por correo.
Un abrazo de
Lucy Wilson

Examiner's comments

A comparatively simple and straightforward letter. All points have been dealt with effectively, so full marks for that. There is some effective use of 'Instant Writing Kit' style phrases (e.g. *la semana pasada, al día siguiente*) and the Spanish is generally very accurate. The grammatical corrections to be made are: (1) *viajé*; (2) *dejé*. A serious point: the beginning and ending are inappropriate for a formal letter (check earlier in this chapter, p. 155) and marks will be lost for that. Overall though, quite a competent performance that scores good marks.

B, A, A* tasks

Question 8 Student's answer

> *Querido José:*
>
> *El lunes passado por la mañana saliba con mi hermana para ir a las tiendas. En el calle cerca el centro cuidad Mary tuvó un accidente porque un perro atacó ella. Se caió del bicicleta y rompió la pierna. El perro era muy grande y era marrón. El hombre con el perro muy asusto y ayudo. Yo llamo la ambulancía que vinó cinco minutos después y llevó Mary al hospital. Mis padres muy asusto. Compran flores y compro uvas. Visitamos Mary en la hospital por la tarde. Está en la hospital por una semana.*
>
> *Un abrazo de*
> *Adrian*

Examiner's comments

This answer is surprisingly easy to understand, in spite of the poor quality of the Spanish, and it will score quite a good mark for Communication. On the other hand, the language really is not good enough for this level. Most of the verbs are wrong and some are in the present tense instead of the preterite. This candidate does not know about the personal 'a', is inconsistent in deciding the gender of *hospital* and has invented the expression *muy asusto* (and used it twice). There are one or two good accurate phrases (e.g. *por la mañana, por la tarde, para ir a las tiendas*) and the description of the dog is entirely accurate! The instructions were quite specific that this was to be a paragraph, not a letter, so the beginning and ending should not have been included. The requirement to express and justify an opinion has not been met.

In the interests of accuracy, here is the same piece of work corrected and extended to include the missing points (though without any attempt to increase the range of expressions used).

> *El lunes pasado por la mañana salí en bicicleta con mi hermana para ir a las tiendas. En la calle, cerca del centro de la ciudad, Mary tuvo un accidente, porque un perro la atacó. Se cayó de la bicicleta y se rompió la pierna. El perro era marrón y muy grande. El hombre que estaba con el perro se asustó mucho y ayudó. Yo llamé para pedir una ambulancia, que llegó cinco minutos después y llevó a Mary al hospital. Mis padres se asustaron mucho. Compraron flores y yo compré uvas. Visitamos a Mary en el hospital por la tarde. Se quedará en el hospital durante una semana. Un accidente como éste no debe ocurrir. Debe ser posible salir sin el peligro de ser atacado. El hombre no debe salir con un perro peligroso.*

PRACTICE QUESTIONS

Specimen answers to several of these questions appear on pages 169–170.

G, F, E tasks

Question 9 List question

Has dejado una bolsa en el autobús. Escribe una lista de 5 artículos diferentes que contenía, con una descripción de cada uno:

	Artículo	*Descripción*
Ejemplo:	*toalla*	*verde*
1.		

2. ______
3. ______
4. ______
5. ______

(*10*)

Question 10 ***Form-filling question***

Rellena el formulario con tu información personal

NACIONALIDAD	(*1*)
ANIMALES EN CASA	(*1*)
ASIGNATURA PREFERIDA EN EL COLEGIO	(*1*)
COLOR DE OJOS	(*1*)
DEPORTE PREFERIDO	(*1*)
PASATIEMPO FAVORITO	(*1*)
OTROS PASATIEMPOS	(*1*)
COMIDA QUE NO TE GUSTA	(*1*)
COMIDA QUE TE GUSTA	(*1*)
BEBIDA QUE TE GUSTA	(*1*)

(*Total: 10 marks*)
(MEG)

Question 11 ***Diary question***

Mandas a tu amigo/a en España una lista de lo que hiciste durante una semana de vacaciones. Escribe una actividad diferente para cada día.

Día	*Actividad*
Lunes	**Ejemplo:** *Jugué al tenis*
Martes	
Miércoles	
Jueves	
Viernes	
Sábado	
Domingo	

(*6*)

Question 12 *Message*

Tu amigo español llegó a tu casa ayer. Esta mañana, tú tienes que salir, pero ¡tu amigo está todavía en la cama! Le escribes un mensaje.

Escribe unas 25 palabras, e incluye la información siguiente:

¿Dónde? Tú

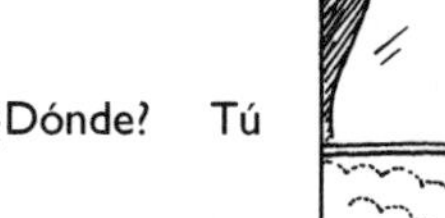

SUPERMERCADO

¿A qué hora?

Desayuno ¿qué? ¿dónde?

Sugerencias para la mañana

¿Qué programa?

(MEG)

Question 13 *Post card*

Estás enfermo/a durante tus vacaciones en Valencia. Ahora no podrás visitar a tu amigo/a en Burgos durante el viaje de vuelta. Escribe una postal contándole lo que ha pasado y qué planes tienes ahora.

(SEG)

Question 14 *Post card*

Escribe una postal respondiendo a las preguntas de tu amigo español.

Valencia, 3 de julio

¿Qué tal? Aquí hace mucho calor. ¿Qué tiempo hace en Inglaterra? ¿Cuándo vas de vacaciones? Y ¿adónde vas? ¿Qué te gusta hacer cuando estás de vacaciones? Yo lo estoy pasando muy bien.

Carlos

Question 15 *Post card (text-completion)*

Escribe un párrafo en español sobre tu casa.
Rellena los espacios de palabras adecuadas (30 palabras más o menos).

Hay que escribir el párrafo entero.

Nuestra casa está situada ___________. Es un edificio ___________________________ .

Tiene ___________ habitaciones (aparte del cuarto de baño). Son ___________ ___________ . En mi dormitorio hay ___________ . Para ayudar a mis padres tengo que ___________ y ___________ .

(20)
(NICCEA)

D, C tasks

You are recommended to ignore any word limits mentioned in the following questions and to work to the word limits set by the examining board for the papers *you* will take. There is an outline answer to Question 16 *only* on p. 169 to give you an idea of what is expected for *all* the questions.

Question 16 *Informal letter*

Tu amiga española te escribe una carta y te pregunta:

¿Dónde recibiste tu experiencia laboral?
¿Qué hiciste exactamente?
¿Cuáles eran tus horas de trabajo?
¿Qué aspectos del trabajo te gustaron?
¿Qué no te gustó?
¿Pasó algo interesante?
¿Qué trabajo buscarás al final de tus estudios?
¿Por qué te interesa ese trabajo?

Escribe una carta contestando a las preguntas de tu amiga.

Question 17 *Informal letter*

Escribe una carta a tu amigo español incluyendo la información siguiente:

- un accidente que tuvo tu hermano
  - lo que ocurrió
  - las heridas que sufrió
  - dónde está ahora
  - tu opinión sobre el hospital
- tus planes para el fin de semana
  - lo que harás
  - dónde
  - con quién(es)

Question 18 *Replying to an informal letter*

Lee esta carta de tu amigo español. Escríbele una carta contestando a todas sus preguntas.

Murcia,
el 15 de julio

¡Hola!
Gracias por tu carta, que recibí ayer. Acabo de pasar dos semanas en casa de mis tíos. Es muy grande. ¿Cómo es tu casa? ¿Prefieres un piso o un chalé? ¿Por qué?
Yo ya estoy de vacaciones. ¿Cómo fueron tus exámenes? ¿Tuviste algún problema? A mí no me gustan los exámenes.
Dentro de dos semanas iremos de vacaciones. Dime algo de tus planes para las vacaciones. ¿Adónde irás? ¿Con quiénes? Y ¿qué harás? ¿Cómo viajaréis? Y ¿dónde os alojaréis?
Escríbeme pronto.
Recuerdos a tus padres.
Un abrazo de
Luis

Question 19 *Formal letter*

Quieres ir a España este verano pero no tienes dinero. Buscas un trabajo en España. En un periódico español, ves este anuncio.

Necesito estudiantes ingleses
para trabajar en hoteles
durante el verano
Se exige ... buena salud
idiomas extranjeros
buenas referencias
Escribe con detalles a:
Sr Moreno
Calle Goya 4-3-A
Madrid

Escribe una carta de unas 100 palabras al Sr Moreno. Incluye la información siguiente:

- información personal, edad, etc;
- tus estudios de español y otros idiomas;
- tu experiencia en otros trabajos que has hecho;
- preguntas sobre el trabajo en el hotel (por ejemplo, dinero, horas . . .);
- las fechas en que puedes trabajar

(MEG)

B, A, A* tasks

Question 20 Tu tío es Director de Turismo de una ciudad o región de Gran Bretaña y quiere mandar un folleto a España para atraer a los turistas españoles.

Escribe el texto del folleto. Tu tío te ha escrito unas notas sobre las posibilidades.

Question 21 Una clase española quiere saber cómo se celebran los cumpleaños en Gran Bretaña. Escribe una carta en español y menciona los detalles siguientes (menciona dos detalles cada vez):

- lo que hacemos aquí para celebrar los cumpleaños
- los regalos que recibiste para tu último cumpleaños y de quién
- cómo pasaste el día de tu último cumpleaños
- lo mejor de tu día
- tus planes para tu próximo cumpleaños

(WJEC)

Question 22 Pasaste las vacaciones en Puerto de la Cruz, en las islas Canarias (donde se habla español). Ahora tu profesor de español quiere que escribas un artículo para la revista del colegio describiendo tus experiencias. Puedes mencionar:

- con quién fuiste;
- dónde te quedaste;
- tus impresiones del pueblo;

- lo que visitaste;
- lo que hiciste;
- la vida nocturna;
- un incidente o accidente que te pasó;
- y otros detalles y descripciones.

Te puedes servir del mapa turístico para ayudarte.

(MEG)

Question 23 Acabas de pasar una semana en un colegio español. Tienes que escribir un artículo para la revista del colegio español, dando tus impresiones y comparándolo con tu propio colegio. Escribe aproximadamente 150 palabras.

Hiciste estas notas:

> **La vida escolar**
>
> Mañana: clases de 9.00 a 12.30, con recreo de 30 minutos.
> Comida: no hay cantina. Los chicos van a casa.
> Tarde: clases de 16.00 a 18.00.
> Dos horas de deberes al día.
> Jueves tarde: no hay clase.
> Sábado mañana: hay clase.
> Vacaciones de verano: desde finales de junio hasta septiembre.
> Dos semanas de vacaciones en Navidad, y dos en Semana

(20)
(Edexcel)

SPECIMEN ANSWERS TO PRACTICE QUESTIONS

The answers that follow are examples of how the Practice Questions could be answered. They are not 'the correct answer' – there are countless correct ways of answering writing questions – but they do communicate all the necessary information and they are written in grammatically accurate Spanish. The language has been deliberately kept quite straightforward.

G, F, E tasks

Question 9 (Answer)

bañador	azul
calcetines	blancos
libro	grande
botella	llena de gaseosa
bolígrafo	pequeño

Question 10 (Answer)

Británica	ir a la discoteca
un perro y un gato	el cine y la televisión
el español	el pescado
azules	hamburguesas con patatas fritas
el tenis	la Coca-Cola

Question 11 (Answer)

Martes:	Fui al parque
Miércoles:	Vi la televisión
Jueves:	Compré un libro
Viernes:	Fui al cine
Sábado:	Salí con mis amigos
Domingo:	Escribí cartas

Question 12 (Answer)

Voy al supermercado.
Vuelvo a la una.
Hay pan, mantequilla y zumo de naranja en la cocina.
Puedes leer o ver el programa de deportes.

Question 13 (Answer)

Valencia, 20 de agosto

¿Qué tal? Lo siento mucho, pero no puedo ir a Burgos. Estoy enfermo. Tengo que estar en la cama durante tres días. Después tengo que volver directamente a Inglaterra.

Peter

Question 14 (Answer)

Sheffield, 13 de julio

Hola. ¿Qué tal? Yo estoy bien. Hace buen tiempo aquí. Voy de vacaciones en agosto. Voy a Francia. Me gusta nadar y bailar.

Mary

Question 15 (Answer)

Nuestra casa está situada en el centro del pueblo. *Es un edificio* pequeño y moderno. *Tiene* cuatro *habitaciones* (*aparte del cuarto de baño*). *Son* dos dormitorios, el cuarto de estar y la cocina. *En mi dormitorio hay* una cama, una mesa y una silla. *Para ayudar a mis padres tengo que fregar* los platos *y* hacer las camas.

D, C tasks

Question 16 (Answer)

Exeter,
el 3 de febrero

Querida Teresa:
Recibí tu carta la semana pasada. Gracias.

Tienes razón – todos tenemos que recibir experiencia laboral. Yo estuve en una compañía de seguros, trabajando de las nueve de la mañana hasta las cinco y media de la tarde. Tuve que escribir cartas, preparar documentos y organizar papeles. Lo más interesante fue salir a ver los coches que había que reparar después de un accidente y lo más aburrido fue poner todas las cartas en sobres por la tarde.

Al final de mis estudios buscaré trabajo en un polideportivo. Me interesan mucho todos los deportes.

Un abrazo de
Karen

B, A, A* tasks

Use the specimen answers to Questions 20 and 21 as a guide on which to model your own answers. No answers have been provided for Questions 22 and 23.

Question 20 (Answer)

Ven a Mytown a pasar las vacaciones. Con 32 hoteles de lujo, a menos de dos horas en autocar del aeropuerto de Londres, Mytown ofrece vacaciones para todos los gustos.

Para las personas activas hay toda clase de posibilidades: golf, tenis, natación, paseos en barco y mucho más.

Las discotecas y salas de fiestas te deleitarán con su ambiente alegre. El año pasado se construyó un cine nuevo con 5 salas y también existe un teatro moderno, donde se pondrá una función diferente cada semana del verano.

Dentro del casco urbano podrás apreciar la arquitectura medieval inglesa, visitando la catedral gótica, que se construyó en el siglo 14, y el castillo, que ofreció protección a la ciudad durante muchas guerras.

Mytown te encantará, porque su playa de arena fina y de aguas transparentes es la maravilla de la costa inglesa, y la región te asombrará con su paisaje incomparable de montañas y mar.

Notes: *At first sight, writing a publicity brochure does not appear to invite the use of different tenses, but, if you are looking for them, you will find plenty of opportunities to refer to past and future. The Grade A expectation of expressing and justifying points of view has been achieved here by saying how the reader will react to Mytown and giving reasons.*

Question 21 (Answer)

Queridos amigos:

Para celebrar los cumpleaños aquí invitamos a los amigos a una fiesta en casa, a una discoteca o a un restaurante.

Desde luego, ¡los regalos también son importantes! Este año mis padres me dieron una cazadora de piel, que me gustó mucho. Mis abuelos me regalaron una radio-cassette.

Ese día tuve que ir al colegio – ¡qué pena! – pero más tarde mis amigos y yo fuimos a un restaurante italiano. Lo mejor del día fue después, cuando fuimos a una discoteca. La discoteca es para mí el mejor sitio que hay, porque tiene un ambiente tan alegre y tan animado.

El año que viene, antes de ir a la discoteca, iremos a un restaurante chino. Yo creo que no debemos volver al mismo restaurante porque eso resulta un poco aburrido. Me gustaría tener un restaurante español aquí, porque me encanta la comida española y quisera invitar a mis amigos a probarla.

Un abrazo para todos de
Chris

Notes: *This question clearly requires the use of past and future tenses. It does not specifically ask for points of view to be expressed and justified but, if you look for them, you will find opportunities to fulfil this expectation of Grade A candidates.*

A STEP FURTHER

Vocabulary practice

Think of a topic area, give yourself a time limit and then see how many words from that topic you can write down in the time you have allowed.

Think of a Spanish word and then see what new word comes into your head next, e.g. *bar, cerveza, botella, vino, camarero, cuenta, tapas, calamares* . . . .This can be an interesting activity to do with a friend.

Practise the strategies for coping with problems.

Improving the quality of your writing

First of all you can draw up your **'Instant Writing Kit'**.

In order to improve the style of your written Spanish, it is a good idea from time to time to note down a dozen everyday nouns (words for things or people). Make sure you include some feminine ones and one or two plurals. Now write a suitable adjective (describing word) with each one, making sure it agrees (e.g. *una falda negra*). Finally, see how many could have an adverb (e.g. *bastante, demasiado, excesivamente*) added to them and still make sense. (Not all can.)

Another practice activity is to write six short and simple sentences involving past action (e.g. *Entré en la cocina*). Now write a suitable adverb or phrase to describe *how* the action was done (e.g. *Entré rápidamente en la cocina*).

Remember, additional adjectives (provided they agree), adverbs and other additional phrases really do improve the style of your written Spanish – and gain you marks.

Practice in writing

If you have contacts in or from Spain or another Spanish-speaking country, use them. Exchange letters and post cards, ask for help, make notes of any vocabulary and expressions they use that you think may help you.

Go over as many specimen questions as you can. There will be many exercises in your coursebook that are similar to those set for GCSE.

Go over and revise exercises you have written in the past and try to do them again, only this time see if you can improve on your previous performance.

Make a note of any particular weaknesses that appear regularly in your writing and try to do something about them. **Ask your teacher for help** if you don't understand, or can't see why you often make the same mistake.

Chapter

8 Coursework

GETTING STARTED

Coursework is a feature of many GCSE subjects. The principal advantage for students is that they can work at their own pace, and, over time, produce considered pieces of work. Many students find coursework challenging, but rise to the challenge and produce excellent work. Other students find examinations nerve-wracking and prefer to work at coursework where they can be certain to have marks 'in the bag' before the final examination. In Spanish, coursework is not compulsory unless you are taking the SEG modular syllabus.

TOPIC	STUDY	REVISION 1	REVISION 2
Introduction			
Advantages and disadvantages of coursework			
Different types of Writing coursework			
Producing coursework at home			
Controlled conditions for coursework			
Writing coursework tasks			
Marking of coursework			
Examples of coursework			
Speaking coursework			
Conclusion			

WHAT YOU NEED TO KNOW

Introduction

Coursework in Spanish will be available to many students for the first time in 1998. For practical reasons, it is only available to students in schools and colleges. Private candidates are not allowed to enter for it.

Four examining boards, Edexcel, MEG, NEAB and WJEC offer the **option** of Writing coursework in place of the Writing examination.

Edexcel has the additional possibility of doing Speaking coursework. However, Edexcel candidates are only allowed to do **one** type of coursework, either Speaking or Writing.

In the SEG Modular examination there is some Speaking coursework at the end of Module 1 (February of Year 10) and some in Module 3 (February of Year 11). Additionally, there is Writing coursework in Module 3 (February of Year 11). In the SEG Modular scheme, there is no choice about coursework; you have to do it.

NICCEA does not offer coursework.

Advantages and disadvantages of coursework

Coursework does have a number of advantages, which may be listed as follows:

- You have more control over the final standard of your work.
- You are not vulnerable to feeling unwell or ill-prepared on the day of the examination.
- You can take as much time as you like over pieces which are done at home.
- You can use a range of reference materials to ensure that your work is good.
- You can take pleasure in working up a piece of work from idea to draft to final version.
- You can often do tasks which interest you particularly.

On the other hand, there are snags to coursework:

- You may find it difficult getting down to work.
- You may not find it easy to write and research pieces of original work.
- You may not be organized enough to ensure that stages of the work are completed on time.
- Your workload may become unpredictable with lots of coursework due from a range of subjects at the same time (February in Year 11 can be a busy time).
- You may move school.
- Your teacher may move school or be ill for an extended period.

Different types of Writing coursework

Most of the boards require that you submit three items of Writing coursework, the exception being SEG, which requires two pieces. Of the three pieces of Writing, two may be done at home in your own time, but at least one must be done under controlled conditions. In practice, many teachers will ask you to do more than the minimum number of pieces of coursework and will then select the best three pieces to send in as your final mark. This should be comforting, as it means that any last-minute disasters are less serious for you.

Producing coursework at home

The boards vary slightly in their regulations about how coursework should be approached, but a typical approach is as follows.

Task training

Your teacher will cover a topic or a unit of work, and let you know that it provides an opportunity for a piece of coursework to be written. The teacher may then wish to do some work on the sort of thing which you might produce, say, a description of your home area. This might include reading and listening to descriptions of other areas in Spanish, and some work on, say, useful adjectives for this topic.

Discussion of task choice

Your teacher may ask you to choose a task, and will then discuss with you how practical your choice is. There is no requirement for all tasks done in a class to be different;

indeed it may be that many of you complete the same task or similar ones. After discussing your choice, your teacher will set you a deadline for either a first draft or an outline. Make sure you have done something about the task by this date so that the next stage is useful.

Discussion of first draft or outline

Your teacher will want to see, and probably take in to read at home, your first draft. This should be as good-quality an effort as you can manage, because then the teacher can concentrate on recommending improvements which you could not have thought up yourself. Your teacher is not allowed to mark the work in detail at this stage. However, he/she will be making comments of a general nature, such as:

- 'This is not long enough to be assessed for grades A*, A or B, although the quality is good.'
- 'Have you thought of checking the gender of the nouns in the dictionary so that you get them right?'
- 'I think you should have another look at the uses of *ser* and *estar*.'
- 'This piece doesn't refer to past, present and future events as it stands.'
- 'You haven't given enough opinions; *bueno* and *me gusta* are not enough on their own: justify your opinions by using *porque*.'

Production of the final piece of coursework

You should re-write your first draft after doing all the checking that your teacher has suggested, as well as any other things that you can think of. It is quite possible, for example, to look up the gender of every noun in a 150-word piece of writing to check that you got it right every time, and that the adjective that goes with it agrees properly. The final piece of coursework should be written on A4-sized paper.

Certificate of authentication

When you hand in the final piece of coursework, you will be asked to sign a statement that the piece of work is your own unaided effort. Your teacher will also have to countersign that statement. In practice, this means that you will have to do without using human reference sources such as other teachers, older brothers and sisters, parents, the Spanish Assistant and so on. Do not attempt to pass off as your own any work that has been corrected or re-worked by anyone else. It is usually noticed and, if the examining board discovers that your signed statement is untrue, you could be disqualified.

Reference materials and other help

All boards allow you to use a Spanish–English dictionary throughout the preparation of coursework. At home, you will also be able to use your textbook, glossaries, exercise books, notebooks, grammars, etc. If you are able to use Information Technology (IT), this can improve the presentation. You will also be able to use a Spanish spell checker if you have one. But you should be aware that Spanish spell checkers require you to have a reasonable knowledge of spelling and of patterns of adjective agreement. Human help, however, should generally be avoided.

Controlled conditions for coursework

As mentioned above, most boards require you to produce at least one of your three pieces of coursework under controlled conditions. This means that the work is produced under the direct supervision of your teacher, in formal test-type conditions. The work should be done in one sitting.

Some of the rules about reference materials are stricter. You will not be allowed to use IT, and some boards restrict you to use of an English–Spanish dictionary only. Check with your teacher beforehand what your board allows.

You will not necessarily know the title of the piece of work you are going to be asked to do beforehand, although your teacher will have given you some indication, such as 'you are going to write a formal letter'. Again, practice varies slightly from board to board, so check carefully with your teacher.

There is no opportunity to have your teacher's comments on your work before you hand it in, and there is limited time available to draft and check the draft. Do make sure you know how long you have been allowed to do the piece of work so that you can produce a neat version on A4 paper at the end of the session.

Writing coursework tasks

Coursework tasks vary somewhat from board to board. Some boards, notably NEAB, have a list of coursework tasks in the syllabus from which all candidates must choose. Other boards give suggestions, but do not insist that you follow them. Because the rules vary somewhat between different boards it is important that you make your choice in consultation with your teacher.

The tasks are divided into three categories, depending on which grade you are aiming for.

Grade G, F, E tasks

Grade G, F, E tasks are usually short, and require between 20 and about 100 words. Examples might include:

- Make a shopping list.
- Fill in a camp site form.
- Make a list of foods you have eaten this week.
- Make a packing list for a walking holiday.

Slightly more ambitious tasks, but still in the grade G, F, E category, might include:

- Write a post card.
- Design a poster about your local area.
- Comment on your school uniform and design a better one.
- Write about a well-known Spanish entertainer.

Grade D, C tasks

Grade D, C tasks will typically require between 90 and 120 words. They could include some of the more ambitious tasks for Grades G, F, E, written at greater length. Other possibilities include:

- My work experience.
- My ideal job.
- A diary of a real or imagined visit to a Spanish-speaking country.
- A job application letter.
- A letter reserving hotel accommodation.
- A diary of a memorable weekend.
- A journey: planning, advantages and disadvantages.

Grade B, A, A tasks*

Grade B, A, A* tasks will typically require between 150 and 170 words. They could include some of the more ambitious tasks for Grades D, C, written at greater length. Other possibilities include:

- An account of a play, film, or book you have enjoyed.
- A report on the structure of Spanish TV, satellite TV and radio.
- A comparison of festivals in Spain and UK (e.g. Christmas).
- An account of an incident you have seen in the street.
- A plan of campaign to tackle an environmental or social issue.

Marking of coursework

Your teacher will mark your coursework usually using grids which measure two or three features of your writing. These are:

- Communication.
- Accuracy.
- Range and variety of language.

Communication is most important at Grades G, F, E, while accuracy and range and variety of language are most important for Grades B, A, A*.

At the simplest level, marks will be awarded for communicating your message, even if the Spanish has many errors.

At the highest level, teachers will be looking for Spanish which is more or less accurate, which uses a range of appropriate tenses, and uses a wide range of adjectives and adverbs. The writing will include your personal opinions, expressed in a mature way, and the justification of those opinions. So if you are aiming for a high grade in your coursework, make sure you include those components.

Examples of coursework

G, F, E task

Escribe una lista de cosas que necesitas para una excursión a pie en el campo.

Student's answer

1. *pan*
2. *queso*
3. *jamón*
4. *naranjas*
5. *lemonada*
6. *cuchillo*
7. *camera*
8. *gafas de sol*
9. *mapo*
10. *mocla*

Examiner's comments

You know your food items well. The first four words are correctly spelt. No. 5 should be *limonada*, but it communicates well. There are no problems with 6 or 8, but 7 is an English word that you should have checked. The expression you wanted is *máquina fotográfica*. You could have got away with *cámara*, but English spellings are not acceptable. No. 9 should have been *mapa*, but your version would be understood by a Spaniard. *Mocla* is meaningless. It is almost certainly an attempt at remembering *mochila*, but it should have been checked in the dictionary.

D, C task

Escribe una carta a tu corresponsal español(a) describiendo una visita que has hecho a España.

Student's answer

Leicester
el 4 de septiembre

Querida Luisa:
¿Qué tal? ¿Cómo están tus padres?

El mes pasado fui a España con mi famillia (1). Hemos salido (2) de casa a las once horas (3) y llegamos en España (4) a las cuatro por la tarde (5). Hemos pasado dos semanas en la costa. Quedamos en un hotel grande (6) cerca Valencia (7). Tenía un restaurante bueno y un disco (8) todas las noches. Hacía muy calor (9) y fuimos a la playa todos los días. Una día (10) fuimos de compras a Valencia, donde compré un bañador muy bonito. Me gusto mucho (11) España. Volveré (12) si puedo el año próximo.

Un abrazo de (13)
Jane

Examiner's comments

1. The correct spelling is *familia*. This could have been checked.
2. The tense is wrong here (though the meaning would be understood by a Spaniard). Instead of the perfect, you should have used the preterite: *salimos*.
3. The word *horas* should be omitted when stating the time of day.
4. There is no doubt about the meaning, but with *llegar* you should use *a* not *en*.
5. This is another error in a time expression. 'In the afternoon' is indeed *por la tarde*, but with the actual time *de* should be used: *a las cuatro de la tarde*.
6. This is a very common mistake. *Quedar* really means 'remain', so this sentence says that you did not go out of the hotel! You should have said *Nos hospedamos en un hotel grande*.
7. Remember that it should be *cerca de ...* .
8. Another typically English error. *Un disco* is a disc or record. For 'a disco' you should use the full word in Spanish: *una discoteca*.
9. The expression should be *Hacía mucho calor*.
10. *Día* is masculine: *un día*.
11. It is not clear here whether you have mis-used the verb *gustar* in the present tense (in which case you should have written: *Me gusta mucho España*) or simply left the accent off *gustó* in the preterite (in which case your sentence was intended to mean 'I really liked Spain').
12. It is good to see the future used here. It ensures that you have met the requirement at this level to use a range of tenses.
13. A correct letter ending, which matches the good beginning.

Overall this letter communicates well. Most of the verbs are correct and there is good use of both the preterite and the imperfect tenses. The final sentence includes verbs in future and present tenses. A number of adjectives have been used and all have the correct agreements. It is a pity that there are quite so many errors, which will pull the mark down rather close to the C/D borderline.

B, A, A task*

'Un incidente que vi en la calle'

Student's answer

'Un incidente que vi en la calle'

El otro día vi un incidente bastante grave en la calle y ahora, como tengo tiempo libre, escribiré los detalles. (1)

Había salido (2) de casa a las nueve para ir de compras. Cuando bajaba (3) la calle vi un coche azul muy grande que salió de una de las otras calles sin parar y atropelló a (4) un chico que paseaba con su perro. El conductor se paró un momento, miró al chico y se fue muy de prisa. Me chocó mucho (5) porque el chico estaba herido. Pero, ¡fíjate qué sorpresa! ¡No se me ocurrió (6) apuntar el número (7) del coche! El chico tenía una pierna rota y le duelía (8) mucho. Fui a una casa donde una mujer, que era alta y delgada y muy simpática, telefoneó para pedir una ambulancia. Llegó la policía y después la ambulancia y llevaron al chicho (9) al hospital. Después tuve que hablar con la policía.

No sé cómo el hombre podía dejar al chico así. Es muy desagradable, ¿no te parece? (10) Después de ver este incidente, he decidido que si un día tengo un coche conduciré con mucho cuidado. Eso me parece verdaderamente importante. No quiero tener accidentes. (11)

Examiner's comments

1. This is a very impressive opening sentence. It includes verbs in the preterite, present and future and has effective use of one adjective (*grave*) and two adverbs (*bastante* and *ahora*).
2. A verb in the pluperfect.
3. The fifth different tense (the imperfect) to be used in the first three sentences. You have already demonstrated a very pleasing command of verbs.
4. It is good to see the personal 'a' being used correctly.
5. A welcome expression of personal reaction to the points being related.
6. A very good use of an idiom with an impersonal reflexive. The use of exclamation marks helps

to communicate your surprise at your own failure to do what you clearly feel should have been obvious.

7. *Número* is not really the correct word here. For a car number the word is *matrícula*.
8. An unexpected mistake here. The imperfect does not have any radical changes. The verb should be *dolía*.
9. An even more surprising error this time. Since the word *chico* has been correctly spelt several times in this piece of writing, it is clear that this is just a slip of the pen (though it should really have been noticed when you checked your work through).
10. At this level we are looking for expressions of opinion and here we have one, linked with an invitation to the reader to respond.
11. Another expression of opinion, linked with an explanation, which gives a logical conclusion to the whole account.

Overall, this is the sort of work that reaches the boundary between Grade A and A*. It has five different tenses, all used correctly, and some effective use of adjectives and adverbs. The narrative flows easily and contains personal reactions and opinions. It invites the reader to react.

Speaking coursework

Edexcel offers the chance to choose speaking coursework. SEG has compulsory Speaking coursework in modules 1 and 3.

Edexcel

The Edexcel coursework option requires you to submit three units of work, each drawn from a different National Curriculum Area of Experience. For each unit you will have to do a role-play-type task and a presentation of a topic. These will be recorded and may be sent off to the board after being marked. The tasks have to be completed by the end of April in the year of the exam, but your teacher may get you to do them at any time during your course.

Edexcel provides example tasks in their syllabus, which your teacher will have a copy of.

If you are a **Foundation Candidate**, for each unit you can expect to do a simple role-play, say, in a shop, similar to those found in the Speaking tests of other boards (see Chapter 5). In addition you can expect to do a presentation and then discuss it. Again, this is similar to the final examination version.

If you are a **Higher Candidate**, for each unit you can expect to do a more complicated role-play, which might be a survey, a negotiation or a presentation of, say, a radio broadcast. In addition you can expect to do a presentation and then discuss it. This is similar to the final examination version.

SEG

SEG candidates have to do Speaking coursework (*see* Table 2.3 on page 10).

Module 1 is assessed in the Spring Term of Year 10. You are asked to produce a short tape-recorded monologue on some aspect of the work you have done. You are not allowed to read from a prepared script, but you can use prompts. You can pause the tape, but it must be recorded on a single occasion.

Module 3 involves the same procedure as Module 1, and is assessed in the Autumn Term of Year 11.

For Speaking coursework, the advice given in Chapter 5 should help you with most tasks.

Conclusion

Coursework has a number of benefits, and, if you take advantage of the extra time in which to do the work, you should be able to produce the grade you deserve with less worry. On the other hand, you should remember that there is much less excuse for poorly planned, inaccurate work when you have had all the time in the world and all possible reference materials to hand. So when you hand a first draft in, make sure it is good, so that the second draft truly is a polished version.

Chapter

9

Grammar

GETTING STARTED

Many people become worried about **grammar** and feel that it is too technical for them to understand. In fact it is simply an explanation of the way in which words are put together to convey meaning. We are using grammar whenever we say or write a sentence and we are also applying our knowledge of grammar to understand what we hear and read. In our own language we apply the 'rules' of grammar without thinking about them – and that should be exactly what we aim to do eventually in Spanish.

You can achieve a great deal by using the expressions you have learnt but a sound knowledge of the main points of grammar will enable you to develop a much wider range of language and also to ensure that you link different expressions correctly. At GCSE the accuracy of your Spanish is marked particularly in Higher Tier Writing and Speaking, but a good knowledge of grammar will improve the quality of your work in all skills.

The grammar section that follows contains fairly brief explanations of the main points of grammar that you will need for the GCSE examinations. You can use it for revision and also for reference.

TOPIC	STUDY	REVISION 1	REVISION 2
Nouns			
Articles			
Adjectives			
Adverbs			
Verbs			
Pronouns			
The personal 'a'			
Dates, times, numbers, question words			

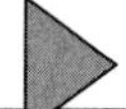

WHAT YOU NEED TO KNOW

Nouns

Gender

All Spanish **nouns** are either masculine or feminine. You need to learn the **gender** with the word.

- All nouns ending in *-aje* are masculine (e.g. el viaje).
- All nouns ending in *-ción* are feminine (e.g. la natación).
- All nouns ending in *-dad, -tad* and *-tud* are feminine (e.g. la verdad).
- All nouns ending in *-umbre* are feminine (e.g. la cumbre).

Almost all nouns ending in *-o* are masculine. Important exceptions: la mano, la radio.

Most nouns ending in *-a* are feminine but there are many exceptions, of which some of the most important are listed below:

el clima	el sofá
el día	el tema
el mapa	el tranvía
el planeta	el telegrama (and all other nouns ending in -grama)
el problema	

Nouns ending in *-ista* can be either masculine or feminine, depending on the sex of the person referred to (e.g. el/la tenista).

Notice also: el policía (*policeman*); la policía (*police force, policewoman*)
el guardia (*policeman*); la guardia (*policewoman, guard duty, protection*).

Plural

Here are some useful 'rules' for forming **plurals.**

- Nouns ending in a **vowel** add -s
  el libro los libros
- Nouns ending in a **consonant** add -es
  la pared las paredes
  – **except** those ending in -s
  el lunes los lunes
  – **but** nouns ending in -s with an accented last syllable do add -es (and lose the accent)
  el inglés los ingleses
  el autobús los autobuses
- Notice the variations in **written accent** (keeping the stress on the same syllable in singular and plural). e.g.
  el joven los jóvenes
  la habitación las habitaciones
- **Remember** also to apply the spelling rules for words ending in -z
  e.g. el lápiz los lápices

Articles

Definite

	Masculine	*Feminine*
Singular	el coche (*the car*)	la casa (*the house*)
Plural	los coches (*the cars*)	las casas (*the houses*)

Notice also the neuter article 'lo', which is used with an adjective to convey the meaning 'the . . . thing' or 'the . . . part', e.g. 'Lo interesante es . . .' *The interesting thing is . . .*; 'Lo mejor es . . .' *The best part is . . . .*

Indefinite

	Masculine	*Feminine*
Singular	un coche (*a car*)	una casa (*a house*)
Plural	unos coches (*some cars*)	unas casas (*some houses*)

There is no word for 'some' in the singular (some coffee: *café*) and in practice the plural indefinite article (*unos/unas*) is usually omitted.

Quiero vino, por favor. *I'd like some wine, please.*
He comprado caramelos. *I've bought some sweets.*

Additional uses of the definite article

- When a noun is used in a **general sense** (so that the sentence could be taken to include every example of that noun that exists). e.g. Me gusta el queso. *I like cheese.* Notice that the sentence could be taken to mean that I like all cheese that exists. Compare that with: Como queso. *I eat cheese* (where the statement clearly refers only to some of the cheese that exists).
- With parts of the **body** and **clothing** when used with a reflexive verb:
  – Me lavo las manos. *I wash my hands.*
  – Se quitó la chaqueta. *He took off his jacket.*
- With **school subjects**: Las matemáticas; la historia.
- With **languages** (except after the verb 'hablar'):
  – El español es un idioma muy importante *but* Hablo español.
- With **prices**: Cien pesetas el paquete. *100 pesetas a packet.*
- **Before titles** (other than *don/doña*) when speaking about someone:
  – El señor Gómez vive en Valencia (*but* Don Ramón vive en Granada).

Omission of the indefinite article

- When saying what someone's job is (*after* ser):
  – Es peluquero. *He is a hairdresser.*
- With 'tener' and 'hay' in the negative:
  – No tengo coche. *I do not have* a *car.*
  – No hay problema. *There isn't a problem.*
- After 'sin' (*without*):
  – Llegó sin chaqueta. *He arrived without a jacket.*
- In exclamations:
  – ¡Qué sorpresa! *What a surprise!*
- Before 'otro', 'tal', 'cierto':
  – Otro tren. *Another train.* Tal libro. *Such a book.*
  – Cierta ciudad. *A certain city.*

Adjectives

Remember to make **adjectives** 'agree' in number and gender with the noun or pronoun they describe.

Adjectives ending in -*o*:

	Masculine	*Feminine*
Singular	un coche blanco	una casa blanca
Plural	unos coches blancos	unas casas blancas

Adjectives ending in any other letter:

	Masculine	*Feminine*
Singular	un edificio grande	una camisa azul
Plural	unos edificios grandes	unas camisas azules

Adjectives of nationality or region:

	Masculine	*Feminine*
Singular	un libro español	una ciudad española
Plural	unos libros españoles	unas ciudades españolas

Apocopation

The following adjectives drop the final *-o* before a masculine singular noun:

bueno:	buen	tercero:	tercer
malo:	mal	alguno:	algún
primero:	primer	ninguno:	ningún

e.g. un buen dia (*but* un día bueno, una buena persona).

Note also that *grande* is shortened to *gran* when used before a singular noun of either gender, e.g.:

un gran hombre, una gran idea (but *unas grandes personas*).
(Remember that in these cases *grande* means 'great'.)

Comparative

Más . . . que . . . *more . . . than . . .*
Menos . . . que . . . *less . . . than . . . (not as . . . as. . .)* e.g.:

Las uvas son más caras que las manzanas.	*The grapes are dearer than the apples.*
El tren es menos rápido que el avión.	*The train is not as fast as the plane.*

Note the **irregular** comparatives:

mejor	*better*	peor	*worse*
mayor	*greater, older*	menor	*lesser, younger.*

Tan . . . como . . . *as . . . as . . .* e.g.:

El libro es tan interesante como la película.	*The book is as interesting as the film.*

Superlative

Madrid es la ciudad más grande de España.	*Madrid is the largest city in Spain.*

Possessive adjectives

Singular		**Plural**		
Masculine	*Feminine*	*Masculine*	*Feminine*	
mi	mi	mis	mis	*my*
tu	tu	tus	tus	*your*
su	su	sus	sus	*his, her, its, your* (Vd.)
nuestro	nuestra	nuestros	nuestras	*our*
vuestro	vuestra	vuestros	vuestras	*your*
su	su	sus	sus	*their, your* (Vd.)

e.g. Mi libro, mis libros.

Demonstrative adjectives

Singular		**Plural**		
Masculine	*Feminine*	*Masculine*	*Feminine*	
este	esta	estos	estas	*this, these*
ese	esa	esos	esas	*that, those**
aquel	aquella	aquellos	aquellas	*that, those*†

* ese *etc. is used for things or persons near the person being spoken to.*
† aquel *etc. is used for things or persons near neither the speaker nor the person spoken to.*

Position of adjectives

Possessive and demonstrative adjectives come before the nouns they describe, e.g.

nuestro coche   este libro

Other adjectives usually follow the nouns they describe, e.g.:

un coche azul un libro interesante

With the following adjectives the position affects the meaning:

	Before the noun	*After the noun*
antiguo	*previous/former*	*ancient*
grande	*great*	*large/big*
pobre	*unfortunate*	*poor (with little money)*

e.g. una gran señora *a great lady*
una señora grande *a large (or tall) lady.*

Adverbs

In most cases, **adverbs** are formed by adding *-mente* to the feminine singular form of the adjective, e.g.:

rápido	rápidamente	*quickly*
cuidadoso	cuidadosamente	*carefully*
probable	probablemente	*probably*

Exceptions include:

bien	*well*	bastante	*fairly, quite*
mal	*badly*	muy	*very*
mucho	*a lot*	demasiado	*too, too much*
poco	*not very (much)*	aquí	*here*
despacio	*slowly*	ahí	*there, near person spoken to*
de prisa	*quickly*	allí	*there, near neither speaker nor person spoken to*
a menudo	*often*		
pronto	*soon*	ahora	*now*
de repente	*suddenly*	luego	*then, next*

Comparative

Comparison of adverbs is very similar to comparison of adjectives:

Habla más de prisa que su hermano. *He speaks faster than his brother.*
Terminó tan pronto como su amigo. *He finished as soon as his brother.*

Note also constructions such as:

Sabe más de lo que crees. *He knows more than you think.*

Superlative

Note the construction:

Anduve lo más rápidamente posible. *I walked the fastest I could.*

Verbs

Present tense

The **present tense** is used for things that happen or are happening at the present time. e.g. 'I eat' or 'I am eating'.

Regular verbs

hablar	*comer*	*vivir*
hablo	como	vivo
hablas	comes	vives
habla	come	vive
hablamos	comemos	vivimos
habláis	coméis	vivís
hablan	comen	viven

Radical-changing verbs

encontrar(ue)	*entender(ie)*	*pedir(i)*
encuentro	entiendo	pido
encuentras	entiendes	pides
encuentra	entiende	pide
encontramos	entendemos	pedimos
encontráis	entendéis	pedís
encuentran	entienden	piden

Common irregular verbs

ser	*estar*	*ir*	*tener*	*hacer*	*venir*
soy	estoy	voy	tengo	hago	vengo
eres	estás	vas	tienes	haces	vienes
es	está	va	tiene	hace	viene
somos	estamos	vamos	tenemos	hacemos	venimos
sois	estáis	vais	tenéis	hacéis	venís
son	están	van	tienen	hacen	vienen

Verbs that are regular apart from the first person singular (*yo* form),

e.g. salir

salgo
sales
sale
salimos
salís
salen

caer: caigo, caes. etc.
traer: traigo, traes, etc.
poner: pongo, pones, etc.
salir: salgo, sales, etc.
ver: veo, ves, etc.
dar: doy, das, etc.
saber: sé, sabes. etc.
ofrecer: ofrezco, ofreces, etc.
(*All verbs ending in* -ecer, -ocer *and* -ucir *follow the pattern of* ofrecer.)

Preterite tense

The **preterite** tense is used to recount events or things that happened in the past. e.g. 'I spoke', 'She went', 'You arrived'.

Regular

hablar	*comer*	*vivir*
hablé	comí	viví
hablaste	comiste	viviste
habló	comió	vivió
hablamos	comimos	vivimos
hablasteis	comisteis	vivisteis
hablaron	comieron	vivieron

Regular – but note spellings

leer	*oír*	*ver*
leí	oí	vi
leíste	oíste	viste
leyó	oyó	vio
leímos	oímos	vimos
leísteis	oísteis	visteis
leyeron	oyeron	vieron

The following verbs are regular in the preterite tense, but note the effects of the spelling rules on the first person singular (*yo* form):

empezar: empecé, empezaste, empezó, etc.
cruzar: crucé, cruzaste, cruzó, etc.
jugar: jugué, jugaste, jugó, etc.
buscar: busqué, buscaste, buscó, etc.

Changes of this sort affect all verbs ending in -zar, -gar, -car.

Radical-changing -ir verbs

sentir (ie)	*dormir (ue)*	*seguir (i)*
sentí	dormí	seguí
sentiste	dormiste	seguiste
sintió	durmió	siguió
sentimos	dormimos	seguimos
sentisteis	dormisteis	seguisteis
sintieron	durmieron	siguieron

There are no radical changes in the preterite of -ar *and* -er *radical-changing verbs.*

'Pretérito grave' verbs

These verbs have no accents in the preterite.

estar	*hacer*	*decir*
estuve	hice	dije
estuviste	hiciste	dijiste
estuvo	hizo	dijo
estuvimos	hicimos	dijimos
estuvisteis	hicisteis	dijisteis
estuvieron	hicieron	dijeron*

andar: anduve, anduviste, etc.
tener: tuve, tuviste, tuvo, etc.
poder: pude, pudiste, pudo, *etc.*
poner: puse, pusiste, puso, etc.
saber: supe, supiste, supo, etc.
querer: quise, quisiste, etc.
venir: vine, viniste, vino, etc.

*Note that there is no *i* in this part of decir. The same pattern is followed by:

traer: traje, trajiste, trajo, trajimos, trajisteis, trajeron
conducir: conduje, condujiste, condujo, condujimos, condujisteis, condujeron

and all verbs that end in -ducir.

Irregular verbs

dar		*ser*		*ir*	
di	dimos	fui	fuimos	fui	fuimos
diste	disteis	fuiste	fuisteis	fuiste	fuisteis
dio	dieron	fue	fueron	fue	fueron

Perfect tense

The **perfect tense** is used when we would use the English past tense with 'have', e.g. 'I have eaten', 'Have you visited Spain?'.

Regular

hablar	*comer*	*vivir*
he hablado	he comido	he vivido
has hablado	has comido	has vivido
ha hablado	ha comido	ha vivido
hemos hablado	hemos comido	hemos vivido
habéis hablado	habéis comido	habéis vivido
han hablado	han comido	han vivido

Irregular

hacer
he hecho
has hecho
ha hecho
hemos hecho
habéis hecho
han hecho

The past participle of regular verbs is formed by removing the infinitive ending (*-ar, -er, -ir*) and replacing it:

for -ar *verbs with* -ado
for -er *and* -ir *verbs with* -ido.

Note the accent required when *-ido* is added to *a, e* or *o*:

caer: caído leer: leído oír: oído.

Remember that you must not put any words between the two parts of the perfect tense. 'Have you eaten?' (addressing the person as 'usted') can be expressed in two ways:

¿Ha comido usted? *and* ¿Usted ha comido?

What you must **not** do is put the word *usted* in the middle (which is where we do put 'you' in English).

Irregular past participles

abrir:	abierto	romper:	roto
cubrir:	cubierto	ver:	visto
decir:	dicho	volver:	vuelto
escribir:	escrito	morir:	muerto
poner:	puesto		

Future tense

The **future tense** is used for future events, e.g. 'I shall go', 'They will arrive'.
The endings of the future tense are the same for all verbs. The stem is normally the infinitive.

Regular

hablar	*dormirse*
hablaré	me dormiré
hablarás	te dormirás
hablará	se dormirá
hablaremos	nos dormiremos
hablaréis	os dormiréis
hablarán	se dormirán

Irregular

decir: diré, etc.
hacer: haré, etc.
poder: podré, etc.
poner: pondré, etc.
querer: querré, etc.
saber: sabré, etc.
salir: saldré, etc.
tener: tendré, etc.
venir: vendré, etc.

'Ir a' + infinitive

You can also express future action by using the verb *ir a* followed by an infinitive, e.g.:

Voy a visitar a mi abuela.	*I am going to visit my grandmother*
Van a reparar el coche para mañana	*They are going to repair the car for tomorrow.*

Conditional

You should understand and be able to use:

Me gustaría . . . e.g. Me gustaría visitar Sevilla *I should like to visit Seville.*
¿Te gustaría . . .? *Would you like . . .?*
¿Le gustaría . . .? *Would you like . . .? (addressing the person as* usted)
Nos gustaría . . . *We should like . . .*

You should also be able to understand and use the conditional of other verbs. The **conditional** is used where in English we use 'would' or 'should', e.g. 'I should like . . .' 'He would do it, if . . .' The endings are the same for all verbs. The stem is the same as for the future tense:

hablar	*divertirse*	*hacer*
hablaría	me divertiría	haría
hablarías	te divertirías	harías
hablaría	se divertiría	haría
hablaríamos	nos divertiríamos	haríamos
hablaríais	os divertiríais	haríais
hablarían	se divertirían	harían

Imperfect

The **imperfect** is used for things that 'used to happen' or 'were happening', e.g. 'When I lived in the North (= used to live . . .)', 'When I was having lunch . . .'

Regular

hablar	*comer*	*vivir*
hablaba	comía	vivía
hablabas	comías	vivías
hablaba	comía	vivía
hablábamos	comíamos	vivíamos
hablabais	comíais	vivíais
hablaban	comían	vivían

Irregular

ser	*ir*	*ver*
era	iba	veía
eras	ibas	veías
era	iba	veía
éramos	íbamos	veíamos
erais	ibais	veíais
eran	iban	veían

Pluperfect

The **pluperfect** is used for what 'had happened', e.g. 'Because I had lost my passport. . .'. The pluperfect is formed by the imperfect of *haber* + the past participle:

hablar		*hacer*	
había hablado	habíamos hablado	había hecho	habíamos hecho
habías hablado	habíais hablado	habías hecho	habíais hecho
había hablado	habían hablado	había hecho	habían hecho

Continuous tenses

Any tense in Spanish can be made **continuous** (e.g. 'He will be eating'). This is done by using the verb **estar** in the tense and form required, together with the present participle, e.g.:

Está hablando	*S/he is speaking.*
Estará comiendo	*S/he will be eating.*
Habían estado trabajando	*They had been working.*

Present participle

The **present participle** is formed by removing the ending (*-ar, -er, -ir*) from the infinitive and replacing it, for *-ar* verbs with *-ando*, and for *-er* and *-ir* verbs with *-iendo*, e.g.:

entrar: entrando comer: comiendo.

The ending *-iendo* has to be added to a consonant. If there is no consonant to add it to, change the *i* to *y*, e.g.:

leer: leyendo ir: yendo.

Any object or reflexive pronouns are placed either before the verb *'estar'* or on the end of the present participle, e.g.:

Lo está leyendo *or* Está leyéndolo.
Se están lavando *or* Están lavándose.

Note the addition of the accent when a pronoun is added to the end of a present participle.

Commands and instructions

Usted/Ustedes commands

These are formed by removing the *-o* from the *yo* form of the present tense and adding these endings:

for *-ar* verbs:	*-e* and *-en*	
for *-er* and *-ir* verbs	*-a* and *-an*	
e.g.: Tomar (tomo):	Tome (usted)	Tomen (ustedes).
Venir (vengo):	Venga (usted)	Vengan (ustedes).

The most important exceptions are:

Ir (voy):	Vaya (usted)	Vayan (ustedes).
Dar (doy):	Dé (usted)	Den (ustedes).

For **negative** commands, simply put '*No*' first, e.g. '*No vaya (usted)*' (Don't go).

Tú commands

These usually have the same form as the 'he/she' form of the present tense, e.g.:

Hablar: Habla (*Speak!*)
Empezar: Empieza (*Begin!*)

The exceptions are:

Decir:	Di.	Salir:	Sal.
Hacer:	Haz.	Ser:	Sé.
Ir:	Ve.	Tener:	Ten.
Poner:	Pon.	Venir:	Ven.

Vosotros commands

These are formed by removing the *-r* from the end of the infinitive and replacing it with a *-d*, e.g.:

Comer: Comed. Salir: Salid.
Ir: Id.

Negative tú and vosotros commands

These all begin with the word *No*. For negative *tú* commands, take the *Vd.* command and add an *-s*, e.g.:

Beber (Beba): No bebas. Ir (Vaya): No vayas.

For negative *vosotros* commands, again take the *Vd.* command and remove the final letter, replacing *-a* with *-áis* and *-e* with *-éis*, e.g.:

Escribir (Escriba): No escribáis.
Ir (Vaya): No vayáis.

Reflexive verbs

These are exactly like other verbs except that they require a reflexive pronoun with them. As an example look at the verb *lavarse* in different tenses and forms.

Present	*Perfect*	*Present continuous*
me lavo	me he lavado	me estoy lavando
te lavas	te has lavado	te estás lavando
se lava	se ha lavado	se está lavando
nos lavamos	nos hemos lavado	nos estamos lavando
os laváis	os habéis lavado	os estáis lavando
se lavan	se han lavado	se están lavando

Tú *command*: Lávate	*Negative*: No te laves
Vd. *command*: Lávese	*Negative*: No se lave (usted).

Gustar

Remember that when the thing that is liked is singular, we use *gusta*; when the thing that is liked is plural, we use *gustan*; when the thing liked is a verb, we use *gusta* + infinitive, e.g.:

Me gusta el café.	*I like coffee.*
Me gustan las uvas.	*I like grapes.*
Me gusta jugar al tenis.	*I like playing tennis.*

Ser and estar

It is important to use the correct verb for 'to be'. The decision depends on what follows the verb.

(a) When the verb is followed immediately by a NOUN or PRONOUN – use **SER**, e.g.:
Mi tío **es actor.**
Madrid **es una ciudad** en España.
¿Qué **es esto**?

(b) When the verb is followed by a PRESENT PARTICIPLE – use **ESTAR**, e.g.:
Cuando llegué, **estaban comiendo.**

(c) When the verb is followed by an EXPRESSION OF PLACE – use **ESTAR**, e.g.:
El libro **está en la mesa.**
Granada **está en el sur de España.**
But don't forget: *Granada es una ciudad en el sur de España* (Rule (a)).

(d) When the verb is followed by a PAST PARTICIPLE:
(i) **SER** tells of the ACTION being done, e.g.:
La puerta **es abierta** por el policía. *The door is opened by the policeman.*
(ii) . . . **ESTAR** tells of the SITUATION RESULTING from the action, e.g.:
La puerta **está abierta.** *The door is open.*

(e) When the verb is followed by an ADJECTIVE:
(i) **SER** tells of an ESSENTIAL or PERMANENT characteristic, e.g.:
El camarero **era simpático.** *The waiter was nice.*
María **es joven.** *Mary is young (an essential, though not permanent, fact about her).*
(ii) **ESTAR** tells of TEMPORARY states, e.g.:
Mi hermano **está enfermo.** *My brother is ill.*

Some adjectives change meaning according to whether they follow '*ser*' or '*estar*':

ser malo	*to be bad*	estar malo	*to be ill*
ser listo	*to be clever*	estar listo	*to be ready*
ser aburrido	*to be boring*	estar aburrido	*to be bored*
ser cansado	*to be tiring*	estar cansado	*to be tired*

Notice also:

ser alegre	*to be cheerful by nature*
estar alegre	*to be happy at the time*

Negatives

(a) For the simple negative, put 'no' before the verb, e.g.:
No tengo paraguas. *I have not got an umbrella.*

(b) With other negatives there is usually a choice of order, e.g.:
Nunca voy a Madrid *or* No voy nunca a Madrid. *I never go to Madrid.*

The same choice is possible with *nadie, nada* and *ni . . .ni . . .*, e.g.:

Nadie me habló *or* No me habló nadie. *Nobody spoke to me.*
Ni el bolígrafo ni el cuaderno estaba en la mesa *or* No estaba en la mesa ni el bolígrafo ni el cuaderno. *Neither the pen nor the exercise book was on the table.*

Pronouns

Personal pronouns

Subject	*Reflexive*	*Indirect object*	*Direct object*	*Disjunctive*
yo	me	me	me	mí
tú	te	te	te	ti
usted	se	le (se)+	le, la	usted
él	se	le (se)+	le, lo	él
ella	se	le (se)+	la	ella
nosotros/as	nos	nos	nos	nosotros/as
vosotros/as	os	os	os	vosotros/as
ustedes	se	les (se)+	les, las	ustedes
ellos	se	les (se)+	les, los	ellos
ellas	se	les (se)+	las	ellas

The **subject pronouns** are usually omitted in Spanish (except for *usted* and *ustedes*). They are used to avoid ambiguity and also for emphasis, e.g.:

> Tengo un hermano y una hermana. Él tiene trece años; ella tiene doce.

The **indirect object form** *se* is used instead of *le/les* if it is followed immediately by *lo, la, los* or *las*.

Disjunctive pronouns are used after a preposition, e.g.:

> Lo he hecho para ella. *I have done it for her.*
> Remember that *conmigo* = with me; *contigo* = with you.

Position of object pronouns

(a) Normally before the verb: *La compré ayer*. I bought it yesterday.

(b) On the end of a positive command: *Tómelo*. Take it.
But not on a negative command: *No lo tome.*

(c) Position optional:
  (i) With a dependent infinitive
  either Lo voy a comprar *or* Voy a comprarlo. *I'm going to buy it.*
  (ii) With a continuous tense
  either La estoy preparando *or* Estoy preparándolo. *I'm preparing it.*

Order of object pronouns

Indirect before direct: *Me lo dieron ayer*. They gave it to me yesterday.
Reflexive before either: *¿Las manos? Sí, me las he lavado*. My hands? Yes, I have washed them.

Tú and usted

Remember that *tú* (plural *vosotros*) is used when speaking (or writing) to:

- Close friends.
- Members of the immediate family.
- People of your own age (at least while in your teens).
- Younger children.
- Pets.

Usted (plural *ustedes*) is used with:

- Older people.
- People to whom you need to show some respect (usually people whom you would address as 'Mr . . .', 'Mrs . . .' or 'Miss . . .').

When addressing someone as *usted*, the verb form you have to use is the 'he/she' form. The form you use with *ustedes* is the 'they' form. Similarly the word for 'your' is *su* (plural *sus*), e.g.:

¿Tiene usted su pasaporte? *Do you have your passport?*

The abbreviations *Vd.* and *Vds.* are often used in writing for *usted* and *ustedes.*

The personal 'a'

Remember that when the direct object of a verb is a person we have to put *'a'* before it, e.g.:

¿Conoces a María?	*Do you know Mary?*
¿A quién viste?	*Who(m) did you see?*
No vi a nadie.	*I saw nobody.*

A more detailed explanation of this point is included in Chapter 6.

Dates, times, numbers, question words

These are all dealt with in Chapter 3, in the section headed 'Key Words and Expressions'.

Index

Page numbers in *italics* refer to practice questions or tasks

accidents 16, 37, *59–60*, 99, *159–60, 177*
accommodation 24–5, 63–5, 98, *101, 139–40, 144*
accounts/reports 150, 157, 175, *177–8*
accuracy 149, 150, 151, 156, 176
acquaintances, making 18, 47
address 41
addresses of examining boards 12
adjectives 151, 176 181–2
adverbs 176, 183
advertising and publicity 23, 61–2, 121, *128–9, 135*, 148
age 17, 41
agreement of adjectives 181
aims of GCSE 8
air travel 22, 58, 82, 99, *141*
alphabet 26
animals 17, 43
announcements 74, 75, *80*
answering questions 72–3, 110–11, 112–17, 122–3, 152–6
apocopation 182
appearance 17, 42
applying for a job *106, 107–8, 166–7*
areas of experience 8, 9, 14, 178
arranging, a meeting 18, 47–8, 99
  to go out 18, 47–8, *83, 104–5*
articles 180–1
asking, directions 19–20, 50–1, *81*, 99,
  for explanations/clarification 14, 31, 40
  questions 111
  the way 19–20, 50–1, *81*, 99
assessment 9, 156
attitudes 75, *88*, 96, 128
attitude to the course 2
authentication 174

bank 14, 21, 55–6, 99
bar/café 14, 17, 38–40, *81*, 98, 99
bathroom 35
bedroom 15, 34
bill, payment of 40
birthday 17, 41, *167*
body, parts of 16, 35–6
box office 17–18, 47
brochure 121, *167*
buses 21–2, *58*, 99

cafés 14, 17, 38–40, *81*, 98, 99
camping 14, 25, 65, 99, *135*
campsites 25, 65, *135*
car 22, *59–60*
cardinal numbers 30–1
careers 23, 60–1
CCEA (= NICCEA) 9, 10, 11, 12, 98, 101, 173
certificate of authentication 174
character 17, 41–2, *87, 143*
checklist 14, 149, 150, 151
chemist's 14, 16, 35–7
cinema 17–18, 46–7, *129–30*
clarifications, requesting 14, 31, 40
cleaning 21, 56–7
clothes 53–4
college 15, 60, 111, *112, 116–17*
colours 31
commands 188
communication 23, 62, 110, 156, 176
comparative, adjectives 182
  adverbs 183
complaining 64, 99
concert 17–18, 46–7
conclusions, drawing 75, 128
conditional tense 186
continuous tenses 187–8
controlled conditions 174–5
conversation 97, 110–19
conversations, understanding 74, 75, *77–8*
coping with, problems 99, 125–6, 156
  words you do not know 125–6
countries 25, 66, 111, *115, 117*
countryside 14, 50
coursework 9, 10, 149, 172–8
  done at home 173–5
  preparing 174
  speaking 178
  tasks 173, *175*
current affairs 25, 67–8
customs 22, *58*, 99

daily routine 43–4, 111, *112, 117*
dates 29
days 29
defined content 8–9
definite article 180, 181
demonstrative adjectives 182
dentist's 14, 36, 99
describing, home 15, 33–5, 112, *116*
  people and pets 17, 41–3, 87, 116, *117*
  places 19, 49–50, *114, 117*
diary entries 153, *158, 164*, 175
dictionaries 2, 11, 25–6, 98, 174
dining room 35
directions *81*, 99
direct object pronouns 190
disjunctive pronouns 190
doctor's 14, *101–2*
drafts 174
drawing conclusions 75, 128
drinks 16–17, 38–40, 111, *112–13, 117*, 121, *128, 158*

eating out 14, 17, 37–8, *80, 84*, 98, 99, *105–6*
Edexcel 9, 10, 11, 12, 110, 118, 173, 178
emotions 28, 75, 96, 128
employment 23, 60–1, *106, 107–8, 115, 117, 166–7*, 175
entertainment 14, 17–18, 46–7, 99, *130*, 175
entry levels 11
environment 19, 49, 67, *146*, 175
estar and ser 189
European countries 25, 66
everyday activities 9, 43–4, 111, *112, 117*
examination, components 8, 10
  rubrics 8, 68–9
  techniques 5–6

examinations (topic) 33
examining board addresses 12
exchange office 14, 21, *55–6*
expressing opinions 115, 126, 154, 170
extras, asking for 40

family 17, 41–3, 111, *113, 117, 118*
festivals 19, 175
finding the way 19–20, 50–1, *81*, 99
fish 38, *100*
fitness 16
flexibility of word order 127, 148
food 16–17, 37–40, *84, 104*, 111, *112–13, 117*, 121, *128–9, 133–4, 136, 158*
foreign countries 25, 66, 111, *115, 117*
foreign exchange office 21, 55–6
formal letters 151, 155–6, *159, 166–7*
form-filling 153, *164*, 175
Foundation Tier 8, 9, 11, 71
free time 17–18, 45–7, 111, *113, 117*
  activities 45–7, *137–8, 134*
friends 17, 41–3, 111, *113, 117*
fruit 38
Full Course 9
further education 22, 60
future plans 23, 60–1, 111, *114, 117*
future tense 74, 126, 154, 186
future with 'ir' 186

garages 14, 99
garden 35, *112*
gender 150, 152, 180
getting around 21–2, 57–8 (see also 'transport')
good-byes 28, 47
grades 11
grammar 3, 179–191
greetings 18, 28, 47
guides 121
gustar 189

hall 35
health 16, 35–7
Higher Tier 9, 11, 71, 149
hobbies 17, 45, 111, *113, 117*
holiday home 25, 65, *139*
holidays 18–19, 48–9, *102*, 111, *113–14, 117, 139, 167–8, 176–17*
home life 14, 15, 33–5, 111, *112, 116–7*
home town 14, 19, 49–50, 111, *114, 117*

hospitality 15
house 15, 33–35
hotel 14, 24, 63–4, 99, *101, 135–6*, 175
hovercraft 22, 58
hygiene 16, 36

illness 16, 36–7, 99
imaginative writing 121, 157
imperfect tense 187
improving listening skills 73–4
indefinite article 181
indirect object pronouns 190
infinitive 186, 190
informal letters 121, 151, 155, *158–9, 166, 176–7*
injury 16, 36–7, 99, *177*
'instant writing kit' 156–7
instRuctions, understanding of 74, 121, 124, 148
  giving 188
interests 111, *113, 117*
international world 14, 25, 66, 111, *115, 117*
ir a + infinitive 186
irregular, future 186
  past participle 186
  verbs 184, 185, 186, 187

jobs 17, 45, 60–1, *106, 107–8, 115, 117, 166–7*, 175
justifying opinions 115, 157, 176, 170

key words and expressions 27–31
kitchen 34–5
knowledge 31

labels 121
language, at work 23
  problems 14–15
  tasks 14–25
  variety 176
learning Spanish 3
learning vocabulary 2, 3, 25, 27
letters, formal 121, 151, 155–6, *159, 166–7*, 175
  informal 121, *137*, 151, 155, *158–9, 166, 176–7*
  semi-formal 155
life at home 14, 15, 33–5, 111, *112, 116–17*
life in other countries 23, 62–3, *115, 117*
liking 189
listening, examination 9, 10, 68–9, 70–96
  place 71
  skills 3–4, 73–4, 96
lists, writing of 152–3, *158, 163*, 175, *176*

livestock 17, 43
living room 35
local environment 19, 49–50, *114, 117*
lost property 14, 21, 56, *105*

magazine articles 121, *145*
maps 121
markets 14, 20, 52–4
marking criteria 156
marks 98, 110, 149
meals 16–17, 37–40, *100, 104, 112–13, 117*
meaning 31
meat 37–8
medical problems 16, 36–7, 99
meeting people 18, 47, 99
MEG 9, 10, 11, 12, 110, 118, 173
memory aids 151
menus 121, 125
messages 121, 151, 153–4, *158, 165*
minimum core vocabulary 8, 74
modular assessment 10
money 21, 55–6
months 29

nationalities 25, 66
nationality 41
nature of the questions/tasks 71, 121–2, 149
NEAB 9, 10, 11, 12, 73, 110, 118, 173
negatives 189
news items 74, 75, *76, 140, 142*, 148
NICCEA 9, 10, 11, 12, 98, 101, 173
notes 121
notices 123–5
nouns 180
numbers 30–1

object pronouns 126, 190
omission of indefinite article 181
opinions 115, 154, 157, 170, 176
order of object pronouns 190
ordinal numbers 31
organization 2

participles, past 185–6
  present 187–8
parts of the body 16, 35–7
party *106–7*
past participle 185, 186
past tenses 74, 115, 126, 154, 184–5, 187
paying the bill 40
people, meeting 18, 47
perfect tense 185–6

personal 'a' 127, 148, 191
personal and social life 9
petrol station 14, 22, *59*, 99, *104*
pets 17, 43
phoning 23, 62, *82*, 99
physical appearance 17, 42, 116, *117*
pictures 71
places of entertainment 17–18, 46–7
places of work 14, 23, 61
planes 22, 58, *82, 141*
planning 5–6
plans for the future 23, 60–1, *114, 117*
plans 121
pluperfect tense 187
plurals 180
pocket money 17, 45
points of view (= opinions) 115, 154, 157, 170, 176
police station 14, *105*
position of: adjectives 182
  object pronouns 190
possessive adjectives 182
post cards 121, 151, 154, *158, 165*, 175
poster 175
post office 20–1, *54–5*, 99
prefix 125
preparation time 97, 98
preparing, coursework 174
  for the speaking test 111
presentations 5, 110, 118
present participle 187–8
present tense 126, 183–4
preterite tense 126, 184–5
pretérito grave 185
price lists 121
private transport 14, 22, 58–60, 61, 111, *114*
problems, coping with 99, 125–6, 152
pronouns 126, 190
publicity 23, 61–2, 121, *128–9, 130, 135*
public notices 123–5, *128–9*
public signs 123–5, 133–4, 148
public transport 14, 21–2, 57–8, 61, *83, 104, 141*

quality of language/expression 98, 115, 149, 156, 170–1
question: types 71, 121–2
  words 31 71–2, 122

radical-changing verbs 184, 185
radio 3, 4, 74, *76, 86–7*
rail travel 22, *57–8*, 61, *83, 104*
range of language 176
reading: examination 69, 120–148
  material 121
  skills 4–5
recordings 71
reference materials 173
reflexive: verbs 188
  pronouns 188, 190
registers 74
regular verbs 183–4, 185, 186, 187
relatives 17, 41–3, *113*
relaxation 2
religion 43
repairs 21, *56–7*, 99
reports/accounts 150, 157, 175, *177–8*
reservations 24, 64
restaurant 14, 17, 37–40, *80, 84*, 98, 99, *100, 105–6*
revision 2–3
road accidents 16, 37, *59–60*
role-plays 97, 98–110
rooms 34–5
routines 43–4, 99, 111, *112, 117*
rubrics 8, 68–9

school 14, 15, 32–3, *76–7, 84, 86–7*, 99, 111, *112, 116–17, 168*, 175
seasons 29
SEG 9, 10, 11, 12, 98, 173
self 17, 41–3, 111, *113, 117*, 118
semi-formal letters 155
ser and estar 189
services 20–1, 54–7
service station 22, *59, 104*
settings 14, 99
shellfish 38
ships 22, 58
shopping 20, 52–4, *80, 82, 83, 85–6*, 99, *103*, 111, *114, 117, 128–9, 133–4, 158*
  for clothes 52–4, 83
  for drinks 38–40, 52–4, *158*
  for food 37–40, 52–4, *80, 82, 85–6, 128–9, 133–4, 158*
shops 14, 20, 52–4, 98, *128–9*
Short Course 9
signs 121, 123–4, *133–4*, 148
skills, weighting of 9, 97
Spanish-speaking countries 25, 66, 121
speaking 4, 69, 97–119
  coursework 178
speed 30
spellings 152
spoken instructions 74
sporting activities 17–18, 46–7
station (railway) *104*
staying with a family *105–6*
subject pronouns 190
suffix 125
superlative, adjectives 182
  adverbs 183

table, asking for 40
targets 3
tasks 14–25
task training 173
taxis 99
telephone messages 74, *75–6, 82*, 98
telephoning 23, 62, *82*, 99
television 3, 74, *117, 134, 141*
telling the time 29
tenses 115, 126, 148, 154, 176, 183–9
  variety of 115, 116
text types for reading 120, 121, 126–7
theatre 17–18, 46–7
tickets 17–18, 22, 47, 57–8, 121
tiers 9, 11
time 29–30
time of day 30, 82
timetable 22, 57–8, 121
timing 5
topics 8, 14–25, 32–68, 99, 110, 111, 150
tourism 23, 63, *167*
tourist office 14, 19, 48–9, *82*, 98, 99, *103*
town 14, 19, 49–50, 111, *114, 117*
traffic reports 74
trains 22, 57–8, 61, *83*, 99, *104*
trams 21–2
transcripts of recordings 91–95
transport 23, 111, *114, 117*
  private 14, 22, 58–60, 61, 99, *104*
  public 14, 21–2, 57–8, 61, *81, 83, 104, 141*
travel 21–2, 23, 58–60, 61, 111, *114, 117*, 175
tú and usted 188, 190

understanding instructions 74, 124
undomesticated creatures 43
unpredictability 98, 101
usted 188, 190

variety, of tenses 115, 116, 154
  of language 176

vegetables 38
verbs 150, 183–9
  irregular 184, 185, 186, 187
  radical-changing 184, 185
village 111, *114, 117*
vocabulary, learning 3, 25, 27, 150, 170
  lists 8, 27–68
  minimum core 8

waiter 40, *84, 100, 105–6*
weather 20, 51–2
  forecast 51–2, 75, *130–1*
weighting of skills 9, 97
welfare 16
wider world 25, 66–8, *115, 117*
WJEC 9, 10, 11, 12, 73, 173
word order 127, 148
work 9, 23, 60–1, *106, 107–8*, 111, *115, 117, 166–7*, 175
world, events 9, 25, 67–8
  issues 9, 25, 67–8, *144*, 175
  of work 9, 23, 60–2, *106, 107–8*, 111, *115, 117*
writing 5, 69, 149–171
  letters 151, 155–6, *158–9, 166–7*
  lists 151, 152–3, *158, 163*
  messages 151, 153–4, *158, 165,*
  post cards 151, 154, *158, 165*, 175

youth hostel 24, 64–5, 99